HIDDEN TRUTHS FROM EDEN

SBL

Society of Biblical Literature

Semeia Studies

Number 76

HIDDEN TRUTHS FROM EDEN

ESOTERIC READINGS OF GENESIS 1–3

Edited by
Caroline Vander Stichele and Susanne Scholz

SBL Press
Atlanta

Library of Congress Cataloging-in-Publication Data

Hidden truths from Eden : esoteric readings of Genesis 1–3 / edited by Caroline Vander Stichele and Susanne Scholz.
p. cm. — (Society of Biblical Literature Semeia Studies ; number 76)
Includes bibliographical references and index.
Summary: "This unique volume features case studies and examples of diverse esoteric interpretive approaches and methodologies focusing on Genesis 1–3 and covering different periods from early Christian discourse through Zoharic, kabbalistic and alchemical literature to modern and post-postmodern approaches"— Provided by publisher.
ISBN 978-1-62837-012-6 (paper binding : alk. paper) — ISBN 978-1-62837-013-3 (electronic format) — ISBN 978-1-62837-014-0 (hardcover binding : alk. paper)
1. Bible. Genesis, I-III—Criticism, interpretation, etc.—History. 2. Bible. Genesis, I-III—Criticism, interpretation, etc., Jewish—History. 3. Creation—Bible teaching. I. Scholz, Susanne, editor. II. Vander Stichele, Caroline, editor.
BS1235.52.H533 2014
222'.1106—dc23 2014027589

Printed on acid-free, recycled paper conforming to
ANSI/NISO Z39.48-1992 (R1997) and ISO 9706:1994
standards for paper permanence.

Contents

Preface

Once upon a time readers did not believe that the search for biblical meanings was limited to historicity or "what the text says." They looked for different levels of meanings that usually began with the sensus literalis but moved quickly to the sensus spiritualis or the "spiritual" sense, which was subdivided into the allegorial, the tropological or moral, and anagogic or mystical meanings. Yet with the emergence of the modern worldview during the sixteenth century C.E. and the predominance of an empiricist scientific epistemology, the valuation of the sensus spiritualis lost traction while the sensus literalis gained popularity and credibility. After several centuries of hermeneutical contestation, historical criticism eventually became the authoritative method for most Protestant scholarly interpretations at the end of the nineteenth century C.E., and many Catholic and Jewish exegetes followed suit by the mid-twentieth century. As a result, spiritual or esoteric interpretations lost their status and were viewed as unscholarly and academically questionable within the field of biblical studies ever since. Yet despite their low regard during the modern era, esoteric biblical interpretations are not limited to that time period but have been emerging even today.

Interestingly, the epistemological and hermeneutical preference for the historicized quest of biblical meaning also consisted of a broad disregard for studying the extensive interpretation history of esoteric readings of the Bible. Accordingly, examinations on the history of esoteric interpretations are few within the field of biblical studies and not on the top of the field's research agenda even today. The only exceptions that have gained respect in the field usually focus on gnostic literature in the early centuries of the Common Era of Christianity and Judaism, because they have led to provocative new views about the study of the biblical gospels and the historical figure of Jesus and were considered important for the reconstruction of early Christianity. Elaine Pagels's bestselling book entitled *The Gnostic Gospels* (1979), investigating texts from the Nag Hammadi library, certainly advanced the study of early Christian "secret" or esoteric literature. At the dawn of the post-postmodern period, then, we want to suggest expanding the exegetical repertoire again and include the study of esoteric biblical readings as part of our disciplinary agenda. We think that such a holistic hermeneutic will give fresh impetus to the academic study of the Bible in our multireligious, increasingly interconnected, and secularized world.

The present volume aims to contribute toward this goal. It includes discussions, comparisons, and analyses of esoteric appropriations of Gen 1–3 from antiquity to the present. The contributors developed essays on creation myths; gender; fate and free will; the concepts of knowledge, wisdom, and gnosis; the origin of good and evil; life and death; the idea of a "fall"; and the afterlife. They consider how esoteric interpretations address gender or race and other social categories, and they explore experiential esoteric approaches to Gen 1–3. As editors, we welcomed theoretical historical-oriented contributions on the integration of esotericism with biblical studies, as well as discussions of past treatments of esoteric approaches to the texts. In sum, we offer a volume that illustrates how future studies may want to proceed so that the vast universe of esoteric biblial readings will become part of the academic discourse in biblical studies. Eventually, the results may also be beneficial to a public that suffers so extensively from the literalist malady.

We would like to express our gratitude to several groups of people who made this volume on esoteric biblical interpretation possible. First, we thank the editorial board and general editor of Semeia Studies for agreeing to include this volume in their series, as well as the staff of SBL Press, especially managing editor Leigh Andersen and Kathie Klein, who worked with us on the publication of this volume, for doing such a wonderful job. Second, we are grateful to the contributors to this volume with whom it was our pleasure to work. We appreciate that they responded quickly and diligently to our correspondence and kept their deadlines. Third, we thank each other for a truly enjoyable collaboration process and our partners and feline friends who kept reminding us that there is more to life than work. Finally, we thank the Perkins School of Theology at Southern Methodist University for supporting the creation of the indices by providing funds for a research assistant in the fall of 2014. We also thank research assistant David A. Schones for his exquisite care and attention in building the indices.

Abbreviations

ACW	Ancient Christian Writers
AJSR	*Association for Jewish Studies Review*
ANF	*Ante-Nicene Fathers*
BETL	Bibliotheca ephemeridum theologicarum lovaniensium
BG	Berlin Gnostic Papyrus
British Library Or.	British Library Oriental Manuscript
CCSA	Corpus Christianorum: Series apocryphorum
CCSG	Corpus Christianorum: Series graeca
FC	Fathers of the Church
GCS	Die griechische christliche Schriftsteller der ersten [drei] Jahrhunderte
HR	*History of Religions*
HTR	*Harvard Theological Review*
HUCA	*Hebrew Union College Annual*
JAAR	*Journal of the American Academy of Religion*
JECS	*Journal of Early Christian Studies*
JHI	*Journal of the History of Ideas*
JJS	*Journal of Jewish Studies*
JJTP	*Journal of Jewish Thought and Philosophy*
JR	*Journal of Religion*
JSJ	*Journal for the Study of Judaism in the Persian, Hellenistic, and Roman Periods*
JSJT	*Jerusalem Studies in Jewish Thought*
JSNT	*Journal for the Study of the New Testament*
JSOT	*Journal for the Study of the Old Testament*
JSOTSup	Journal for the Study of the Old Testament: Supplement Series
LCL	Loeb Classical Library
MS Vatican ebr.	Vatican Library Hebrew Manuscript

NHC	Nag Hammadi Codices
NovTSup	Novum Testamentum Supplements
NRSV	New Revised Standard Version
Oxyr.	Oxyrhynchus Papyrus
PL	Patrologia latina
Proof	*Prooftexts: A Journal of Jewish Literary History*
SA	*Scientia Aeterna*
SAC	Studies in Antiquity and Christianity
SBLSP	*Society of Biblical Literature Seminar Papers*
SC	Sources chrétiennes
SHR	Studies in the History of Religions
SS	*Scientia Sacra*
TJ	*Trinity Journal*
TU	Texte und Untersuchungen
VV	Világválság (World Crisis)
ZAC	*Zeitschrift für Antikes Christentum/Journal of Ancient Christianity*
ZKT	*Zeitschrift für katholische Theologie*

Introduction

Caroline Vander Stichele and Susanne Scholz

Esoteric interpretations of the Bible are a largely neglected research area in biblical studies. With this volume we want to draw attention to the knowledge that remains hidden in what for many scholars and readers of the Bible still is a *terra incognita*. In that light it may well be appropriate to start with the opening chapters from the Bible. Undoubtedly, Gen 1–3 is a key text for Jews and Christians. It had an enormous impact on Western thought in terms of the emergence as well as the rejection of science, attitudes towards human nature, and constructions of sociopolitical and cultural norms. Moreover, the opening chapters from Genesis were also widely commented upon in esoteric circles from antiquity to the present. Important topics that have been addressed time and again include creation myths, gender, fate and free will, concepts of gnosis, the origin of good and evil, life and death, the idea of a "fall," the afterlife, as well as experiential approaches of Gen 1–3. As Elaine Pagels notes in her introduction to *Adam, Eve, and the Serpent*,

> Our spiritual ancestors argued and speculated over how God had commanded the first man and woman to "be fruitful and multiply, and fill the earth," and how he instituted the first marriage; how Adam, after he found among the animals no "helper fit for him" (Genesis 2:20), met Eve, with well-known and disastrous consequences. Such interpretations of the first three chapters of Genesis, as we can see, engaged intensely practical concerns and articulated deeply felt attitudes. (1990, xix)

This holds true for the whole spectrum of interpretations, including esoteric ones. In this volume some of these interpretations are discussed.

Yet perhaps it is wise to begin with a clarification of terminology, especially since the adjective *esoteric* is so loaded in colloquial usage. When people say that something is esoteric, they usually do not mean it as a compliment. Rather, they indicate that the matter under consideration is difficult to understand, requiring highly specialized expertise that is not of general relevance and broad reach. Depending on the particular situation, the adjective esoteric may even include derogatory connotations. Such is, of course, not the usage of the term in this book. Derived from the Greek word ἐσωτερικός (*esōterikos*), a compound of ἔσω (*esō*; "within, in"), the word contrasts with *exoteric* (outside, out). As such it is often used to refer to an inward mode of thinking or being. However, if the adjective esoteric dates from antiquity, the substantive *esotericism* was only used since the end of the eighteenth century to denote a wide variety of movements from antiquity to the present. As such, the term is a modern concept, covering philosophical traditions, among them Hermeticism, traditional sciences such as alchemy, and theological speculative thought as found in Jewish and Christian kabbalah. "Western esotericism," then, "is not a natural term, but an artificial category, applied retrospectively to a range of currents and ideas that were known by other names at least prior to the end of the eighteenth century" (Hanegraaff 2013, 3). In more popular use today, it is often applied to those religious phenomena and movements that are inner-oriented, sometimes identified as the "mystical" path, and differentiated from the "outer" processes of the world. Yet at other times, this distinction is not considered to be all that meaningful, as esotericism is also understood as an investigation about the various levels of consciousness and being.

In the modern Western era, esoteric thinkers and movements often found themselves on the margins of institutionalized religions. Nevertheless, many examples of esoteric religious practices and theories still exist, such as alchemy, astrology, Anthroposophy, Gnosticism, Neoplatonism, Rosicrucianism, or Christian Theosophy. In the Western and European world, esoteric thinkers such as Jacob Böhme (1575–1624), Emanuel Swedenborg (1688–1772), Eliphas Lévi (1810–1875), Helena Blavatsky (1831–1891), Rudolph Steiner (1861–1925), George Ivanovitsj Gurdjieff (ca.1866–1949), and René Guénon (1886–1951) are among the key figures of Western esoteric thought. Other religious traditions, especially on the Asian continent but also among the indigenous peoples on the American and African continents, also exhibit great esoteric sensitivities, knowledge, and wisdom. Examples can be found in Sufism, Taoism, Buddhism, Tantra, or various traditions in what is called Hinduism. Western esoteric twentieth-century thinkers, such as Frithjof Schuon (1907–1998), integrated many of the traditionally non-Western esoteric insights into their own philosophical, religious, and spiritual studies.

In esoteric thought and practice, the Bible surfaces all the time, as Western esoteric thinkers sought to uncover its esoteric meaning. The creation stories of Gen 1–3 have been popular texts in esoteric Bible readings, but Western biblical studies has shown little interest so far in investigating this particular branch of the Bible's history of interpretation. This lacuna is hardly surprising, because modern Western academia as a whole emerged in refutation of everything it regarded as "unscientific," irrational, and in opposition to its own empiricist scientific principles of knowledge. So far, this volume on esoteric interpretations of Gen 1–3 is unique in academic biblical studies, and no comparable volume exists that concerns itself with a cross-historical investigation of the esoteric interpretation history of the Bible. We certainly hope that in due time this situation will change.

In the meantime and with the goal to inspire additional work, this collection contains nine case studies and examples from the wealth of esoteric approaches and methodologies. The volume introduces the topic to the academic field of biblical studies and invites scholars to explore esoteric approaches in relation to other biblical texts. Yet it also aims to awaken interest in esoteric perspectives, methodologies, and thinkers in general. A unique feature of our volume is that it brings together an array of different approaches and theoretical lenses to esotericism and the Bible by scholars in the field of both biblical studies and esotericism.

The included essays are intentionally diverse in method and scope, although all of them focus on Gen 1–3. The material is arranged in three parts, covering different periods of the reception history. This arrangement demonstrates the continued but also changing cultural impact of the creation stories. The first part deals with the different ways in which early Christian discourse engages these stories. In the first essay, Anna Rebecca Solevåg argues that the Acts of Andrew offers an esoteric interpretation of Gen 2–3, which values inner experience and a search for revealed knowledge mediated by the apostle Andrew, and that the relationships and actions among the main characters of the Acts of Andrew are presented as a symbolic reenactment of the so-called "fall" in which the tragic outcome is reversed. Next, Tuomas Rasimus explores why an eagle rather than a serpent appears to Eve and Adam in the gnostic Apocryphon of John, influencing them to eat of the tree of knowledge. In his view, the author draws more specifically on Roman imperial propaganda to represent Christ as an eagle offering salvation. In the third essay Peter W. Martens investigates

Origen's approach to another element from the story, notably the "garments of skin" (Gen 3:21) with which God clothed Adam and Eve. His reconstruction shows that Origen's literal and allegorical interpretations represent God in a way that befits him.

In the second part of the volume, the focus shifts from early Christian texts to interpretations found in the zoharic, kabbalistic, and alchemical literature. Elliot R. Wolfson examines the construction of gender typologies that emerge from the narrative accounts of the creation of woman and man, the nature of sin, and the implicit sense of rectification elicited from the Sefer Hazohar. In his view, the deep structure undergirding the kabbalistic construction of gender, including possible subversions of that structure, is that of a masculine androgyny. In the following article, Peter J. Forshaw begins with a discussion on the exegetical techniques used in kabbalistic texts, such as the Bihar and Zohar. He focuses on the opening words of Gen 1:1 ("In the beginning God created heaven and earth") and then examines Christian appropriations in the pioneering work of the Italian aristocrat and philosopher Giovanni Pico della Mirandola and several related Christian commentators. The essay by Georgiana (Jo) Hedesan highlights the notion of the uncreated *mysterium magnum* used by God to make the world in the interpretation of creation advanced in the treatise *Philosophia ad Atheniensis,* attributed to Paracelsus. Hedesan also investigates some of the most significant responses to *Philosophia ad Atheniensis* to explain how Paracelsian followers and opponents made sense of this ambiguous text.

The third part moves from modern to post-postmodern esoteric approaches. In her essay Susanne Scholz concentrates on the esoteric hermeneutics used by Emanuel Swedenborg, Rudolph Steiner, and Samuel D. Fohr to interpret Gen 1–3. She maintains that their esoteric interpretations may well provide a way out of the rigidly literalist worldviews, whether religiously or secularly defined, that are dominant in our post-postmodern age. László-Attila Hubbes in turn presents the work of Béla Hamvas, a Hungarian esoteric thinker, who sought to understand and actualize the message of Eden. Hamvas asserted that the *status absolutus* of the unspoiled human of the original creation appears in all narratives of origin. According to Hubbes, Hamvas's work should be read as a poetics of creation, which enriches our understanding of the biblical tradition with new insights. Finally, the programmatic essay by Hugh R. Page Jr. uplifts yet another marginalized tradition in Western thought, that of Africana esotericism. According to Page, more scholarly attention needs to be paid to this largely neglected field. In light of the important role the Bible plays in the construction of Africana esoteric cosmologies and epistemologies, abundant opportunities exist for interdisciplinary research that have yet to be fully explored. This includes the relationship between African esoteric sources and their relationship to Gen 1–3.

Finally, in their responses to this volume, Elaine Pagels and Samuel D. Fohr engage the nine essays from their respective positions as a scholar of early Christianity and Gnosticism and as a philosopher, who reads, translates, and writes esoteric works.

This volume draws attention to largely marginalized esoteric discourses in the field. A lot of this material has hardly received attention as modern scholars have often concentrated on early Christian materials in their reconstructions of Christian origins and histories. Even then, however, one can observe the existence of a canon within the extracanon, as some texts have received much more scholarly attention than others. Boundaries have shifted, but they have not been questioned. As Elisabeth Schüssler Fiorenza notes, in order for a real paradigm shift to take place in the field of biblical studies, a critical rhetorical investigation of interpretation is needed to "understand the bible and biblical interpretation as a site of struggle over authority, values and meaning" (2007, 254). Putting esoteric biblical interpretations on the agenda, this volume aims to contribute to such a paradigm shift.

As editors, we hope that this collection encourages other scholars to view esoteric approaches to the Bible as an academically serious, intellectually rich, and culturally important area for further scholarly research. We therefore look forward to further investigations of this culturally, theologically, literary, and historically exciting material.

Works Cited

Hanegraaff, Wouter. 2013. *Western Esotericism: A Guide for the Perplexed*. London: Bloomsbury.

Pagels, Elaine. 1990. *Adam, Eve, and the Serpent*. London: Penguin.

Schüssler Fiorenza, Elisabeth. 2007. *The Power of the Word: Scripture and the Rhetoric of Empire*. Minneapolis: Fortress.

Part 1
Early Christian Explorations

Adam, Eve, and the Serpent in the Acts of Andrew

Anna Rebecca Solevåg

How did early Christians understand and use the stories about the creation and fall of Adam and Eve? Different communities undoubtedly employed these stories in many different ways. Within one tradition (what eventually became dominant or orthodox Christianity), Eve was often depicted as weak and easily deceived and was used to subordinate women (see, e.g., 1 Tim 2:13–14; Tertullian, *Cult. fem.* 1.1.1–2). Traditions reflected in the Nag Hammadi texts show a different interpretation of the Genesis story, pointing to Eve as a revealer of knowledge and representing a higher principle than Adam (see, e.g., Orig. World 115–116; Hyp. Arch. 89, 13–17; Hobgood-Oster 1999, 51; Pagels 1989, 66). In the apocryphal Acts of Andrew, we find an example of an early Christian interpretation of Genesis that is quite extraordinary. In this second or third century C.E. narrative,[1] the relationships and actions among the main characters are presented as a symbolic reenactment of the fall in which the tragic outcome is reversed. I will argue that this is an *esoteric* interpretation of Gen 2–3, which values inner experience and a search for revealed knowledge mediated by the apostle Andrew.[2]

The Western esoteric traditions can be traced back to the first centuries C.E. Esoteric strands of thought may be found within Neopythagoreanism, Stoicism, Hermeticism, Neoplatonism, and Gnosticism (Faivre 1993a). According to Arthur Versluis, a central characteristic throughout the period is gnosis, and thus he chooses gnosis as the defining characteristic of esotericism: "a term referring to cosmological or metaphysical religious or spiritual knowledge that is restricted to or intended for a limited

1. For a second-century C.E. date, see MacDonald 1994, 59; and Prieur 1989, 413–14. For a third-century C.E. date, see Elliott 1993, 236; and Klauck 2008, 116.
2. See also Solevåg 2013.

group" (2002, 10). Antoine Faivre has developed a typology of esotericism with four important characteristics (1993b): (1) the idea of correspondences between a higher divine reality, the universe, the earthly realm, and human beings; (2) the idea of a living, ensouled, or animated universe; (3) notions of spiritual intermediaries in the form of hierarchies, planes, and angels acting as a ladder of descent and ascent between higher and lower worlds; (4) and the idea of the human soul's transmutation through reawakening and returning to these higher worlds (Faivre's typology as presented in Goodrick-Clarke 2008, 15).

In this essay I will consider the use of Gen 3 in the Acts of Andrew. It is particularly in a speech to the female convert Maximilla that the story of the fall is referred to. The apostle Andrew compares and contrasts Maximilla with Eve and himself with Adam:

> I rightly see in you Eve repenting [τὴν Εὕαν μετανοοῦσαν] and in me Adam converting [τὸν Ἀδὰμ ἐπιστρέφοντα]. For what she suffered through ignorance [ἔπαθεν ἀγνοοῦσα], you—whose soul I seek—must now redress through conversion. The very thing suffered by the mind [νοῦς ἔπαθεν] which was brought down with her and slipped away from itself, I make right with you, through your recognition [τῇ γνωριζούσῃ] that you are being raised up. You healed [ἰάσω] her deficiency by not experiencing the same passions [τὰ ὅμοια παθοῦσα], and I have perfected [τετέλεκα] Adam's imperfection [ἀτελές] by fleeing to God for refuge. Where Eve disobeyed [παρήκουσεν], you obeyed [ἤκουσας]; what Adam agreed to, I flee from; the things that tripped them up, we have recognized [ἐγνωρίζαμεν]. For it is ordained that each person should correct his or her own fall [πταῖσμα]. (Acts Andr. 37)

What is the temptation Maximilla must resist? What is it she must recognize or learn (γνωρίζω)? How can she correct her fall, and is this the way to salvation for all believers? I will use an intersectional approach to tease out some of the nuances in the narrative's esoteric use of Gen 3. The Acts of Andrew has often been interpreted as an encratite text, meaning that salvation is made dependent on sexual continence (Prieur 1989, 323). I will show that its concern for sexual renunciation is complicated if we deploy an analysis that pays attention to gender and class. But before describing the method, I will briefly introduce the text.

The Acts of Andrew

The Acts of Andrew tells the story of the miracles, speeches, and martyrdom of the apostle Andrew. It belongs to the apocryphal acts, a group of narratives popular among early Christians. Theologically as well as thematically, these narratives share many features with one another. They have a common interest in chastity, and they ascribe a significant role to the apostle as a mediator between humans and God. The stories in these acts focus on the missionary activities of particular apostles, their preaching, and their miracle working, and the stories usually end in martyrdom. They may be fruitfully compared to ancient Greek novels (Söder 1969; Perkins 1995; Cooper 1996), but they also bear resemblance to Greek historiography and biographies of philosophers (Klauck 2008, 8). The latter is particularly true of the Acts of Andrew, which is considered the most philosophical of the apocryphal acts (Nasrallah 1999, 237; MacDonald 1994). Andrew is depicted as a new Socrates, and influence from Middle Platonic philosophy seems strong. Still, traits from the genre of Hellenistic novels can be found in the use of certain literary *topoi*, such as a travel motif and a love triangle (Pervo 1994, 244–46).

Only parts of the Acts of Andrew are preserved in the original Greek (the beginning of the text is only preserved in a late Latin redaction). In this essay it is the Greek Acts of Andrew—based on MacDonald's (1990) reconstruction of the Greek text—that will be considered. Sometimes referred to as the Greek Acts of Andrew (AAGr) or the Passion of Andrew, this text narrates the events of Andrew's second visit to Patras in Achaia, leading up to and culminating into his martyrdom. In the story the apostle Andrew persuades his convert, the rich and influential Maximilla, to abstain from sexual relations with her husband Aegeates, who is the proconsul of the province of Achaia. This spurs the subsequent chain of events: Maximilla pays her slave, Euclia, to sleep with her husband. When the conspiracy is discovered, Aegeates kills the slave girl and arrests Andrew. Aegeates tells Maximilla that he will kill the apostle unless she returns to the marriage bed, but Andrew persuades Maximilla to resist. As a result, Andrew is crucified. Towards the end of the story, while in prison awaiting his martyrdom, Andrew gives a lengthy speech to Maximilla, which contains several references to the story of the fall in Genesis, including Adam, Eve, the serpent, and Cain. Through her sexual renunciation, Andrew explains, Maximilla can amend the fall (see quote above).

An Intersectional Perspective

Intersectionality is a growing interdisciplinary field that combines feminist, gender, antiracist, postcolonial, and class sensitive modes of analysis (McCall 2005; de los Reyes and Mulinari 2005; Nasrallah and Schüssler Fiorenza 2009). The main insight is that identity categories and power structures are irreducibly complex, and that analyzing only one axis of differentiation or discrimination will never lead to a comprehensive understanding. Here I will use the category of class, or more particularly slave/free, to examine the text in addition to gender. The character of Maximilla and her relation to Eve is particularly interesting to study from an intersectional perspective. While previous scholars have assumed that her commitment to celibacy reflects an encratite theology (Klauck 2008, 135; Prieur 1989, 323), I suggest we reconsider how she is represented and whom she may represent (Solevåg 2013). In the text, Maximilla's renunciation of sexual relations with her husband is described with three different types of imagery. She becomes the chaste bride of Christ, a new Eve, and male.

Maximilla as Chaste Bride of Christ

As noted above, the apocryphal acts share many features with Greek novels. Among them is a concern for love and chastity (Pervo 1994, 244). The mutual love between the main characters—the hero and the heroine—is a recurring motif in the novels. The story is driven by the complications and temptations for the couple on their way to marriage—the happy ending of the novels (Perkins 1995, 62). In the Acts of Andrew it is, more particularly, the *topos* of the love triangle that is employed. As Saundra Schwartz explains: "The catalyst for this noble martyrdom is paradoxical for its sheer banality: it is a love triangle—specifically, an adulterous triangle—although, ironically, without the sex" (2007, 268).

The conflict in our story is caused when the apostle Andrew forms a relationship with Maximilla that upends her marital relations with Aegeates. She refuses to have sex with her husband but invites Andrew to her bedroom, "so that he may come here to pray and lay his hands on me while Aegeates is sleeping" (Acts Andr. 15). Hence a love triangle is formed, with Maximilla as adulterous wife, the apostle as secret lover, and the proconsul as cuckolded husband (Schwartz 2007, 296).[3] The twist in the plot is

3. For different analyses of the triangles, see Rodman 1997, 35; Bolyki 2000.

that Maximilla is not in love with Andrew but with God. Her love is not external and carnal, but internal and pure. The object of Maximilla's love is an "inner man"—Jesus—not Andrew. She admits to her husband when she is asked: "I am in love, Aegeates. I am in love, and the object of my love is not of this world and therefore imperceptible to you" (Acts Andr. 23). Maximilla is in love with Jesus, but Andrew is his earthly representative, and so it is him she admits repeatedly into her bedroom.

Just as Andrew represents Jesus, Maximilla's husband also represents something more than himself. Through Andrew's speeches we learn about the true nature of Aegeates: that he is the devil in disguise (Pesthy 2000, 48). He is called "that insolent and hostile snake" (Acts Andr. 16) and "the enemy" (62). There are also suggestions that he is the son of the serpent (40) as well as the devil (40; 63).[4] Early in the story, Andrew comes to Maximilla's bedroom at night to pray for her while her husband is away. This is an excerpt of his prayer:

> With respect to our savage and unbearable enemy [ἐχθρὸν], cause her to sleep [κατακοίμησον] apart from her visible husband and wed [ἅρμοσον] her to her inner husband [τῷ ἔσω ἀνδρί], whom you above all recognize, and for whose sake the entire mystery of your plan of salvation [σου μυστήριον τῆς οἰκονομίας] has been accomplished. (Acts Andr. 16)

In this quotation Andrew redefines the love triangle on a typological level.[5] By introducing the image of marriage with Christ, Christ becomes Maximilla's inner husband. Her alliance is shifted from Aegeates/the devil to Andrew/Christ. Thus, having sexual relations with Aegeates (the outer husband) becomes adultery. Sex between Aegeates and Maximilla is further made repulsive since the story links Aegeates to the ultimate enemy—the devil.[6] Thus, Maximilla's choice is whether she should remain faithful to Jesus, who is her true husband, or cheat on him by sleeping with Aegeates. Maximilla avoids sexual intercourse with her husband, Aegeates, but as noted above, at first she does not tell him directly. Rather, she uses one

4. As I will elaborate below, the references to Gen 2–3 also connect Aegeates to the devil.

5. Schwartz does not consider this typological level of the triangle.

6. The word ἐχθρόν was used in early Christianity as an epithet for the devil. See Lampe 1961.

of her slaves, Euclia, as a surrogate body, as also Jennifer Glancy has noted (Glancy 2002, 22). This passage describes the subterfuge:

> Just as a woman customarily adorns herself to look like her rival, Maximilla groomed Euclia in just such finery and put her forward to sleep with Aegeates in her stead. Having used her as his lover, he let her go to her own bedroom, just as Maximilla used to. By so doing Maximilla escaped detection for some time, and thereby got relief, rejoiced in the Lord, and never left Andrew. (Acts Andr.17)

While Maximilla's conversion is described as a new marriage union, the other main conversion story is described with very different imagery. Aegeates's brother, Stratocles, is also persuaded by Andrew's message. In contrast to the proconsul, who is described as a violent and unlikeable character, Stratocles is a well-liked man, interested in philosophy. His conversion is described as a Socratic birthing process. Andrew is the midwife when Stratocles gives birth to his new inner being through discourse: "Bring to birth the child you are carrying and do not give yourself over to labor pains alone. I am no novice at midwifery and divination. I desire what you are bearing. I love what you are suppressing. I will suckle what is within you" (Acts Andr. 7).

It is particularly in the conversion of Stratocles and the ensuing friendship between the convert and the apostle that the Platonic influences in the text become clear. The use of Socratic birthing imagery casts Andrew in the role of a Christian Socrates, as MacDonald (1994) has observed. According to Caroline Schroeder, the *eros* of the Greek novels, which is consummated in sexual passion, marriage, and procreation, is transformed in the Acts of Andrew into Platonic *eros*, whose fulfillment comes through "an understanding of the inner self, a unification with the divine, and a lasting sense of peace and rest" (2006, 49–50). It should be noted, however, that in Stratocles's conversion, sexual renunciation, which is so important in the discourse concerning Maximilla, is not an explicit concern. Rather, Stratocles declares that he will rid himself of all *possessions* and live with the apostle (Acts Andr. 8). Stratocles, too, has fallen in love with Andrew's teaching but the response focuses on Stratocles's sincere, almost extreme interest in learning from Andrew's words of salvation. This relationship, too, plays on the erotic element. Stratocles spends day and night with the apostle and seeks him out to receive private instructions. They declare their love for each other, but their intercourse is not passionate lovemaking; it is Socratic dialogue (Schroeder 2006, 50). On the eve of Andrew's martyrdom, Stratocles laments the apostle's imminent departure:

> But after this, where and in whom will I seek and find your concern and love? I received the seeds of the words of salvation while you were my sower; for them to shoot up and reproduce requires no one else but you, blessed Andrew. (Acts Andr. 44)

The role of the apostle for both Stratocles's and Maximilla's conversion is therefore paramount. The apostle serves as intermediary between the divine realm and the earthly and almost takes over the soteriological role of Christ (Klauck 2008, 135). As noted, the notion of spiritual intermediaries is a characteristic of esoteric writings. This trait may be recognized in the Acts of Andrew in the importance given to the apostle as an almost divine revealer of cosmic knowledge. Another esoteric trait, which I will come back to, is the emphasis on knowledge and understanding.

Both Maximilla and Stratocles, who are upper-class converts, go through a process of transformation in their conversion. However, two further converts are named in the Acts of Andrew. They are Stratocles's slave, Alcman, and Maximilla's slave, Iphidama, but they receive less attention in the story than the two upper-class converts. Alcman is at the center in the beginning of the story, when he is healed by Andrew (Acts Andr. 2–4); then he fades out of the picture. Iphidama is Maximilla's obedient handmaid, running to summon Andrew on her mistress's request and always behaving dutifully and faithfully (28). Euclia, the slave who is put forward to sleep with Aegeates instead of Maximilla, to the contrary, is portrayed with bad characteristics: she boasts, flatters herself, steals, and threatens her mistress (18–22). Even Euclia's body shape betrays her sexual licentiousness: "She [Maximilla] summoned a shapely and exceedingly wanton servant-girl named Euclia and told her what she delighted in and desired" (17).

Euclia is presented as the opposite of Maximilla, as she supposedly takes delight in her sexual encounters with Aegeates. She is Maximilla's fleshly counterpart, her "evil twin," as Schwartz observes (2007, 301). She is portrayed as a braggart and a thief who is concerned with her looks, whereas Maximilla has eyes only for her purity and her eternal fate. Euclia's main character flaw is her hubris. She thinks she can rise above her station in life, and she wants too much. Aegeates kills her because she has boasted and betrayed family secrets (Acts Andr. 22). As James Albert Harrill argued, early Christian narratives used slave *topoi* well known in classical culture: "From one side came the 'faithful slave' of familial loyalty; the flip side brought the 'enemy slave' of domestic betrayal" (2003, 232). We can also recognize this type/antitype in the Acts of Andrew. Iphidama and Alcman are thus presented as "faithful slaves," whereas Euclia, on the other hand, fits the stereotype of the "enemy slave."

Because slaves in antiquity were habitually used as sexual outlets by their owners, and as prostitutes, sexual renunciation could not be a tenable lifestyle for an enslaved woman (Osiek 2003). If slaves were included in the soteriological economy of encratite groups at all, this would have implied that slaves were expected to live chastely in order to be saved. Prieur asserts that the Acts of Andrew is encratite, but the representation of slaves indicates that sexual renunciation is not significant for their conversion. The two believing slaves in the Acts of Andrew—Alcman, who is male, and Iphidama, who is female—are both the favorite slaves of their masters. Obedience to their master's will is the most important aspect of these slaves' conversion. They are not freed, and we are not informed whether they lived chastely or not. Their auxiliary function in the story gives them no personality, and obedience is their only trademark. As Harrill has shown for the martyrdom stories, this story, too, reinforces ancient ideologies of slavery, stressing the "faithful slave's" obedience to the master's will (2003, 253).

Maximilla as New Eve

As noted already, Maximilla is likened to Eve and Andrew to Adam. Maximilla's resistance to Aegeates's sexual invitation represents "in you Eve repenting, and in me Adam converting" (Acts Andr. 37). Maximilla does right what Eve did wrong, just as Andrew perfects Adam's imperfection. The quotation from Andrew's speech to Maximilla at the beginning of this essay refers to suffering and healing, misconception and understanding. Maximilla is an enlightened Eve, who understands (γνωρίζω) what Eve did not. The question is, however, what Eve's misdeed consisted of and how Maximilla, through her superior understanding, can amend it. Several scholars, such as Elaine Pagels and Hans-Josef Klauck, have suggested that in the Acts of Andrew original sin is understood as sexual intercourse and that sexual continence overcomes this sin (Pagels 1989, 21; Klauck 2008, 205). I agree that the fall entails *carnal* knowledge, but I would suggest that it refers to Eve's illicit sexual union with the serpent, not with Adam. As noted earlier, Aegeates is called a snake—he is the devil personified. This "snake" is making sexual advances towards Maximilla, so if she refuses him, she corrects the fall. It seems reasonable to assume that the original sin, then, involved sex with the serpent.

Such an understanding of the fall—that Eve was sexually seduced by the serpent—is not unaccounted for in Hellenistic Judaism or early Christianity. This tradition appears in texts such as 4 Maccabees, 2 Corinthians, 1 Timothy, the Protevangelium of James, and the Mishnah (Hanson 1968). For example, in 4 Maccabees, the mother of the seven sons contrasts her own chaste behavior as a young woman to that of Eve: "I was a pure virgin and did not go outside my father's house; but I guarded the rib from which woman was made. No seducer [λυμεών] corrupted me on a desert plain, nor did the destroyer, the deceitful serpent [λυμεῶν ἀπάτης ὄφις], defile the purity of my virginity [τὰ ἁγνὰ τῆς παρθενίας]" (18:7–8). The notion of sexual seduction also emerges in the Protevangelium of James (150–200 C.E.). This narrative elaborates on the story of Mary's conception of Jesus, highlighting her virginity as the central issue. Joseph married Mary but promised to preserve her as a virgin. When he returns from a journey and finds her pregnant, he likens his situation to Adam's, saying: "For as Adam was absent in the hour of his prayer and the serpent came and found Eve alone and deceived [ἐξηπάτησεν] her, so also has it happened to me" (Prot. Jas. 13.5, Hock 1995). In my view the Genesis interpretation in the Acts of Andrew is in line with this tradition.

Justin Martyr, a contemporary of the author of the Acts of Andrew, also alludes to a sexual union between the serpent and the primordial woman in his *Dialogue with Trypho*:

> He [i.e., Christ] became man by the Virgin, in order that the disobedience which from the serpent might receive its destruction in the same manner in which it derived its origin. For Eve, who was a virgin and undefiled, having conceived the word of the serpent, brought forth disobedience and death. (*Dial.* 100)

In the Protevangelium of James and Justin's *Dialogue with Trypho*, the difference between Eve and Mary is further developed. In the Acts of Andrew, Mary has no role to play, but Maximilla takes on a role similar to the one Justin awards the virgin Mary: her actions undo Eve's sin. As a result, Maximilla's actions have a cosmic counterpart.

A further indication that the Acts of Andrew is familiar with the idea that Eve's sin consisted in having sex with the serpent is a reference to Cain in Andrew's speech to Maximilla. Andrew admonishes her to keep herself "unsympathetic to the works of Cain [τὰ τοῦ Καίν ἔργα]" (40). Rabbinic and gnostic traditions hold that Cain was Eve's offspring generated through her intercourse with Satan. These traditions are mainly found in texts dated later than the Acts of Andrew (Luttikhuizen 2003, 209; Pearson 1990, 100). For example, in the Gospel of Philip, dated about a hundred years later than the Acts of Andrew, it is claimed:

> First adultery came into being, afterward murder. And he was begotten in adultery, for he was the child of the serpent. So he became a murderer, just like his father, and he killed his brother. Indeed every act of sexual intercourse which has occurred between those unlike one another is adultery. (Gos. Phil. 61:5–10, Isenberg 1990)

The reference to Cain in the Acts of Andrew shows affinities with these ideas. It ends a long list of vices and virtues that distinguish the pure and the holy from "anything foreign to us." In the Acts of Andrew, the believers are called "kindred" (συγγενής). Since God is their father, believers are spiritual siblings. On the flip side, whoever is opposed to Andrew's message is kindred to the snake (ὄφθεως συγγενής, 42; see Bovon 2000, 91). The exhortation to Maximilla to keep herself unsympathetic, unmoved by feelings, for the works of Cain is a warning to keep herself away from those who are not believers, those who are not spiritually "kindred." If the logic is similar to that of the Gospel of Philip, it goes as follows: Eve's union with the serpent generated Cain, who became a murderer and is thus a symbol of all evil. The potential offspring of a union with Aegeates—that is, "the serpent"—is nothing to strive for. By keeping her distance to Aegeates, Maximilla reverses the spiral of evil, murder, and death that pertains to Cain, Aegeates, and all the devil's sons—a spiral started by too much passion on Eve's part.

If Eve's seduction by the serpent constituted her wrongdoing, and if Maximilla, as the new Eve, can undo it by abstaining from sexual relations with her husband, what then was Adam's wrongdoing, and how can Andrew amend it? What Andrew must resist, it seems, is not the temptation to indulge in sexual intercourse but the temptation to choose life over a martyr's death. Andrew urges Maximilla to abstain from intercourse with Aegeates, and if she follows Andrew's advice, it will inevitably imply Andrew's death. In the narrative he elaborates on this point as follows:

> Scorn Aegeates' threats, Maximilla … remain chaste. Let him not only avenge himself on me with the tortures of captivity, let him also throw me to the beasts, burn me with fire, and throw me off a cliff. So what? Let him destroy this body as he will, for it is only one body and it is akin to him. (Acts Andr. 39)

In the creation myth of Genesis and in the apocryphal tale of Andrew, the woman holds the key to life and death. Eve's seduction led to Adam's (and her own) death (Gen 3:3, 19), and if Maximilla consents to sex with her husband, Andrew will ultimately be destroyed and suffer eternal death. As he explains:

> If I am driven from here, perhaps I can help others of my kindred because of you, but if you become won over by the seductions of Aegeates and the flatteries of the serpent, his father, so that you return to your former sexual acts, know this: I will be punished there because of you. (Acts Andr. 40)

In my view, the use of Gen 3 in the Acts of Andrew is similar to Nag Hammadi uses of Adam and Eve. In both cases, Gen 3 is "understood as spiritual allegory—not so much *history with a moral* as *myth with meaning*" (emphasis original; Pagels 1989, 64). On the one hand, the story of the fall is interpreted typologically in order to give meaning to events in the present. The fall is not something "that happened" but a divine reality that corresponds to the challenges at hand. On the other hand, from a gender-analytical perspective, the interpretation of Genesis resembles those of other mainstream or proto-orthodox Christian interpretations. Eve is portrayed as weak and as succumbing to the seduction of the devil. The use of Genesis in the Acts of Andrew shows that in the second century the lines between gnostic and othodox were blurry, or even nonexistent. For that reason, *esoteric* is probably a better label than *gnostic* when it comes to the Acts of Andrew. In particular, the Maximilla-Eve typology reflects the notion of correspondences between divine reality and the earthly realm, a typical characteristic of esoteric writings.

Maximilla as Male

In his speech to Maximilla, Andrew also refers to her as a man and appeals to her mind and intellect. In juxtaposition to Maximilla (the man), there is Stratocles (the childbearer) and Andrew (the midwife). One wonders if there is not a complete gender reversal in the Acts of Andrew, as some interpreters have suggested. According to MacDonald: "Perhaps here, more than in any other early Christian text, one finds a conscious articulation of gender transformation, one bordering on gender reversal" (1994, 237). At the end of his long exhortation to Maximilla, Andrew finally appeals to her as a "wise man" (τοῦ φρονίμου ἀνδρὸς) with a "clearsighted mind" (εὔοψις νοῦς) and begs her to assist him in becoming perfect (τέλειος γένωμαι, Acts Andr. 41). It could be argued that Maximilla thus "becomes male," transformed through Andrew's words. She becomes male as a sign of her spiritual progress towards salvation. According to Kari Vogt the "sex-change metaphor" is common in early Christian literature (1995, 182). She notes that

> "becoming male" or becoming "perfect man" involves both sexes and refers to a metasexual sphere; "man" and "male" can therefore describe human nature (in what is common to the sexes) and relate to a state in which sex is transcended. "Woman" and "female" on the other hand always refer in such contexts to the inferior beings in this world. All this literature redefines and spiritualizes the category "sex": belonging to one or the other sex is not something given; it has to be achieved by the inner man, in this context, "sex" depends on spiritual progress, and it has a decisive role in attaining salvation. (1995, 183)

As Vogt observes, the sex-change metaphor is a spiritualized usage of the category *sex*. Maximilla's designation as a man signals her spiritual progress toward salvation. In contrast to Eve, whose mind fell because she was swayed by passion (Acts Andr. 37), Maximilla is described as having a clear-sighted mind that stands firm (41). Her "becoming male" moreover serves to effeminize and ridicule her husband Aegeates, who is portrayed as less than a woman in his rage, fear, and sensuality. However, even though she is called a "wise man," she is also still female, as the images of her marriage to Christ and her role as a second Eve indicate.

It is clear that Maximilla's conversion also signifies a display of male features. We may recognize the ancient protocols of masculinity in the description of her male characteristics. As a man she has a rational mind and controls her body (Ivarsson 2007, 156–166). However, she does not become a perfect man in every respect. For example, she does not dominate others except her slaves, and she does not speak outside the house. On the contrary, she remains quiet and dutiful even after her conversion. She just shifts in allegiance from one husband to another. She goes from her husband's authority to Christ's (that is, to Andrew who functions as his earthly representative). Throughout the story she is obedient to Andrew's words: she listens rather than speaks and always seeks his advice.

When Maximilla leaves the prison after Andrew's speech, his words have transformed her: "For when she heard the words that applied to her and in some way was changed by them, she became what the words signified [γενομένη τοῦτο ὅπερ οἱ λόγοι ἐδείκνυον]" (Acts Andr. 46). It is at this point that Maximilla finally has worked up the courage to defy her husband. She goes directly from the prison to Aegeates's *praetorium* and tells him that she will not sleep with him. Aegeates then decides that Andrew will be crucified. When Maximilla becomes "what the words signified," it means that she takes on the chastity that Andrew has preached. Maximilla's transformation is an embodiment rather than an articulation of her salvation. In contrast to Stratocles, who gives birth to saving words and starts to speak them, Maximilla's transformation is a *mute* act, displayed by her actions. Rather than birthing her understanding in discourse, her understanding has to be transformed into something physical, something bodily. Andrew's words are transcribed onto her chaste body. Thus, Maximilla's marriage to Christ is not as fruitful as Stratocles's childbearing is. While Maximilla embodies words, Stratocles generates words. In the narrative Stratocles is transformed, growing into a new community leader after Andrew's death. Maximilla continues her patronage role, but the narrative emphasizes her continued bodily integrity, as she rejects Aegeates's sexual invitations until he commits suicide.

Maximilla is addressed as both man (ἀνήρ) and human being (ἄνθροπος) in Andrew's speech, and she is also described as a new Eve. Kenneth Wagener asks whether the Acts of Andrew conveys "the idea of a restoration of the pristine innocence and return to Paradise" (1991, 354). Does Maximilla overcome the primordial gender divide and restore the "androgynous image" according to Gen 1:26–27 (see Meeks 1972, 185–89)? I suggest that the Acts of Andrew is neither interested in eschatology nor in cosmic restoration of the fall but rather in the individual's conversion and salvation. For this reason, the passage ends with an exhortation stressing that everyone should correct his or her own fall (Acts Andr. 37).

As already noted, the idea that salvation entails understanding (gnosis) is important in the Acts of Andrew, and so the verb γνωρίζω occurs frequently. Sometimes, it refers to an act of God, who recognizes or knows a believer ("we have been recognized by him," Acts Andr. 33; "The person who belongs to Jesus and who has been recognized by him in the end cannot be punished," Acts Andr. 55). Sometimes, the verb refers to the act of the believer, who understands or recognizes his or her true place in the universe ("The savior through whom we have recognized the destroyer," Acts Andr. 33; "You may recognize your true nature," Acts Andr. 41). Salvation thus seems to entail some form of *mutual recognition* by both believer and deity, mediated by the apostle. This emphasis on gnosis, on the knowledge that "the kindred" have received from Andrew, grounds the Acts of Andrew firmly as part of the Western esoteric tradition.

According to the Acts of Andrew, the achievement of gnosis is possible for all believers, male as well as female. Maximilla, although secured in her femininity through the imagery of marriage with Christ, also achieves male understanding (νοῦς, Acts Andr. 41). There is thus no ontological difference between male and female. Still, there is a gender difference in how such an understanding should be embodied and articulated. Thus, Maximilla's sexual continence is emphasized. However, not only is there a gender difference, class also plays a role in the embodiment of salvation. In this respect it should be noted that Iphidama, Maximilla's faithful slave, does not experience any transformation toward maleness in her conversion. For instance, the short prayer that Andrew offers on Iphidama's behalf, characterizes her as a courageous "fellow servant" (συνδούλος, Acts Andr. 29); there is no "becoming male" imagery. The same goes for Alcman, who is repeatedly called παίς (Acts Andr. 2; 3; 4), a word that can interchangeably refer to both children and slaves and thus deprives male slaves of their masculinity (Glancy 2002, 24). As a result, just like sexual renunciation, laudatory masculinity is an upper-class prerogative.

Conclusion

This intersectional reading of the Acts of Andrew has demonstrated that there are some inconsistencies in the encratite ideology of the text. Only in the case of Maximilla is *sexual renunciation* deemed necessary, while neither in the case of Stratocles and Andrew, the two believing men in the story, nor in the case of the slaves, is chastity a concern. *Masculinity*, as a marker of salvation, is also distributed unevenly among the characters. Both the upper-class man and the upper-class woman move towards maleness on the male-female continuum. As male philosophers, Stratocles and Andrew are close to becoming perfect men, while Maximilla balances her inner man and her outer woman. She deserves to be called man, due to her high understanding, but, as a woman, she is responsible for correcting the fall of Eve. A slave's salvation, however, does not depend on rising in any hierarchy, whether it is the male-female or the slave-free hierarchy, but in remaining obedient and staying in the socially defined place of a slave. Thus, *esoteric* is perhaps a better label than *encratite* to describe the soteriology of the Acts of Andrew.

Both male and female, slave and free, are included in the group surrounding Andrew. They are the receivers of esoteric knowledge and thus ultimately of salvation. There is nevertheless a difference between slave and free. Both Stratocles and Maximilla receive direct instruction from the apostle. The slaves, Alcman and Iphidama, are present but do not display any change in character or behavior. They are not transformed in the same way as the upper-class converts. They simply continue being good slaves. The soteriological economy of this text thus distributes different routes to salvation determined by gender and class. A hierarchy of bodies emerges. At the top are Andrew, the mediator of God's saving words, and Stratocles, who speaks words of salvation. On a middle level is Maximilla, who must become what the words signify through bodily chastity. At the bottom of the hierarchy are slaves, such as Iphidama and Euclia, whose bodies may be used for the purpose of their owners' pursuit of salvation. Hence, Iphidama's and Alcman's salvation is assured only through their submissive slave behavior. Euclia's salvation is of no concern to the narrator who does not lament her fate. Instead, her story serves as an instructive tale about a slave who wants too much.

The Acts of Andrew also displays characteristics typical of the Western esoteric tradition. Following Faivre's typology presented at the beginning of this article, I find three out of four characteristics. First, the idea of correspondences between the divine realm and the earthly is present in the typology that links Maximilla with Eve, Andrew with Adam and Christ, and finally Aegeates with the devil. As I have argued, the references to the fall do not regard it as a past event, but rather as a cosmic reality that has consequences in the present. Second, the notion of spiritual intermediaries that act as a ladder between the upper and lower worlds is present in the importance given to the apostle Andrew. The apostle's role can hardly be overemphasized. Without Andrew's "saving words" (Acts Andr. 9), there is no salvation. Finally, the idea of the soul's transformation through reawakening is found in the emphasis on gnosis and the recognition of eternal truths through Andrew's preaching. The soteriology found in the Acts of Andrew may be called a salvation by *mutual recognition*, wherein the believer understands his or her cosmic situation through gnosis and, simultaneously, is recognized and reclaimed by God as his own, his "kindred."

The stories about Adam and Eve from Gen 2–3 were popular in early Christianity. Different groups interpreted and used the stories about creation and the fall in different ways. When it comes to the Acts of Andrew's reading of Genesis, the Jewish-Christian *topos* about Eve's illicit sex with the serpent is used. This tradition is in line with the proto-orthodox emphasis on Eve as weak and easily deceived. However, the text also resembles Nag Hammadi sources that depict the story of the fall as a myth to be reenacted rather than as a historical tale. This reading is an esoteric interpretation of Gen 2–3, in which the main characters of the narrative reenact the primordial drama. When Maximilla, the new Eve, chooses Andrew, that is, Christ, instead of Aegeates, "the snake," she succeeds where Eve failed—she corrects the fall (Acts Andr. 37).

Works Cited

Bolyki, János. 2000. Triangles and What is Beyond Them: Literary, Historical and Theological Systems of Coordinates in the Acts of Andrew. Pages 70–80 in *The Apocryphal Acts of Andrew*. Edited by Jan N. Bremmer. Leuven: Peeters.

Bovon, François. 2000. The Words of Life in the Acts of Andrew. Pages 81–95 in *The Apocryphal Acts of Andrew*. Edited by Jan N. Bremmer. Leuven: Peeters.

Cooper, Kate. 1996. *The Virgin and the Bride: Idealized Womanhood in Late Antiquity*. Cambridge: Harvard University Press.

Elliott, J. K., ed. 1993. *The Apocryphal New Testament: A Collection of Apocryphal Christian Literature in an English Translation*. Oxford: Clarendon.

Faivre, Antoine. 1993a. Ancient and Medieval Sources of Modern Esoteric Movements. Pages 1–70 in *Modern Esoteric Spirituality*. Edited by Antoine Faivre and Jacob Needleman. London: SCM.

———. 1993b. Introduction. Pages xi–xxii in *Modern Esoteric Spirituality*. Edited by Antoine Faivre and Jacob Needleman. London: SCM.

Glancy, Jennifer A. 2002. *Slavery in Early Christianity*. Oxford: Oxford University Press.

Goodrick-Clarke, Nicholas. 2008. *The Western Esoteric Traditions: A Historical Introduction*. Oxford: Oxford University Press.

Hanson, Anthony Tyrell. 1968. *Studies in the Pastoral Epistles*. London: SPCK.

Harrill, James Albert. 2003. The Domestic Enemy: A Moral Polarity of Household Slaves in Early Christian Apologies and Martyrdoms. Pages 231–54 in *Early Christian Families in Context: An Interdisciplinary Dialogue*. Edited by David L. Balch and Carolyn Osiek. Grand Rapids: Eerdmans.

Hobgood-Oster, Laura. 1999. Another Eve: A Case Study in the Earliest Manifestations of Christian Esotericism. *Esoterica* 1:48–60.

Hock, Ronald F., ed. 1995. *The Infancy Gospels of James and Thomas*. Scholars Bible 2. Santa Rosa, Calif.: Polebridge.

Isenberg, Wesley W., trans. 1990. The Gospel of Philip. Pages 141–60 in *The Nag Hammadi Library in English*. Edited by James M. Robinson and Richard Smith. San Francisco: HarperSanFrancisco.

Ivarsson, Fredrik. 2007. Vice Lists and Deviant Masculinity: The Rhetorical Function of 1 Corinthians 5:10–11 and 6:9–10. Pages 162–84 in *Mapping Gender in Ancient Religious Discourses*. Edited by Todd C. Penner and Caroline Vander Stichele. Leiden: Brill.

Justin Martyr. 2001. *Dialogue with Trypho*. Translated by Philip Schaff. *ANF* 1. Grand Rapids: Christian Classics Ethereal Library.

Klauck, Hans-Josef. 2008. *The Apocryphal Acts of the Apostles: An Introduction*. Translated by Brian McNeil. Waco, Tex.: Baylor University Press.

Lampe, G. W. H. 1961. *A Patristic Greek Lexicon*. Oxford: Clarendon.

Luttikhuizen, Gerard P. 2003. Gnostic Ideas about Eve's Children and the Salvation of Humanity. Pages 203–17 in *Eve's Children: The Biblical Stories Retold and Interpreted in Jewish and Christian Traditions*. Edited by Gerard P. Luttikhuizen. Leiden: Brill.

MacDonald, Dennis Ronald, trans. 1990. The Acts of Andrew. Pages 326–441 in *The Acts of Andrew and the Acts of Andrew and Matthias in the City of the Cannibals*. Texts and Translations 33. Christian Apocrypha Series 1. Atlanta: Scholars Press.

———. 1994. *Christianizing Homer: The Odyssey, Plato, and the Acts of Andrew*. New York: Oxford University Press.

McCall, Lesley. 2005. The Complexity of Intersectionality. *Signs* 30:1771–1800.

Meeks, Wayne A. 1972. The Image of the Androgyne: Some Uses of a Symbol in Earliest Christianity. *HR* 13:165–208.

Nasrallah, Laura S. 1999. "She Became What the Words Signified": The Greek Acts of Andrew's Construction of the Reader-Disciple. Pages 233–58 in *The Apocryphal Acts of the Apostles*. Edited by François Bovon, Ann Graham Brock, and Christopher R. Matthews. Cambridge: Harvard University Center for the Study of World Religions.

Nasrallah, Laura, and Elisabeth Schüssler Fiorenza, eds. 2009. *Prejudice and Christian Beginnings: Investigating Race, Gender, and Ethnicity in Early Christian Studies*. Minneapolis: Fortress.

Osiek, Carolyn. 2003. Female Slaves, *Porneia*, and the Limits of Obedience. Pages 255–74 in *Early Christian Families in Context*. Edited by David L. Balch and Carolyn Osiek. Grand Rapids: Eerdmans.

Pagels, Elaine. 1989. *Adam, Eve, and the Serpent*. New York: Vintage.

Pearson, Birger Albert. 1990. Cain and the Cainites. Pages 95–107 in *Gnosticism, Judaism, and Egyptian Christianity*. Edited by Birger Albert Pearson. Minneapolis: Fortress.

Perkins, Judith. 1995. *The Suffering Self. Pain and Narrative Representation in the Early Christian Era*. New York: Routledge.

Pervo, Richard I. 1994. Early Christian Fiction. Pages 239–54 in *Greek Fiction: The Greek Novel in Context*. Edited by J. R. Morgan and Richard Stoneman. New York: Routledge.

Pesthy, Monika. 2000. Aegeates, the Devil in Person. Pages 47–55 in *The Apocryphal Acts of Andrew*. Edited by Jan N. Bremmer. Leuven: Peeters.

Prieur, Jean-Marc, ed. 1989. *Acta Andreae*. CCSA 5–6. Turnhout: Brepols.

———. 1991. The Acts of Andrew: Introduction. Pages 104–18 in *New Testament Apocrypha*. Edited by Wilhelm Schneemelcher and R. McL. Wilson. Cambridge: James Clarke.

Reyes, Paulina de los, and Diana Mulinari. 2005. *Intersektionalitet: Kritiska reflektioner över (o)jämlikhetens landskap*. Stockholm: Liber.

Robinson, James M., and Richard Smith, eds. 1990. *The Nag Hammadi Library in English*. San Francisco: HarperSanFrancisco.

Rodman, Rosamond C. 1997. Who's on Third? Reading Acts of Andrew as a Rhetoric of Resistance. *Semeia* 79:27–43.

Schroeder, Caroline T. 2006. The Erotic Asceticism of the Passion of Andrew: The Apocryphal Acts of Andrew, the Greek Novel and Platonic Philosophy. Pages 47–59 in *A Feminist Companion to the New Testament Apocrypha*. Edited by Amy-Jill Levine with Maria Mayo Robbins. London: T&T Clark.

Schwartz, Saundra. 2007. From Bedroom to Courtroom: The Adultery Type-Scene in the Acts of Andrew. Pages 267–311 in *Mapping Gender in Ancient Religious Discourses*. Edited by Todd Penner and Caroline Vander Stichele. Leiden: Brill.

Solevåg, Anna Rebecca. 2013. *Gender and Class in Early Christian Childbearing Discourse*. Leiden: Brill.

Söder, Rosa. 1969. *Die apokryphen Apostelgeschichten und die romanhafte Literatur der Antike*. Darmstadt: Wissenschaftliche Buchgesellschaft.

Versluis, Arthur. 2002. What is Esoteric? Methods in the Study of Western Esotericism. *Esoterica* 4:1–15.

Vogt, Kari. 1995. "Becoming Male": A Gnostic and Early Christian Metaphor. Pages 170–86 in *Image of God and Gender Models in Judaeo-Christian Tradition*. Edited by Kari Elisabeth Børresen. Minneapolis: Fortress.

Wagener, Kenneth C. 1991. "Repentant Eve, Perfected Adam": Conversion in the Acts of Andrew. Pages 348–56 in *Society of Biblical Literature 1991 Seminar Papers*. Atlanta: Scholars Press.

Imperial Propaganda in Paradise? Christ as Eagle in the Apocryphon of John*

Tuomas Rasimus

According to the classic gnostic[1] revelation treatise, the Apocryphon of John, Christ appeared to Adam and Eve in the guise of an eagle and influenced them to eat of the tree of knowledge to attain salvation:

> I appeared in the form of an eagle on the tree of knowledge, which is Reflection from the Providence of pure light, that I might teach them and awaken them out of the depth of the sleep. For they were both in a fallen state and they recognized their nakedness. (Ap. John 2, 23.26–33)[2]

Although animal symbolism attached to Christ was fairly common in early Christianity—famous examples include the lamb of God, the lion of Judah, and the fish (ἰχθύς)—the idea of Christ as an eagle is a rare one. While, for example, Hippolytus explained that an eagle with spread wings can symbolize Christ on the cross with stretched hands (*Antichr.* 61),[3] and Pseudo-Ambrosius of Milan could compare a soaring eagle to the resurrected Christ ascending back to the Father (*Sermon* 46.1–2), the Apocryphon of John does not give any apparent explanation as to why Christ

* This essay is based on a paper I read at the Christian Apocrypha section of the 2009 Society of Biblical Literature Annual Meeting. I wish to thank the anonymous gentleman in the audience for his questions and comments that made me rethink and improve some of my arguments. Thanks are also due to Jean-Michel Roessli and the editors of this volume for helpful comments and to Tim Pettipiece for improving my English.

1. For a definition of Gnosticism, see the section "The Apocryphon of John and Gnosticism" below.

2. The translations of the Apocryphon of John are from Waldstein and Wisse 1995.

3. Similarly Acts Phil. 3.5–9 (see below for discussion).

should have assumed an eagle's form in paradise. What is more, Genesis does not know of eagles in Eden, nor is such an idea attested in the writings of the New Testament. Even other classic gnostic texts related to the Apocryphon of John do not depict the revealer as an eagle, but rather as having used the serpent as a vehicle. In fact, the idea of Christ in the form of an eagle in paradise seems to be confined to the Apocryphon of John.[4]

Eagle symbolism in itself, of course, abounded in the Greco-Roman world, including Second Temple Judaism and early Christianity. The eagle was the bird of Zeus and Jupiter, a divine messenger, a sign of military and imperial power, one of the four living creatures around the throne of YHWH, and so forth. In interpreting the Apocryphon of John's eagle symbolism and discussing various parallels, I make use of Umberto Eco's theory of the model reader and its concept of the cultural encyclopedia. In the following, I first discuss the Apocryphon of John and its eagle episode. I then consider other scholars' interpretations of the eagle symbolism in question, and in so doing, I search for a better explanation in the cultural encyclopedia of the Apocryphon of John. Finally, I discuss the ritual implications of my interpretation. But before entering the discussion about the eagle, a few words are needed on the definition of Gnosticism.

The Apocryphon of John and Gnosticism

The Apocryphon of John is generally considered a chief representative of so-called Sethian Gnosticism—often considered the earliest and classic form of Gnosticism, represented by sixteen documents from Nag Hammadi and related codices, as well as from heresiological literature.[5] In Sethian Gnosticism, Adam's third son Seth often appears as an important savior figure.[6] After the attacks on the term and category *Gnosticism* by

4. The idea itself that Christ appeared in paradise, as well as various forms of Adam Christology, were common in early Christianity. See Rasimus 2009, 176–77.

5. Apocryphon of John (NHC II,1; III,1; IV,1; BG 8502,2), Hypostasis of the Archons (NHC II,4), Gospel of the Egyptians (NHC III,2; IV,2), Apocalypse of Adam (NHC V,5), Three Steles of Seth (NHC VII,5), Zostrianos (NHC VIII,1), Melchizedek (NHC IX,1), Thought of Norea (NHC IX,2), Marsanes (NHC X), Allogenes (NHC XI,3), Trimorphic Protennoia (NHC XIII), the Untitled text in the Bruce Codex, and the accounts of Irenaeus, *Haer.* 1.29 ("Barbeloites") and Epiphanius, *Pan.* 26, 39, and 40 ("libertine gnostics," "Sethians," and "Archontics," respectively). See Schenke 1981.

6. On Sethianism, or Classic Gnosticism, see especially Schenke 1981, as well as Sevrin 1986; Layton 1987; Pearson 1990; Turner 2001; and Rasimus 2009.

Michael Williams (1996) and Karen King (2003, 1–19, 218), many scholars have been reluctant of speaking of Gnosticism and may, for example, speak simply of *Sethianism*. While Williams suggests we abandon the misused term and category Gnosticism completely and start afresh with a new one, *biblical demiurgy* (in itself an artificial category), King is still ready to speak of Gnosticism as long as one clearly defines the purpose, nature, and discursive situation of the term.

I agree that to use Gnosticism as a wide umbrella term for a large variety of—or to treat it as identical with—"heretical" forms of Christianity is inappropriate. However, from Clement of Alexandria's own testimony and from other heresiological literature,[7] we know that many Christians in antiquity did claim the title *gnostic* for themselves. In addition, Sethian and closely related teachings became generally known as teachings of *the* gnostics already in antiquity, because their influential opponents, Irenaeus and Epiphanius, reserved the term gnostic specifically for Sethian and related myths.[8] If we thus are entitled, as I believe, to use the term gnostic of the Apocryphon of John and closely related texts, it seems to me, however, that the standard definition of Sethianism—developed by Hans-Martin Schenke (1974, 1981)—is in need of revision.

I have recently argued that the Sethian corpus should not only be expanded but also that the Sethian mythology consists of *three* distinct clusters of mythological ideas that are attested in various combinations in texts of the expanded corpus: (1) "Sethite" speculations about the biblical Seth, (2) "Barbeloite" speculations about the first principles in middle- and neoplatonic fashion, and (3) "Ophite" speculations about the

7. For Clement, see especially Lilla 1971. For the purported self-designations, see Irenaeus, *Haer.* 1.25.6; Hippolytus, *Haer.* 5.2; 5.6.4; 5.11.1; and Epiphanius, *Pan.* 31.1.1–5. A certain Justin (in Hippolytus, *Haer.* 5.28.1) was labeled "pseudognostic" by the heresiologists, which suggests that he had called himself a gnostic.

8. Irenaeus's list of heresies culminates in three entries (in *Haer.* 1.29–31), which he simply labels "gnostics," "others (among gnostics)," and "yet others (among gnostics)." All previous entries in the catalog received a specific name from Irenaeus, such as the teachings of Simon, Mendander, Saturninus, or Marcion. Even certain followers of Marcellina that reportedly called themselves gnostics (1.25.6) are rather labeled *Marcellinians* and *Carpocratians* by Irenaeus. Epiphanius does the same. Even though he says that many heresiarchs such as Basilides and Valentinus were really gnostics (*Pan.* 31.1.1–5), Epiphanius reserves the title gnostic for one specific entry in his catalog of eighty heresies, that of *Pan.* 26, which is generally considered to contain Sethian teachings.

rewritten Genesis paradise story.[9] The Apocryphon of John includes elements from all three clusters, including Ophite paradise material where the eagle appears. The main features of the Ophite mythology, based on a reversed paradise exegesis of Gen 1–3, are: (1) eating from the tree of knowledge is considered positive, although the snake is usually distinguished from the true revealer; (2) seven archons with specific names (Yaldabaoth, Yao, Sabaoth, Adonaeus, Eloeus, Oreus, and Astaphaeus, or the like) appear; (3) Sophia/Eve figures make up the female aspect of the true Godhead; and (4) heavenly man/Adam figures make up the male aspect of the true Godhead. I call this expanded and remodeled Sethian corpus the "classic gnostic" corpus.[10] Thus, I use the term *gnostic* as a convenient reference tool, to denote a constructed corpus that includes texts whose advocates became known as *the* gnostics in antiquity. Instead of Sethianism—which only reveals part of a larger whole—one should speak of Classic Gnosticism whose chief representative is the Apocryphon of John.

The Eagle in the Apocryphon of John

The Apocryphon of John exists in four Coptic manuscripts, two of which represent the so-called short recension (NHC III,1; BG, 2) and the other two the so-called long recension (NHC III,1; IV,1). The eagle (ἀετός) appears both in the short and long recension. While both recensions relate

9. The strange-sounding names are borrowed from heresiologists, although I use them somewhat differently, as convenient reference tools. See Rasimus 2009, 9–62.

10. In addition to Schenke's Sethian texts, I include the following ones in my classic gnostic corpus: On the Origin of the World (NHC II,5; NHC XIII,2; British Library Or. 4926[1]), Eugnostos the Blessed (NHC III,3; V,1), Sophia of Jesus Christ (NHC III,4; BG,3; Oxyr. 1081), Irenaeus, *Haer.* 1.30, and Origen, *Cels.* 6.24–38. Ophite material is also attested in the Sethian Hypostasis of the Archons, Apocryphon of John, and Epiphanius, *Pan.* 26. See Rasimus 2009, esp. 9–62. Schenke's original (1974) list of Sethian features contains: (1) the self-understanding of the gnostics that they are the pneumatic seed of Seth; (2) Seth as the heavenly-earthly savior of his seed; (3) the heavenly triad of Father, Mother Barbelo, and Son Autogenes; (4) the four lights of the Son called Harmozel, Oroaiel, Daveithe, and Eleleth, who are also dwelling places of heavenly Adam, Seth, and his seed; (5) the evil creator god Yaldabaoth who tries to destroy the seed of Seth; and (6) the division of history into three ages and the appearance of the savior in each age, related to the four lights of Autogenes. Schenke added more features later (1981).

that a divine being in the form of an eagle appeared in paradise and taught Adam and Eve to eat of the tree of knowledge (II,23.26–35 par.), it is only the long recension that identifies this being as Christ (II,23.26–27).[11] The short recension, which in all likelihood is the earlier one,[12] identifies this being as a "reflection (ἐπίνοια) of light," a spiritual Eve. However, apart from the different identities of the eagle, the two recensions relate the primordial drama in a very similar manner. The following recapitulation applies to both recensions. Unless a distinction between the two is required, I will simply speak of the Apocryphon of John or its author in the singular—by "author" I mean the empirical author, not the model author.[13]

The whole text is framed as a revelation from the risen Christ to John, son of Zebedee. The revelation begins with a description of the divine fullness on top of which there is a supreme triad of the Father, Mother Barbelo, and their son Christ Autogenes. After the emanation of all the divine entities is complete, the youngest divinity, Sophia, acts rashly. She gives birth to a demonic hybrid of a lion and a snake, who is called Yaldabaoth and who represents both YHWH and the devil.[14] This demonic creator then takes a great divine power from Sophia and produces offspring, the archons, to whom he boasts to be the only, jealous God (cf. Isa 46:9) (II,9.25–11.22 par.). The supreme Godhead (Father in the short recension, the Mother Barbelo in the long recension) intervenes and reveals its own luminous human image (εἰκών) in the primordial waters (II,14.13–34 par.). Yaldabaoth and the archons see the image and decide to create Adam after the divine model they have seen (cf. Gen 1:26–27). They construct a body out of soul-substance (cf. Gen 2:7), but it remains lifeless (II,15.1–29; 19.10–15 par.).

---

11. "I appeared in the form of an eagle." The first person singular identifies the speaker with Christ of the frame story.

12. E.g., Waldstein 1995, 388–93; Barc and Painchaud 1999; Turner 2001, 141.

13. On the model author, see the section "Eagles in the Cultural Encyclopedia of the Apocryphon of John" below.

14. Yaldabaoth is YHWH: he claims to be the only God (II,13.8–9 par.; cf. Isa 46:9); he breathes the spirit into Adam (II,19.23–32 par.; cf. Gen 2:7); he puts Adam in paradise (BG 55.18–20 par.; II has here the rulers in plural; cf. Gen 2:15); and he casts him out with Eve (II,24.6–7 par.; cf. Gen 3:23–24). Yaldabaoth is the devil: he is called Samael (only in the long recension: II,11.16–18 par.), which is the devil's name in Tg. Ps.-J. Gen 4:1–2; Midr. Rab. Exod 18:5; Midr. Rab. Deut 11:10; Ascen. Isa. 2:1–2; 7:9; and he rapes Eve (II,24.8–34 par.), a deed attributed to the devil in Tg. Ps.-J. Gen 4:1–2; b. Yebam. 103b; b. Šabb. 146a.

Sophia, for her part, wants to rescue the power Yaldabaoth took from her and begs for the true God's help. By a holy "decree" (ⲱⲟϫⲛⲉ; II,19.19 par.), the merciful supreme Godhead (Father in the short recension, Barbelo in the long recension) sends luminaries[15] to fool Yaldabaoth into blowing the stolen, spiritual power into Adam—a play on Gen 2:7. When Adam receives the power, he immediately becomes luminous and wiser than his creators (II,19.15–20.7 par.). The archons become jealous of Adam and cast him into the lowliest matter (II,19.34–20.9 par.), which probably means the mortal body in which Adam and his spiritual power are later said to have been imprisoned (II,20.35–21.13 par.). The merciful true God, on the other hand, has sent Adam a helper (βοηθός; cf. Gen 2:18) who is a "reflection (ἐπίνοια) of light" and life (ζωή; cf. Gen 3:20). This spiritual Eve is hidden inside Adam and teaches him about his origin and salvation and restores him to his perfection (II,20.9–28; 22.3–7 par.). She is identified as the tree of knowledge itself (II,22.3–5 par.).

Yaldabaoth, for his part, wants to regain the divine power he lost to Adam by bringing it out of his rib. The Apocryphon of John stresses that things did not happen as Moses told them.[16] The "trance" (ἔκστασις, LXX Gen 2:21) did not result in actual sleep (LXX: ὕπνωσεν) but in veiled perception, and in reality the woman was not created out of Adam's rib, but out of his power. When Adam first sees the newly created woman, the reflection immediately lifts the veil over his mind (II,22.18–23.16 par.). As the reflection is identified both as a spiritual Eve (inhabiting now the earthly Eve created by Yaldabaoth) and the tree of knowledge, the Genesis stories of Adam's awaking from the sleep and his eyes opening after eating of the tree, have here been combined. Already in Genesis, Eve was present at both of Adam's "awakenings," and here in the Apocryphon of John these two events have become one due to an appraisal of Eve's role as a savior figure.

Although Yaldabaoth had suppressed Adam's divine light and thinking through the creation of the mortal body and the veiling of his mind, reflection restored Adam's perfection and awakened his thinking, a message that

15. Autogenes and the four luminaries (Harmozel, Oroiael, Daveithe, and Eleleth, see BG 32.19–34.9 par.) in the short recension (BG 51.8–10; the text of NHC III seems slightly corrupted here, but appears to be closer to the long version), five luminaries in the long recension (II,9.18–19 par.).

16. Christ repeatedly tells John that "it was not as Moses said" (II,13.19–20; 22.22–24; 23.3–4; 29.6–7 par.).

the Apocryphon of John keeps repeating (II,20.9–28; 22.3–7; 23.26–35 par.). According to the Apocryphon of John, the snake had nothing to do with this revelatory event and only taught Adam and Eve to eat out of wickedness. Instead, there was an eagle on the tree, which taught Adam and (the earthly) Eve to eat of knowledge so that they might remember their perfection because they had fallen into ignorance (II,22.9–15; 23.26–35 par.). While the identity of the eagle is different in the two recensions, as noted earlier, both recensions do state that Christ orchestrated the events leading to Adam and Eve's eating (II,22.9 par.).

The tree of knowledge—that is, reflection—is further juxtaposed with the so-called tree of life, which in reality is a tree of death. This tree of death is also a counterfeit spirit of the archons (II,21.16–22.9 par.). As such, it is the opposite of the spirit of life, which equals the divine presence in Adam/humanity, that is, reflection. Thus, while eating of the archontic tree of life leads to the acquisition of the counterfeit spirit, eating of the tree of knowledge leads to the acquisition of the spirit of life—the tree of knowledge is simultaneously the *real* tree of life. In a section that follows later in the text, John asks Christ about the fates of human souls. Christ explains that those who have the spirit of life will be saved, but those into whom the counterfeit spirit enters will fall into ignorance. Such people can, however, be brought back to saving knowledge through providential care (ἐπισκοπή) and proper teaching (II,25.16–27.21 par.). Only apostates, who abandoned the knowledge they had acquired, are condemned (II,27.21–31 par.).

Such exegesis and rewriting of the first chapters of Genesis is common in gnostic texts containing Ophite material (e.g., Hypostasis of the Archons, On the Origin of the World, and Irenaeus's sources in *Haer.* 1.30). However, all these texts apart from the Apocryphon of John explain that the revelation was mediated to Adam and Eve through the serpent: it was either an unwitting instrument of Sophia (*Haer.* 1.30) or of the Spirit (Hypostasis of the Archons), or the true teacher was simply called the "beast" by the lying archons (without having used the serpent or assumed a serpentine shape, as in On the Origin of the World).[17] With the serpent present in the text of Genesis itself, one needs to ask why the Apocryphon of John depicts the revealer in the shape of an *eagle*.

17. Similar interpretations are also hinted at in Origen, *Cels.* 6.27–28 and in Epiphanius, *Pan.* 26.2.6. For details, see Rasimus 2009, 65–101.

Eagles in the Cultural Encyclopedia of the Apocryphon of John

The interpretation of this symbolism requires "inferential walks" into the cultural encyclopedia (Eco 1979, 31–33) in which the Apocryphon of John was produced. While the encyclopedia contains *all* of a given culture's formulations, including its literature and art (both "high" and "low" forms),[18] and as such is potentially infinite, a text is a limited instantiation of the encyclopedia and actualizes only certain parts of it (Eco 1979, 18–19, 23; 1984, 80). The reader's first task is to identify the historical period in which a text was produced in order to read it in light of the correct encyclopedia (Eco 1979, 16–17; 1990, 5, 59–60). In the case of the Apocryphon of John, we know it is a Christian text probably written in the second century C.E. somewhere in the Roman Empire.[19]

Eco, situating himself between radical "open" reader-response and "closed" structuralist interpretative methods,[20] also assumes that each text has its own embedded intention (*intentio operis*), which guides its interpretation (Eco 1979, 9; 1990, 52). At given points, a text may intend the model reader[21] to actualize specific items from the cultural encyclopedia. The model reader interprets the text as he or she goes by taking the aforementioned walks into the cultural encyclopedia and decides which parts of the encyclopedia are to be actualized as relevant and which parts should be kept "narcotized" as unessential (Eco 1979, 23). These decisions are often based on a further reading of the text. When a potential explanation to a given textual problem is found, for example, through the actualization

18. Apart from literature, also visual arts and "lower" art forms such as newspaper comic strips are included in the encyclopedia, see Eco 1979, 21–22, 70–72.

19. While the Coptic manuscripts come from the fourth (Nag Hammadi) and fifth (BG 8502) centuries, Irenaeus (*Haer.* 1.29) paraphrased a version of the Apocryphon of John ca. 180 C.E.—either in Rome or in Lyons—and the Greek *Vorlagen* of the four Coptic versions are customarily dated to the second century. Possible places of composition include Alexandria, Rome, or Asia Minor, perhaps Ephesus. See Tardieu 1984, 10, 37–39; Turner 2001, 257–92; King 2006, 10; Rasimus 2009, 259–77. See also Logan 1996, 26–69, 191, 283.

20. Huizenga 2009, 23. My use of Eco is influenced by Leroy Huizenga's monograph on Isaac typology in the Gospel of Matthew.

21. The model reader is an ideal construct by the author, "a model of the possible reader … supposedly able to deal interpretatively with the expressions in the same way as the author deals generatively with them" (Eco 1979, 7).

of a specific intertextual frame,[22] the model reader tests this hypothesis in light of the narrative context (Eco 1979, 32; 1990, 59, 148–49). If it does not make sense, a new walk is required. If it does make sense, a working hypothesis is found, which may be further confirmed (but also disproved) by other sections of the text. This theoretical framework allows the consideration of a wide range of parallels (including such that might otherwise go unnoticed, like popular art forms), but effectively limits their use to only those that make sense in light of the narrative context, thus providing protection from "parallelomania" (see Huizenga 2009, 11, 21–41).

In what follows, I first discuss the two principal solutions that have been proposed for the Apocryphon of John's eagle imagery. The first solution is advanced by Bernard Barc. In his forthcoming commentary on the long recension of the text, Barc suggests that the Apocryphon of John, claiming the authority of John son of Zebedee, makes here a conscious allusion to John's animal symbol, the eagle. That the four living creatures around the throne of God (lion, ox, man, eagle), known, for example, from Ezek 1:10 and Rev 4:7, became identified with the four canonical evangelists is well-known (see, e.g., Culpepper 1994, 167–68, 260, 292). There was, however, considerable variance among early Christian authors in connecting the four living creatures with the four evangelists, and John was not always connected with the eagle (see Culpepper 1994, 167–68; Osborne 2002, 232–36). What also makes Barc's suggestion unpersuasive is the fact that John's authority, or visions of the throne of God, do not seem very relevant for making sense of the Apocryphon of John's paradise story, because it is not John who is the eagle, but reflection or Christ.

A second solution is proposed by István Czachesz, who has argued that Christ's eagle shape here would be an example of the tradition of Christ's metamorphoses encountered in other early Christian literature and that, specifically, the Apocryphon of John's eagle symbol would be based on Homer, whose gods could occasionally change themselves into birds (Czachesz 2007, 162–82). Apollo and Athena could appear as vul-

22. On "common" and "intertextual" frames, see Eco 1979, 20–22. For Eco, "intertextuality" approximates the encyclopedia (1984, 187) and includes not only texts, but also, for example, movies, comic strips, and pictures (see, e.g., 1979, 21–22, 70–72). Huizenga (2009, esp. 43–74), working specifically with the Gospel of Matthew and ancient Judeo-Christian Isaac traditions, clarifies Eco's theory with respect to intertextuality by evoking—and slightly modifying—Richard Hays's (1989) seven criteria of scriptural echoes.

tures sitting on a tree (e.g., *Iliad* 7.58–61), and Athena—whose well-known attribute was the owl—could also assume the shape of a swallow (*Odyssey* 22.239–40). Zeus could change himself into a swan to seduce Leda or into an eagle to abduct Ganymede and Europa, as is the case on some Cretan coins (Czachesz 2007, 162, 169–70).[23] However, the suggested Homeric metamorphoses do not seem to clarify the meaning of the Apocryphon of John's episode, and one does not find here meaningful echoes of the stories about Leda, Ganymede, or Europa either. The model reader can therefore narcotize the bird traditions proposed by Barc and Czachesz, because, although present in the cultural encyclopedia, they do not illuminate the Apocryphon of John's eagle episode in a satisfactory way.

Czachesz has, on the other hand, gathered and discussed a large amount of sources—both Greco-Roman and Judeo-Christian—that deal with eagles (Czachesz 2007, 162–82), and I will briefly go through them (and some additional evidence) here in order to assess whether any of them might shed light on the Apocryphon of John's symbolism. In antiquity, eagles often appeared as messengers from gods, especially from Zeus/Jupiter, but also from YHWH—even though the eagle (*nesher; ἀετός*) was counted among the unclean animals in Deut 14:12. In Rev 8:13, an eagle proclaims, "Woe, woe, woe to the inhabitants of the earth, at the blasts of the other trumpets that the three angels are about to blow!" (NRSV). In 2 Baruch (77; 87), the eponymous scribe sends his letters by an eagle, and in 4 Bar. 6.15–7.23, possibly dependent on 2 Baruch (Herzer 1994, 72–77), an angel of YHWH sends an eagle to deliver Baruch's letter promising deliverance from the Babylonian captivity to Jeremiah. The eagle awaits Jeremiah on a post or a tree (ξύλον), asks him to gather the people, and revives a corpse as a sign so that the people might believe that the same God who appeared to them through Moses during the Exodus from Egypt is still with them. An allegorical story with similarities can be found in the Syriac version of the Hymn of the Pearl (see Poirier 1981 and Drijvers 2003). In this text, a prince left his homeland for Egypt to snatch a pearl from a serpent, but instead became enslaved through oblivion. The king sent him a letter to awaken him from his deep sleep. The letter flew like an eagle and became a word whose voice awoke the prince. He remembered who he was and seized the pearl for which he had come. The prince then

23. Usually, however, Zeus was thought to have abducted Europa in the form of a bull.

put off his filthy clothes and set out for a journey toward his true home, guided by the letter.

Both 4 Baruch and the Hymn of the Pearl speak of an eagle as a divine courier who awakens a sleeper/corpse and is connected to deliverance from Egypt. However, one can also detect interesting parallels in the Hymn of the Pearl to the eagle episode in the Apocryphon of John. While the divine messenger is not, or does not carry, a letter, it is, nonetheless, compared to an eagle that awakens a sleeper by reminding him of his origins. Moreover, the sleeper's enemy in both texts is the serpent, although the serpent's roles are somewhat different in the two texts. Drijvers interprets the Hymn of the Pearl as an allegory of Adam's departure from paradise where he returns after the Exodus (2003, 331–32).[24] In addition, the removing of clothes in the Hymn of the Pearl may well be a baptismal allusion, and the long recension of the Apocryphon of John contains clear baptismal language (see below). Unfortunately, the respective dates of composition of these two texts are not known with accuracy—perhaps the best we can say is that both probably come from the second century C.E.[25] Therefore, it lies within the realm of possibility that the author of the Apocryphon of John knew the Syriac Hymn of the Pearl and was influenced by it. If, however, a conscious intertextual allusion to or an echo of the Hymn of the Pearl was intended in the Apocryphon of John, the model reader would expect to find something in it that, in the words of Richard Hays, would "illuminate the surrounding discourse" and "produce for the reader a satisfying account of the effect of the intertextual relation" (1989, 31).

I fail to see how the allegory of the Hymn of the Pearl, which is at least one more step removed from Genesis than the Apocryphon of John, would illuminate the paradise story in the latter. That the "gnostic call" to awakening was addressed prototypically to Adam and related to baptismal imagery is certainly not restricted to these two texts. The serpent's presence can be explained on the basis of Gen 3, and the two authors may well have developed their respective eagle symbols independently of each other, out

24. Drijvers sees the parables of the Prodigal Son (Luke 15:11–32) and the Pearl (Matt 13:45–46) being here interpreted in light of Gen 3 and Exodus, but he also views the Hymn of the Pearl as a general allegory of humanity's expulsion from and return to paradise/immortality after Satan's power is conquered through Jesus's gospel.

25. For the second-century date of the Apocryphon of John, see above. For the date of the Hymn of the Pearl in the late second or early third century, see Drijvers 2003, 330–33.

of different materials. In fact, the eagle in the Hymn of the Pearl is a *letter* that is delivered to someone in the *Egyptian captivity*. These motifs are missing from the Apocryphon of John, but are known from traditions surrounding the figure of Baruch. However, the motif itself of the eagle as a messenger does seem relevant for the Apocryphon of John's imagery, and I will return to this idea below.

Another theme that occurs in certain early Christian texts is that of the eagle with spread wings symbolizing Christ on the cross. The Acts Phil. 3.5–9[26] relates how the apostle Philip sat under a tree when he saw an eagle, whose wings were spread like the true cross. This turned out to be a manifestation of Jesus, who "spoke to Philip as if from the mouth of the eagle" (ὁ δὲ Ἰησοῦς τῷ Φιλίππῳ ὡς ἐκ στόματος τοῦ ἀετοῦ εἶπεν; 3.8.1).[27] Hippolytus, commenting on Rev 12:14 ("But the woman was given the two wings of the great eagle," NRSV),[28] compares the eagle's two wings to Christ with stretched hands on the cross:

> The Church … possessed of no other defence than the two wings of the great eagle, that is to say, the faith of Jesus Christ, who, in stretching forth His holy hands on the holy tree, unfolded two wings, the right and the left, and called to Him all who believed upon Him, and covered them as a hen her chickens. (*Antichr.* 61)

Czachesz also points out certain artifacts (a fourth-century sarcophagus, a seventh-century stele) that depict an eagle sitting on a cross (2007, 165–66), although it is not certain that in these cases the eagle actually stands for Christ. While both the tree of life and tree of knowledge could symbolize Christ's cross in other early Christian texts,[29] the Apocryphon of John does not seem to assign any importance to the crucifixion, nor does the text speak of stretched wings. Thus, the parallels concerning Christ's stretched hands on the cross do not seem very relevant to the interpretation of the

26. Text in Bovon, Bouvier, and Amsler 1999, 89–95.

27. Amsler believes that 4 Baruch might be a source of this episode, as Baruch and Philip were both considered scribes (1999, 172).

28. Revelation 12:14 may refer to Exod 19:4: "You have seen what I did to the Egyptians, and how I bore you on eagles' wings and brought you to myself" (NRSV).

29. Tree of life: e.g., Justin Martyr, *Dial.* 86; Clement of Alexandria, *Strom.* 5.72.2–4; Gos. Phil. II,73.8–19; *Teach. Silv.* VII,4.106.21–22. Tree of knowledge: e.g., Gos. Truth I,3.18.21–31; Gos. Phil. II,74.1–12; see also Irenaeus, *Haer.* 5.19.1; 5.23.1–2.

Apocryphon of John's eagle episode, and the model reader may narcotize them as well.

In still other early Christian texts, Christ appears as an eagle to fight the devil. In the Acts of Xanthippe and Polyxena 17–18, a certain Probus has a dream in which an eagle seizes the kingdom from a king who rules the world (and whose weakness is symbolized by a raven), destroys the king's power with a staff, and protects and washes those who flee from the king. The wise men Barandus and Gnosteas explain that the king is the devil, the eagle is Christ, and the staff is the cross.[30] Pseudo-Ambrose of Milan (*Sermon* 46.1–2), commenting on Prov 30:19, explains that the eagle in the sky and the snake on the rock are Christ and the devil: Christ, after his resurrection, soared back to the Father like an eagle and protects his church with his wings like an eagle its nest, having killed the serpentine devil. The notion of the hostility between eagles and snakes with the eagle being victorious was common currency in the Greco-Roman world.[31] Because this notion is missing from the passage in Proverbs, Pseudo-Ambrose seems to have read it in there, no doubt guided by the traditional Judeo-Christian idea of the devil as a serpent[32] and the Christian notion of Christ as his conqueror. Also in the Apocryphon of John, the eagle is an enemy of the serpentine Yaldabaoth, who stands for both YHWH and the devil. While the notions of the eagle as the conqueror of the serpent and a messenger from God seem to account for some aspects of the Apocryphon of John's symbolism, they alone cannot completely explain it. There is, however, one important parallel in the Apocryphon of John's encyclopedia, which completes the picture and provides a satisfactory overall interpretative frame.

Since the Apocryphon of John was in all likelihood written within the borders of the Roman Empire during the principate, one should look at Roman eagle symbolism, especially the imperial one. The eagle had become an important symbol of Rome's military power already during the republic. According to Pliny the Elder (*Nat.* 10.16), Gaius Marius (in 104 B.C.E.) rejected other, previously used animal images and chose the eagle as the sole standard for the legions (Czachesz 2007, 170–71). Pliny continues

30. As Czachesz (2007, 165) points out, similar eagle dreams are found in Ezek 17 (where two eagles stand for Babylon and Egypt), 4 Ezra 11–12, and the Acts Thom. 91.

31. See, e.g., Aristotle, *Hist. an.* 609a4; Pliny the Elder, *Nat.* 10.17; Virgil, *Aen.* 11.751–757; Cicero, *Div.* 1.106. See Küster 1913, 52–55, 127–28.

32. E.g., Rev 12:9; Wis 2:24; Gos. Phil. NHC II,61.5–10; 2 En. 31; 3 Bar. (Slavonic) 4:8; Justin, *Dial.* 103.

(10.17) with the story known throughout the Greco-Roman world about an eagle defeating a serpent. Moreover, the Romans saw the eagle as a messenger from Jupiter, and through augury its flight could be interpreted, for example, as an omen of victory or ascension to power. Suetonius relates how an eagle enfolded Domitian's statue on the day of his victory over Lucius Antonius (*Dom.* 6) and how an eagle landed on Claudius's shoulder (*Claud.* 7) when he entered public life (Peppard 2009, 232).

Augustus's life was full of bird omens.[33] In his youth, an eagle once snatched bread from his hands, ascended high, and then returned the bread (Suetonius, *Aug.* 94.6). The rupture between Augustus (Octavian), Antony, and Lepidus was foretold by an eagle defeating two ravens on top of Augustus's tent (*Aug.* 96). Augustus's death and future divinity was likewise revealed by an eagle. While sacrificing in the Campus Martius, an eagle flew several times around Augustus and then landed on the first letter of Agrippa's name inscribed on the temple. At the same time, a flash of lightning melted away the first letter of his own name (Caesar) from an inscription of his statue and this was taken to mean that he would only have a hundred days left to live (*Aug.* 97). But most importantly, an eagle was released from Augustus's funerary pyre and was thought to take the dead emperor to heaven with Jupiter (Dio Cassius 56.34, 42). This practice became standard for imperial funerals, and the motif appeared in imperial iconography. By adopting the theme of an eagle as a psychopomp,[34] especially for the rich and the powerful (see Artemidorus, *Oneirocritica* 2.20), the imperial propaganda made the king of birds a vital part in the process of the emperor's (and the empress') apotheosis, which was itself decreed by the Senate.[35]

The role of the eagle in the imperial apotheosis finally throws sufficient light on the Apocryphon of John's symbolism. In the Apocryphon of John, the eagle teaches Adam and Eve to eat from the tree of knowledge

33. For these and other Roman bird omens, see Peppard 2009, 231–35.

34. See Cumont 1917, 35–71; Friedman 2000, 50–52, with additional bibliography in note 22. Gradel (2002, 316–20), however, thinks Augustus himself may have invented the concept of an eagle as a psychopomp, as the presence of the concept in pre-Augustan evidence is somewhat unclear.

35. While in iconography the empress could ascend with the help of a peacock—it was the bird of Hera/Juno, just as the eagle was the bird of Zeus/Jupiter—in actual practice an eagle must have been released from the funerary pyre, since peacocks do not fly very well. Some monuments, such as the statue base of Antonius Pius (see below), indeed depict an eagle aiding the empress to ascend (Gradel 2002, 307–10).

that awakens their thinking and leads them to perfection and salvation; this makes Adam and Eve better than their creators by virtue of possessing the previously suppressed but now activated divine light and intelligence. In other words, *the eagle here plays a crucial role in what amounts to an apotheosis of Adam and Eve*. Let us take a closer look at the imperial apotheosis and the eagle's role in it.

Apotheosis and Worship of the Emperor

The study of emperor worship has undergone major developments in recent years, most notably by Simon Price (1984) and his student Ittai Gradel (2002). Price, by discarding Christianizing views of God and religion, revolutionized the research on emperor worship by showing that the divinity of the emperor was a matter of relative power, not of absolute essence. Price also showed how local elites competed for the building of officially sanctioned provincial temples to gain social prestige and influence (see, e.g., 1984, 62–65, 89–90, 122–32, 234–48). Price concentrated on the worship in the province of Asia Minor, and many scholars have added pieces to the puzzle by concentrating on other provinces[36] or other sectors of society.[37] Nonetheless, until a few years ago, the common assumption was that while the living emperor could be worshipped in provinces, this did not happen in Italy or Rome itself where only dead emperors were given divine honors. However, Gradel has convincingly shown that also the living emperor was worshipped in Rome and that his worship there took place in every context other than the official, "constitutional" state cult.[38]

Throughout the empire, the worship of the emperors—often including the living emperor and occasionally other members of the imperial family alongside several posthumously deified emperors—took many forms

36. For a bibliography, see Peppard 2009, 79.

37. For example, Harland (2003) has studied the role that associations, including Jewish synagogues and Christian congregations, played in the worship of the emperor.

38. According to Gradel (2002, e.g., 142–44), the main reason that the worship of the living emperor was excluded from the official cult was the strong association between deification and death: Caesar had been murdered soon after he had been declared a god, and Augustus and Romulus had been declared gods only after their deaths. Presumably the emperors felt uneasy about this association and hence refused *official* divine honors during their lifetime, but felt comfortable as long as the worship took place in the private sphere.

(sacrifice, hymns, prayers, etc.), existed on many levels (state, provincial, municipal, private), and was considered a natural part of the web of power relations in society. What matters for the present purpose is that "good" emperors, and sometimes empresses, were not only widely considered divine already during their lifetime, but were posthumously *decreed* gods (*divus*/*diva*) by the Senate, with an eagle released from the funerary pyre to symbolically take the emperor or the empress to heaven.

Most scholars have not accepted Dio Cassius's description (56.34, 42) according to which the release of the eagle was performed already at Augustus's funeral, although there is a consensus that the practice became standard at some later point.[39] What seems to support the authenticity of Dio's description, however, is the existence of the iconography of the eagle apotheosis already in the first century C.E. The evidence discussed by Gradel includes: (1) a coin (ca. 36 C.E.) showing a radiate head of the deified Augustus on the obverse and an eagle with spread wings on the reverse; (2) a cameo (ca. 54 C.E.) depicting Claudius's apotheosis with the emperor sitting on the back of an eagle soaring heavenwards; (3) the statue base of Antoninus Pius (d. 161 C.E.), where the emperor and empress Faustina Maior sit on the back of the god Aion and ascend to heaven aided by two eagles; and (4) examples of private funerary monuments from the first and second centuries where the imperial imagery has been mimicked (2002, 291–95, 305–20).

To this evidence, one should add (5) the Arch of Titus (ca. 85 C.E.) in the Roman Forum—not to be confused with the Arch of Titus that once stood in the nearby Circus Maximus[40]—showing the deified Titus on the back of an eagle. Whether or not Dio's description of the release of an eagle at Augustus's funeral is anachronistic—and together with Gradel, I believe it is not—the iconography of the eagle apotheosis was, in any case, well established in the first century C.E. It is important to note, however, that the eagle rite was simply a part of the process of the apotheosis since the deification was actually decreed by the Senate (Gradel 2002, 261–371). The Senate's decree was what ultimately mattered, although the eagle remained symbolically important (299–304).[41] In addition, since the emperor was

39. Suetonius does not mention the eagle (*Aug.* 100.4) in his earlier description, so Dio might be anachronistic. See Gradel 2002, 291–304.

40. On the arch in the circus, see Humphrey 1986, 97–100.

41. Sometimes the formal decree was issued before and sometimes only after the

widely seen as divine already during his lifetime, the Senate's decree, together with the eagle rite, merely confirmed or fulfilled his divinity.

Just like the emperor and empress, Adam and Eve were already inherently divine, according to the Apocryphon of John, but it was the eagle and its message that led them to salvation and to the restoration or fulfillment of their divine nature. Thus, themes of the eagle as a divine messenger and a psychopomp[42] are here combined with its role as a helper in the process of apotheosis (the divine nature of humanity having already been decreed by the supreme Godhead's decision to send luminaries to fool Yaldabaoth into blowing the lost divine power into Adam). Symbolism relating to imperial apotheosis was in all likelihood common knowledge, at least in Rome itself, and quite possibly in the provinces as well. Therefore, it was very likely known to the author of the Apocryphon of John and was, in fact, an important part of the cultural encyclopedia. The model reader should thus actualize the frame "imperial Roman eagle symbolism" to interpret the Apocryphon of John's eagle symbolism. This frame not only includes the notion of the eagle as a helper in the process of apotheosis, but also the ideas of the eagle as a messenger from god, as an enemy of the serpent, and as a psychopomp (all ideas well-known to the Romans). While the parallelism is not exact, I believe it is close enough to warrant the idea that the Apocryphon of John is making use here of a concept borrowed from the imperial propaganda. What is more, the theoretical framework of *colonial mimicry* can explain why the concept differs from its imperial archetype.

Ritual Implications

Although developed in the context of modern European and American colonialism, various forms of postcolonial theory can provide fruitful results when applied to the study of early Christianity in the Roman Empire.[43] According to postcolonial theorist Homi Bhabha, colonial power

---

funeral and its eagle rite. In any case, the *decision* to deify the emperor had already been made before the funeral by the Senate, following the emperor's will.

42. On Christ as a psychopomp, see Friedman 2000, 38–85.

43. Among others, see Friesen's study (2001, theoretical discussion on 15–22) on emperor worship and Revelation with insights from Edward Said's seminal postcolonial writings (1978; 1994), as well as Liew's article (1999) on the Gospel of Mark and colonial mimicry; and Peppard's dissertation (2009), where he argues that the Gospel of Mark presents Jesus's baptism in terms of colonial mimicry of the adoption of the

produces "mimicry" (1994, 85–92, 112–14, 120–21).[44] On the one hand, the Western colonizer, as part of the authoritative discourse, represents the colonized as mere "mimic men" who are "almost the same [as Westerners], but not quite." On the other hand, such discourse enables resistance on the part of the colonized, because it simultaneously allows their own "denied knowledges to enter upon the dominant discourse" (Bhabha 1994, 114). Mimicry can also be construed as a form of critique, where the colonial power is fought with its own terms:[45] the colonized adapts and reproduces (i.e., mimics) the discourse of the colonizer while renouncing it. The adaptation is *almost the same, but not quite.*[46]

Seen in this perspective, the Apocryphon of John seems to mimic the imperial eagle symbolism and present an alternate version of it. It is not just the members of the imperial family who can fully actualize their divinity with the help of the eagle, but *all* who have the spirit of life and eat of the tree of knowledge. This is, in theory, open to everyone because even those in whom the counterfeit spirit has entered will be saved once they have acquired the proper knowledge.[47]

How does one, then, come in the possession of the spirit of life and eat of the tree of knowledge? First, both the short and long recensions of the Apocryphon of John place emphasis on proper teaching, which can be acquired from someone who already possesses the spirit of life (BG 69.12–70.8 par.). The chain of transmission goes back to Christ who

emperor as a son of god (the most famous example of which was the adoption of Octavius [Augustus] by Caesar).

44. See also the discussion in Young 2004, 181–98.

45. One can, of course, mimic the dominant culture without criticizing it. See Peppard 2009, 82 n. 201. Williams (1996, 103–13) suggests that some second-century Christian groups, such as Valentinians, tended toward a low-tension sociocultural accommodation to the surrounding Greco-Roman culture, for example, by attending gladiatorial shows and making heavy use of Platonic philosophy in their teachings.

46. Peppard 2009, 245. The expression, "almost the same, but not quite," comes from Bhabha (e.g., 1994, 86, 89).

47. Only the apostates are denied salvation, and this, in a way, corresponds to the *damnatio memoriae* suffered by "mad" emperors, who, from the viewpoint of the Senate, had abused their powers and were denied apotheosis. (On the other hand, many "mad" emperors, e.g., Caligula, Nero, Caracalla—not all of them received the *damnatio memoriae*, though—were loved by the common people, because they built baths and were dedicated to the spectacles and the distribution of grain. See Mittag 1999, 133–37.) One, of course, does not need to evoke colonial mimicry to explain the damnation of apostates per se, but an interesting parallel, nevertheless, exists here.

taught John and asked him to pass on the content of the revelation to his fellow spirits who are from the immovable race (BG 22.2–16; 75.15–77.7 par.). However, already in the short recension there are hints at a baptismal context. The supreme God is the spring of living water (BG 26.15–27.1 par.), and before the creation of the world, he anointed his son Christ who thus became perfect (τέλειος) (BG 30.14–31.1 par.). Likewise, souls who receive the spirit of life will be saved and become perfect (τέλειος) (BG 65.3–6 par.).

The baptismal context, however, becomes much clearer in the long recension. It is also no accident that in the long recension the eagle is identified as Christ. Perhaps the most important difference between the short and long recensions of the Apocryphon of John is the concluding Providence Hymn at the end of the long recension (II,30.11–31.25 par.). This hymn—which is not without parallels to the prologue of the Fourth Gospel[48]—relates three descents of divine Providence, who is elsewhere in the text identified as Mother Barbelo (II,4.32). Since the concluding Providence Hymn is told in a first person singular, this effectively identifies Providence also with Christ, who likewise speaks in the first person singular in the narrative frame story. And indeed Christ tells John that the Father, Mother Barbelo, and the Son are ultimately one (II,2.13–15 par.). While the first two descents of Providence shook the foundations of chaos and she had to return to the light, her third descent culminates in a sleeper's awakening and baptism with five seals.

As Bernard Barc and Louis Painchaud have demonstrated (1999), the addition of the Providence Hymn has caused the author of the long recension of the Apocryphon of John to rewrite the paradise story in order to harmonize it with the hymn's three descents. According to Barc and Painchaud, the hymn's third descent is identified with the eagle's appearance in paradise.[49] In comparison to the short recension, the long recension of the Apocryphon of John presents a slightly different version of the

48. See Waldstein 1995; Rasimus 2009, 261–77; Turner 2010.

49. Barc and Painchaud (1999) identify the first two descents with the appearance of the luminous image of the supreme Godhead in the waters and with the advent of reflection as a helper to Adam, respectively. Turner (2010, 120) follows them in this regard, but identifies the third descent as Christ's appearance to John in the frame story.

eagle episode, and the differences clearly connect it with the hymn's third descent through verbal and thematic parallels:[50]

> Short Recension's (BG) Eagle Episode
> From the tree, in the form of an eagle, she [reflection] taught him [Adam] to eat of knowledge, so that he might remember his perfection, for both [Adam and Eve] had (undergone) the fall of ignorance.
>
> Long Recension's (NH II) Eagle Episode
> *I* appeared in the form of an eagle on the tree of knowledge, which is *Reflection from the Providence of pure light*, that I might teach them and *awaken them out of the depth of the sleep*. For they were both in a fallen state and they recognized their nakedness.

Christ here tells John that it was he ("I") who appeared as the eagle, which, first of all, allows the identification between the eagle and the first person speaker of the hymn. The long recension also connects reflection here with the "light of Providence," a theme recurrent throughout the concluding hymn (II,30.15, 23–24, 30–31, 33–34; 31.1–2, 11–12 par.). However, what specifically connects this episode with the *third* descent is that the Christ-eagle awakens Adam and Eve *from the depth of the sleep* (ⲃⲟⲗ ϩⲙ̄ ⲡϣⲓⲕ ⲙ̄ⲡϩⲓⲛⲏⲃ). This clearly evokes Providence's declarations in the course of her third descent, "He who hears, let him arise *from the deep sleep* (ⲉⲃⲟⲗ ϩⲙ̄ ⲫⲓⲛⲏⲃ ⲉⲧϩⲟⲣϣ)" (II,31.3–6 par.), and "Be watchful of *the deep sleep* (ⲡϩⲓⲛⲏⲃ ⲉⲧϩⲟⲣϣ)" (II,31.20–21 par.). In the hymn, the description of the third descent culminates in the sealing of the awakening one "in the light of the water with five seals in order that death might not have power over him from this time on" (II,31.23–25 par.). Closely related classic gnostic texts, such as the Gospel of the Egyptians (NH III,2; IV,2), describe this baptism of five seals in great detail.[51] What is more, the hymn's declaration, "He who hears, let him arise from the deep sleep," may be an allusion to Eph 5:14 ("Sleeper, awake! Rise from the dead, and Christ will shine on you!" NRSV), which in itself may be a fragment from a baptismal hymn.[52] Thus, having the spirit of life and eating of the tree of knowledge—two

---

50. For the comparison, see Barc and Painchaud 1999, 331.

51. On the Sethian baptism of five seals, see especially Sevrin 1986, as well as Schenke 1981, Turner 2001, and Rasimus 2009, 243–79.

52. Ferguson (2009, 316–17): "The quotation of Ephesians 5:14 … in a context of exhortation to 'become little children and be *regenerated* [ἀναγεννηθῆτε],' lends sup-

sides of the same coin—are baptismal images, at least in the long recension of the Apocryphon of John. Eating of the tree of knowledge is thus presented as a primordial prototype of the catechetical teaching leading to the baptism of five seals, which restores one's original, divine perfection (the spirit of life).

The image of the eagle was borrowed from imperial propaganda where it symbolically helped in the posthumous apotheosis of the emperor or the empress (which completed and officially accepted his or her inherent divinity). Since early Christian baptism generally was loaded with symbolism of death (and rebirth),[53] the eagle's presence at baptism does not seem out of place.

In the imperial propaganda, the eagle could also herald the adoption or ascension of the new emperor, the new "son of god," as noted above.[54] This raises the question whether in the Apocryphon of John, too, the eagle symbolism might have been borrowed from this aspect of the imperial propaganda. However, the narrative context of the Apocryphon of John rather seems to favor the apotheosis interpretation. Creation of the *mortal* body temporarily "deactivated" Adam's divine essence until he ate of the tree of knowledge; and Providence-Christ is said to have descended into Hades (II,30.35–31.1, 20–22 par.) and sealed the awakening one "in the light of the water with five seals in order that *death* might not have power over him from this time on." And although *Jesus's* own baptism in Jordan can be seen in terms of adoption or ascension, the baptism of *Christians* is rather connected with images of death and rebirth in various forms of early Christianity, including the Apocryphon of John.

To conclude, the author of the short recension of the Apocryphon of John probably invented the idea that the revealer appeared to Adam and Eve in the form of an eagle instead of a serpent. The idea was borrowed from the imperial propaganda—part of the cultural encyclopedia—according to which an eagle, as a psychopomp, took the emperor,

port to the suggestion that this passage in Ephesians quotes from a baptismal hymn" (emphasis original).

53. See Rom 6:1–14; Col 2:12; John 3:3–7; Herm. *Sim.* 9.16.1–6; Justin, *1 Apol.* 61.3; *Apos. Con.* 3.17.

54. Michael Peppard (2009, esp. 170–260) has argued that the Gospel of Mark presents Jesus's own baptism in terms of colonial mimicry: Jesus was the true Son of God, whose adoption was heralded by a bird of peace, the dove (and not the eagle, a symbol of Rome's military power). I think his basic argument is convincing.

and occasionally the empress, to heaven and thus helped in the process of apotheosis. Imperial Roman eagle symbolism also carried with it the notions of the eagle as a messenger from god and a victorious enemy of the serpent, and thus the activation of this interpretative frame is able to illuminate all the main aspects of the Apocryphon of John's eagle imagery. The author of the short recension of the Apocryphon of John mimicked the imperial eagle and presented an alternative version according to which *Christians* generally can attain divinity if they acquire proper, saving knowledge and probably also a special baptism. The author of the long recension of the Apocryphon of John made the baptismal connection clearer by adding the Providence Hymn to the text. Christ-Providence's final, third descent, which culminated in the sleeper's awakening from the deep sleep, accompanied by the baptism of five seals, came to be identified with Adam's awakening from his deep sleep with the help of the eagle. This meant that the eagle had to have been none other than Christ himself.

Works Cited

Amsler, Frédéric. 1999. *Acta Philippi: Commentarius*. CCSA 12. Turnhout: Brepols.

Barc, Bernard. Forthcoming. *Le Livre des secrets de Jean: Recension longue*. Bibliothèque copte de Nag Hammadi. Quebec: Presses de l'Université Laval.

Barc, Bernard, and Louis Painchaud. 1999. La Réécriture de l'Apocryphon de Jean à la lumière de l'hymne final de la version longue. *Le Muséon* 112:317–33.

Bhabha, Homi K. 1994. *The Location of Culture*. New York: Routledge.

Bovon, François, Bertrand Bouvier, and Frédéric Amsler, eds. 1999. *Acta Philippi: Textus*. CCSA 11. Turnhout: Brepols.

Culpepper, R. Alan. 1994. *John, the Son of Zebedee: The Life of a Legend*. Columbia: University of South Carolina Press.

Cumont, Franz. 1917. *Études Syriennes*. Paris: Picard.

Czachesz, István. 2007. "The Grotesque Body in Early Christian Literature: Hell, Scatology, and Metamorphosis." Habilitationsschrift, Ruprecht-Karls-Universität Heidelberg.

Drijvers, Han J. W. 2003. The Acts of Thomas: Introduction. Pages 322–39 in *Writings Relating to the Apostles; Apocalypses and Related Subjects*. Edited by Wilhelm Schneemelcher. English translation edited by Robert MacLachlan Wilson. Vol. 2 of *New Testament Apocrypha*. Revised Edition. Louisville: Westminster John Knox.

Eco, Umberto. 1979. *The Role of the Reader: Explorations in the Semiotics of Texts*. Bloomington: Indiana University Press.

———. 1984. *Semiotics and the Philosophy of Language*. Bloomington: Indiana University Press.

———. 1990. *The Limits of Interpretation*. Bloomington: Indiana University Press.

Ferguson, Everett. 2009. *Baptism in the Early Church: History, Theology, and Liturgy in the First Five Centuries*. Grand Rapids: Eerdmans.

Friedman, John. 2000. *Orpheus in the Middle Ages*. Syracuse, N.Y.: Syracuse University Press.

Friesen, Steven. 2001. *Imperial Cults and the Apocalypse of John: Reading Revelation in the Ruins*. Oxford: Oxford University Press.

Gradel, Ittai. 2002. *Emperor Worship and Roman Religion*. Oxford Classical Monographs. Oxford: Clarendon.

Harland, Philip. 2003. *Associations, Synagogues, and Congregations: Claiming a Place in Ancient Mediterranean Society*. Minneapolis: Fortress.

Hays, Richard B. 1989. *Echoes of Scripture in the Letters of Paul*. New Haven: Yale University Press.

Herzer, Jens. 1994. *Die Paralipomena Jeremiae: Studien zu Tradition und Redaktion einer Haggada des frühen Judentums*. Tübingen: Mohr Siebeck.

Huizenga, Leroy A. 2009. *The New Isaac: Tradition and Intertextuality in the Gospel of Matthew*. NovTSup 131. Leiden: Brill.

Humphrey, John H. 1986. *Roman Circuses: Arenas for Chariot Racing*. London: Batsford.

King, Karen L. 2003. *What is Gnosticism?* Cambridge: Belknap Press of Harvard University Press.

———. 2006. *The Secret Revelation of John*. Cambridge: Harvard University Press.

Küster, Erich. 1913. *Die Schlange in der griechischen Kunst und Religion*. Religionsgeschichtliche Versuche und Vorarbeiten 13. Giessen: Töpelmann.

Layton, Bentley. 1987. *The Gnostic Scriptures: A New Translation with Annotations and Introductions*. Garden City, N.Y.: Doubleday.

Liew, Tat-siong Benny. 1999. Tyranny, Boundary and Might: Colonial Mimicry in Mark's Gospel. *JSNT* 73:7–31.

Lilla, Salvatore R. C. 1971. *Clement of Alexandria: A Study in Christian Platonism and Gnosticism*. Oxford: Oxford University Press.
Logan, Alastair. 1996. *Gnostic Truth and Christian Heresy: A Study in the History of Gnosticism*. Peabody: Hendrickson.
Mittag, Peter F. 1999. *Alte Köpfe in neuen Händen: Urheber und Funktion der Kontorniaten*. Antiquitas Series 3: Abhandlungen zur Vor- und Frühgeschichte, zur klassischen und provinzial-römischen Archäologie und zur Geschichte des Altertums 38. Bonn: Habelt.
Osborne, Grant O. 2002. *Revelation*. Baker Exegetical Commentary on the New Testament. Grand Rapids: Baker Academic.
Pearson, Birger A. 1990. *Gnosticism, Judaism, and Egyptian Christianity*. SAC. Minneapolis: Fortress.
Peppard, Michael L. 2009. The Christian Son of God in the Roman World. Ph. D. diss., Yale University.
Poirier, Paul-Hubert. 1981. *L'hymne de la perle des Actes de Thomas: Introduction, Texte, Traduction, Commentaire*. Homo Religiosus 8. Louvain-la-Neuve: Centre d'histoire des religions.
Price, Simon R. F. 1984. *Rituals and Power: The Roman Imperial Cult in Asia Minor*. Cambridge: Cambridge University Press.
Rasimus, Tuomas. 2009. *Paradise Reconsidered in Gnostic Mythmaking: Rethinking Sethianism in the Light of the Ophite Evidence*. Nag Hammadi and Manichaean Studies 68. Leiden: Brill.
Said, Edward W. 1978. *Orientalism*. New York: Pantheon.
———. 1994. *Culture and Imperialism*. New York: Knopf.
Schenke, Hans-Martin. 1974. Das sethianische System nach Nag-Hammadi-Handschriften. Pages 167–73 in *Studia Coptica*. Edited by Peter Nagel. Berliner Byzantinistische Arbeiten 45. Berlin: Akademie-Verlag.
———. 1981. The Phenomenon and Significance of Gnostic Sethianism. Pages 588–616 in *Sethian Gnosticism*. Edited by Bentley Layton. Vol. 2 of *The Rediscovery of Gnosticism*. SHR 41. Leiden: Brill.
Sevrin, Jean-Marie. 1986. *Le dossier baptismal séthien*. Bibliothèque Copte de Nag Hammadi: "Études" 2. Quebec: Presses de l'Université Laval.
Tardieu, Michel. 1984. *Écrits Gnostiques: Codex de Berlin*. Paris: Cerf.
Turner, John D. 2001. *Sethian Gnosticism and the Platonic Tradition*. Bibliothèque Copte de Nag Hammadi: "Études" 6. Quebec: Presses de l'Université Laval.
———. 2010. The Johannine Legacy: The Gospel and *Apocryphon* of John. Pages 105–44 in *The Legacy of John: Second-Century Reception of the*

Fourth Gospel. Edited by Tuomas Rasimus. NovTSup 132. Leiden: Brill.
Waldstein, Michael. 1995. The Providence Monologue in the Apocryphon of John and the Johannine Prologue. *JECS* 3:369–402.
Waldstein, Michael, and Frederik Wisse, eds. 1995. *The Apocryphon of John: Synopsis of Nag Hammadi Codices II,1; III,1; and IV,1 with BG 8502,2*. Nag Hammadi and Manichaean Studies 33. Leiden: Brill.
Williams, Michael A. 1996. *Rethinking "Gnosticism": An Argument for Dismantling a Dubious Category*. Princeton: Princeton University Press.
Young, Robert J. C. 2004. *White Mythologies: Writing History and the West*. 2nd ed. New York: Routledge.

A Fitting Portrait of God: Origen's Interpretations of the "Garments of Skins" (Gen 3:21)

Peter W. Martens

The opening chapters of Genesis captivated Origen's scholarly attention throughout his literary career. His monumental thirteen volume *Commentary on Genesis* was his most ambitious philological study of Gen 1–3, although he also preached one homily on these chapters and dispersed brief exegetical notes on them throughout his voluminous writings.[1] Unfortunately, only scattered remains of the *Commentary on Genesis* survive today, due in large measure to the sixth-century condemnations of Origen and his followers. Yet despite the fragmentary evidence, the picture emerging from this lacunose work is that Origen was convinced that the opening scenes in Genesis coded "certain mysteries" through the semblance of historical events (*Princ.* 4.3.1).[2]

One of the most perplexing mysteries in the opening pages of Scripture was the episode that transpired after Adam and Eve's trespass in the garden of Eden: God ostensibly clothed this couple with "garments of skins" (Gen 3:21). Many years after finishing his *Commentary on Genesis*, Origen responded to Celsus's incredulity about this passage by insisting

1. Origen began his *Commentary on Genesis* around 229 while still in Alexandria and completed it around 234, after he had moved to Caesarea Maritima. For descriptions of its content, scope, and theological concerns, see Heine 2003, 63–73; Heine 2005, 122–42; Metzler 2005, 143–48. Among the remarks on Gen 1–3 found elsewhere in his writings, the lengthiest is his first homily on Genesis, delivered sometime in the 240s. For dates of these and other writings attributed to Origen, see Nautin 1977, 409–12.

2. See Görgemanns and Karpp, 1992, 732; *Princ.* 324.4. On the esoteric/exoteric distinction in Origen's thought, see Heine 2010, 222–26.

that it ought to be read allegorically, since it enjoyed "a certain secret and mysterious meaning [ἀπόρρητόν τινα καὶ μυστικὸν ἔχει λόγον]" (*Cels.* 4.40).

In the following essay, I reconstruct Origen's interpretation of these garments of skins.[3] However, this is a notoriously difficult task. The textual basis is meager, as there are only three passages in his surviving corpus that directly address his interpretation of these garments. Moreover, a later scholar, Theodoret of Cyrus, excised a promising fragment from Origen's *Commentary on Genesis*, but this excerpt almost certainly does not convey everything he wrote about the garments in that work.[4] The challenge of this scant evidence is further compounded by the daunting realization that Origen's views of the garments were implicated in some of his more enigmatic theological positions, in particular, his accounts of Edenic paradise and the preexistence, the fall, and the subsequent embodiment of souls. Yet what makes Origen's interpretation of these garments arguably most difficult to reconstruct is that he appears to have made conflicting statements about them, a point many scholars have overlooked.

The episode in which God clothed Adam and Eve with garments of skins had already elicited much commentary during Origen's day, both in Jewish and Christian circles.[5] Origen was aware of this exegetical plurality and wrestled (as far as we can determine) with four different interpreta-

---

3. For previous discussions of this topic, see Simonetti 1962, 370–81; Beatrice 1985, 448–54; Pisi 1987, 322–35; Vogt 1985a, 100–103; Noce 2002, 99–108; Dechow 1988, 315–33; Reuling 2006, 74–76; Tzvetkova-Glaser 2010, 98–108.

4. In his *Questions on the Octateuch* composed sometime in the 450s, Theodoret of Cyrus posed the question of how the garments of skins in Gen 3:21 should be understood (the thirty-ninth question). In his answer he juxtaposed two passages from earlier (and rivaling) exegetical traditions, both of which served as a foil for his own view. The first passage he attributed to Theodore of Mopsuestia, who argued that the garments were composed from the bark of trees; the second he attributed to Origen, who represented the allegorical view that these garments symbolized mortal flesh. The edited texts for these fragments can be found in Petit 1986, texts 120 and 121 (pp. 123–26). While we cannot simply assume on the authority of Theodoret that this latter fragment is authentically Origenian (it could, for instance, be attributed to a later Origenist), as Hermann-Joseph Vogt and several others have argued, there are many clues in this passage that suggest that it does, in fact, trace back to Origen. For the arguments, see Vogt 1985b, 86–87; Strutwolf 1993, 254 n. 265; Metzler 2010, 190 n. 260. I, too, accept this attribution and with most scholars suspect that this passage was excerpted from his *Commentary on Genesis*.

5. For discussions of the much debated garments in antiquity, see Smith 1965–1966, 217–38; Daniélou 1967, 355–67; Brock 1982, 11–40; Beatrice 1985, 433–84;

tions. As we will see below, two of these he rejected: a literal view that an anthropomorphic God fashioned actual garments out of animal hides for the first couple and an allegorical view that saw these "garments" as narrative symbols of mortality. Yet two he also endorsed: first, that God clothed Adam and Eve with literal animal hides, which in turn were symbolic of their mortality (a view conspicuously close to the two rejected interpretations above); and second, that these "garments" were an allegory of the bodies that God had given to originally discarnate human souls.

In the course of this essay, several questions arise from an examination of these four interpretations of Gen 3:21. Did Origen, in fact, make conflicting statements about the garments? What was the theological vision that his exegetical decisions promoted? And perhaps most interesting, what was the criterion he invoked to adjudicate between these disparate exegetical options? Since the textual basis for this topic is so thin, it is important to draw upon additional sources in attempting to answer these questions, beginning with the circumstantial evidence dispersed throughout his corpus. It is also helpful to sift through the hostile reports of his later critics, even if they recoiled at his interpretations of these opening chapters of Genesis and did not always present his views fairly. Finally, Philo's interpretation of Gen 3:21 plays a role. He appears to have shaped Origen's exegetical strategy and even suggested some of his own interpretive conclusions.

This essay has three sections. First I discuss Origen's allegorical interpretation of the garments. In two of the three passages where he commented directly on Gen 3:21, he endorsed the view that the "garments" referred figuratively to the bodies God bestowed on previously incorporeal souls. He proposed this interpretation in his *Commentary on Genesis* (a relatively early work), as well as in *Against Celsus* (one of his latest writings), thereby suggesting that it was an interpretation he considered viable throughout his scholarly career.[6] Second, I discuss the two interpretations of the garments that Origen explicitly rejected. In the final section, I turn to the third passage from the *Homilies on Leviticus* where he commented directly on Gen 3:21. Here he endorsed yet another interpretation that seemingly conflicted with the views he had earlier rejected.

Lambden 1992, 74–90; Valevicius 1995, 163–75; Anderson 2001a, 101–43; Anderson 2001b, 117–34; Reuling 2006, 74–76; Toepel 2010, 62–71.

6. On the dating of the *Commentary on Genesis*, see n. 1 above. *Against Celsus* is dated ca. 248 (Chadwick 1953, xiv–xv).

Position One: The "Garments of Skins" Symbolize Bodies

Origen opens his reflection on Gen 3:21 in the *Commentary on Genesis* by asking: "How ought one to understand the 'garments of skins [δερματίνους χιτῶνας]' " (124.2)?[7] His answer canvasses several interpretations that were in circulation in his day. One of these contended that the garments signified "nothing other than the body" (οὐκ ἄλλους εἶναι τοῦ σώματος; 125.7–8). This allegorical view had already achieved some prominence by the early third century. Origen does not mention who held it, but we know that Philo proposed that the garments pointed figuratively to human bodies (*QG* 1.53.).[8] Additionally, from the middle of the second century this same interpretation of the Edenic garments had been widely promulgated in Valentinian circles.[9] The attractiveness of this allegorical interpretation lay, no doubt, in the similitude between its referent—the body—and the actual garments. According to Genesis, these were not made from cloth but from the skins or *bodies* of animals, and thus to allegorize them as human bodies evidently did not come across as an artificial move to many interpreters.

Origen not only reported this allegory, he espoused it. There is a significant reception history of his interpretation of this verse that claims he endorsed this reading of the garments. Origen was a controversial figure at the turn of the fifth century. Among other things, he was presented as having a negative view of the body and an arbitrary reading of Genesis—thus the fixation on his interpretation of the garments as bodies only

7. All the translations below from this section of the *Commentary on Genesis* are mine, based on the critical edition of Petit 1986. This question is probably indicative of the genre of Origen's *Commentary on Genesis*: it belonged to the ancient "questions and answers" form of inquiry where problems concerning the biblical text were raised (either by commentators themselves or by others prior to them) and then subsequently answered. Recall Origen's description of the contents of his *Commentary on Genesis* in *Cels.* 6.49, where he summarizes his exegetical work on Gen 1:1–6 in terms of the questions he asked and answered. Note as well fragments from the *Commentary on Genesis* that reflect this genre: e.g., on Gen 1:14 (Metzler 2010, D7) or Gen 1:16–18 (Metzler 2010, D9). See esp. Perrone 1995, 151–64, and Heine 2003, 68.

8. See also *Alleg. Interp.* 3.22(69) and *Post.* 41(137). For this interpretation in later rabbinic circles, see Anderson 2001b, 124–26.

9. This view of the "garments of skins" was attributed to Valentinus (Hippolytus, *Haer.* 10.13.4), his pupils Ptolemy (Irenaeus, *Haer.* 1.5.5) and Theodotus (Clement of Alexandria, *Exc.* 55.1), as well as others (Clement of Alexandria, *Strom.* 3.95.2; Tertullian, *Res.* 7 and *Val.* 24.3).

bestowed as a result of/after sin. Two of his earliest critics, Peter of Alexandria and Methodius of Olympus, attributed this teaching to him, and toward the end of the fourth century, Epiphanius of Salamis and Jerome also repeatedly leveled this charge against him.[10] We should certainly be reticent about accepting at face value the reports of his critics. None of them acknowledged, for instance, that he debated alternative interpretations of this contentious passage or, as we will see below, that he elsewhere adopted a different view. But this evidence ought not to be summarily dismissed. Corroborating this *Rezeptionsgeschichte* are several pieces of evidence in Origen's own corpus that confirm his identification of these garments with bodies.[11]

Bodies in Paradise?

We begin with a clue in the previous extract from the *Commentary on Genesis*. Origen raises a single objection to the interpretation of the garments as bodies: while such an interpretation is "persuasive and able to gain approval," he writes, "it is not clear if it is true. For if these garments of skin are flesh and bone, how does Adam earlier say, 'This now is bone from my bones and flesh from my flesh'?" (125.8–12; see Gen 2:23). The objection concerns the prior embodiment of Adam and Eve. A surface reading of the Genesis narrative that precedes the bestowal of garments suggests that the first couple was *already* embodied before they were clothed with the garments of skins. Prime evidence for this is Adam's description of Eve as "bone from my bones" in Gen 2. But if this is the case, the objection runs, then it is hardly clear how one could interpret the bestowal of garments in Gen 3 as symbolic of the embodiment of Adam and Eve, since such an interpretation appears to make God bestow bodies redundantly on the first couple.[12]

10. See Procopius of Gaza, *Comm. Gen.* Gen 3:21; Methodius, *Res.* 1.4.2, 1.29.1; Epiphanius, *Anc.* 61.7–62.9; *Pan.* 64.4.9, 64.63.5–64.66.6; *Letter to John of Jerusalem* (= Jerome, *Letter* 51.5.2, 51.5.6); Jerome, *Jo. Hier.* 7.

11. It is significant that a noted *proponent* of Origen, Didymus, also read the garments as bodies. See Didymus, *Comm. Gen.* 106.10–254, 108.16, plus Reuling 2006, 72–77 and Layton 2007, 14–22.

12. Note that Tertullian earlier raised the same objection in *Res.* 7, as would Epiphanius (*Letter to John of Jerusalem* [=Jerome, *Letter* 51.5.2]), among others.

Toward the end of this fragment from the *Commentary on Genesis*, however, Origen offers two rebuttals to this objection, thereby strongly suggesting that he endorsed this allegorical interpretation of the garments of skins.[13] His first response to this critique is indirect, focusing not on the exegesis of "bone from my bones," but on the nature of the Edenic paradise. He contends that it was not a corporeal place and on this basis draws a conclusion about the constitution of its inhabitants. He writes: "But also if paradise is some sort of divine place [τι χωρίον ἐστίν], let them say how each of the body parts there which were not created in vain, performs its own proper activity" (125.20–23).

To help us interpret this argument, it is important to decipher Origen's view of paradise. This is difficult since he not only offered several different allegorical interpretations of it, but also entertained the notion of multiple paradises—Edenic, ecclesiastical, and eschatological—that are not easy to demarcate from one another. Nevertheless, his reflections on Eden demonstrate that it was *not* some corporeal place on earth to him.[14] In *Prayer*,

13. Tzvetkova-Glaser 2010, 103 argues that Origen "decidedly rejects" the allegorical interpretation of the garments as bodies in this fragment. This conclusion appears to rest upon a mistranslation (instead of the interpretation being "persuasive and able to gain approval," she renders it, "klingt dies plausibel, kann aber nicht überzeugen" ["this sounds plausible but does not convince"]). Borret reads the objection to this allegorical interpretation (based on the reference in Gen 2:23 to "bone from my bones") as coming from Origen himself (1981, 271). But this too is difficult since Origen claims this view of the garments is "persuasive" and defends it with his account of paradise as a divine place (more on this below). Most of the scholarship, in fact, sees Origen advocating bodies in this passage (Simonetti 1962, 370–81; Beatrice 1985, 448–54; Vogt 1985a, 101–3; Bammel 1989, 72; Dechow 1988, 316–18; Strutwolf 1993, 253–54; Heine 2010, 114). Note as well that Theodoret of Cyrus, who transmits Origen's fragment from the *Commentary on Genesis*, understood him in this extract to be endorsing the view that the garments referred to bodies (Vogt 1985a, 100–103).

14. Several scholars have argued, puzzlingly, that the Edenic paradise for Origen *was* a corporeal place here on earth. See esp. Rauer 1961, 253–29, who argued most staunchly for this position, though in fact he wrongly attributed his main evidence (a catena fragment on 258–59) to Origen. This fragment actually constituted part of Epiphanius's critique of Origen (Bammel 1989, 89 n. 46). Curiously, Edwards 2002, 119, esp. n. 93, follows Rauer's conclusion; moreover, Edwards reads Origen's fragment on Gen 3:21 as if he were *denying* paradise was a "divine place," whereas Origen actually asserts that it was so. Bockmuehl 2010, 204–6, also sees Origen situating the Edenic paradise on earth. Yet intriguingly, in the same volume his coeditor, Stroumsa, opposes this view, arguing that "Origen's position seems to deny any real 'historical' significance to the paradise story" (2010, 11). Others, notably Bammel, offer a slightly

for instance, Origen expounds on the opening phrase in the Lord's Prayer, "Our Father in heaven," and unequivocally rejects the idea that God is a corporeal being who resides in a correspondingly spatial-physical realm. He refers to his *Commentary on Genesis* where he dealt with the same problem—or rather, the absurdity—of an historico-geographic paradise in Eden in which God is portrayed as walking around in search of Adam (see Gen 3:8). Such a conception of Eden, Origen argues, would require that God be not only corporeal, but also modest in stature, as he would have been confined to such a diminutive place. Rather, Origen contends, the reference to God dwelling in paradise ought to be heard spiritually as follows: that God dwells among the saints in an incorporeal realm or simply in these saints (*Or.* 23.3–4; 25.3).[15]

We find a related passage in the second book of Origen's *Commentary on John*, written concurrently with his earlier volumes on the *Commentary on Genesis*. There he wrestles with the verse, "There was a man sent from God, whose name was John" (John 1:6; *Comm. Jo.* 2.175–192, Heine 1989). Origen is inquisitive about John's origin, since the gospel claims that he was already filled with the Holy Spirit in his mother's womb (Luke 1:15). Origen proposes a solution to the difficulty that a fetus is filled with the Holy Spirit and not, as is usual in the Bible, an adult by relying on a current philosophical theory concerning the soul, namely, "that it has not been sown with the body but exists before it and for various reasons is clothed with flesh and blood" (*Comm. Jo.* 2.182, Heine 1989). Here he alludes to his

different position: they contend that the Edenic paradise was in fact a real place for Origen, but not a place on this earth (1989, 63–64). Although this is not the place to survey the various interpretations of paradise, including the Edenic paradise, in Origen's writings, it seems to me that the evidence points strongly to the Edenic paradise as *not* being a corporeal place here on earth for him. Origen offers several unambiguous statements that reject precisely the literal interpretation that would see it as such (in addition to the passages discussed below, note his repeated denial that this paradise contained actual trees: *Princ.* 4.3.1; *Hom. Gen.* 2.4; *Comm. Gen.* [Metzler 2010, D18]; *Hom. Lev.* 16.4.1; *Cels.* 4.39). The only passage I have found where he explicitly speaks of any sort of paradise as a place on earth occurs at *Princ.* 2.11.6, but here he is referring to an *eschatological* paradise and not the Edenic paradise. I am, thus, more inclined to accept Bürke's conclusion that the paradise of Genesis was less a historical-geographic and more a religious reality (1950, 25 and 27; followed by Bietz 1973, 31–32). For an overview of some of the different interpretations of paradise in Origen's writings, still valuable are Rauer 1961 and Bürke 1950, esp. 25–28.

15. See also *Hom. 1 Reg.* 1.1; *Hom. Jer.* 1.16.3; *Cels.* 6.64.

account of the fall of preexistent souls and their subsequent embodiment. Origen argues that "John must have been sent from some other region when he was placed in a body.... John's soul, being older than his body and subsisting prior to it, was sent to the ministry of testimony concerning the light" (*Comm. Jo.* 2.180–181, Heine 1989). Origen then substantiates this claim by turning to Adam's dismissal from paradise in Gen 3:

> Perhaps just as it has been written of Adam, "And the Lord God sent him out of the paradise of pleasure to work the earth from which he was taken" (Gen 3:23) so also John was sent, either from heaven, or from paradise, or from whatever other place there may be besides this place on earth, and he was sent "that he might give testimony of the light." (*Comm. Jo.* 2.175–176, Heine 1989; see John 1:7)

The claim here, as in *Prayer*, is that the Edenic paradise was not to be envisioned as a place on earth, but as an incorporeal realm in which souls or minds, prior to their embodiment, dwelt in communion with God.[16]

Both of these passages help us understand what Origen meant when he called paradise a "divine place" in the *Commentary on Genesis.* His defense of the identification of the "garments" with bodies—against the view that earlier passages in Genesis already suggested corporeality—rested upon his conception of paradise as an incorporeal realm. "But also if paradise is some sort of divine place, let them say how each of the body parts there which were not created in vain, performs its own proper activity" (125.20–23).

Origen makes two points here. First, he stresses that the nature of paradise had ramifications for the constitution of its inhabitants. Since it was an incorporeal realm, it would have been impossible for its residents to have been *corporeal* creatures, for what could their "proper activity" as corporeal beings have been in an incorporeal realm? Second, Origen underscores how unfitting bodies in paradise were for his view of God. If

---

16. For a similar account of the Edenic paradise, see *Hom. Num.* 12.3.4 and esp. *Cels.* 4.40, which is discussed in more detail below. There the whole "human race" resided in paradise before it was given garments of skins and cast out into this corporeal world. This parallels *Princ.* 3.6.3, where Origen describes the eschatological Eden as the mind's engrossing contemplation of God, a final state that restores the condition of rational creatures when they resided in the protological Eden. On this interpretation of Edenic paradise, see Bürke 1950, 25–28; Bietz 1973, 31–34; and Ledegang 2001, 472.

God had created bodies for this divine paradise, it would have been done inappropriately, in other words, "in vain."[17] The strong implication in the *Commentary on Genesis*, then, is that whatever Gen 2:23 meant, it could not refer to bodies (i.e., literal bones and flesh) in a prelapsarian, incorporeal, paradisal realm. Rather, the bodies signified by the garments of Gen 3:21 were bestowed for the first time *after* souls had fallen and were about to depart this realm for the corporeal world.

The preceding argument is Origen's first reply to the objection that bodies had already been present in paradise prior to the fall and bestowal of "garments." Further below I will turn to his second, and more direct, response to this objection. There we will see his alternative exegesis of those passages that suggested Adam and Eve were corporeal prior to the gift of their garments. But in order to appreciate this exegetical move, it is important to first turn to the passage in *Against Celsus* where he again develops the interpretation of the Edenic garments as bodies. This passage not only mirrors his earlier interpretation in the *Commentary on Genesis*, but it also gives us a clearer picture of the larger theological narrative that this association of the garments with bodies bolstered.

Gen 3:21 and the Doctrine of Preexistence

In the preceding discussion of the Edenic paradise, and particularly in the passage from *Against Celsus* to which I now turn, Origen strongly insinuates that the garments symbolized the bestowal of bodies on previously incorporeal souls. In other words, he links Gen 3:21 to his doctrine of preexistence. This doctrine, or drama, played a significant role in his theology.[18] Concisely sketched, Origen claimed that God, through the agency of his Word or Wisdom, fashioned a number of incorporeal rational beings ("intelligent natures," "minds," or "souls"). These were equal and alike to one another and endowed with the power of choice. In their prelapsarian state of bliss, they lived in an original unity and harmony as they contemplated God and divine Wisdom. With the notable exception of Jesus's soul, most, if not all, other souls fell away from their contemplative state. Whether through sloth, weariness, or satiety, they abandoned their first activity in varying degrees of severity and in so doing immersed

17. For a similar reading of this passage, see Vogt 1985a, 101–2.

18. For important literature on Origen's doctrine of the preexistence of souls, see Gasparro 1978, 45–82; 1981, 231–73; Harl 1985, 238–58.

themselves in varying degrees of evil. A just judgment ensued, in which God used the newly emerged postlapsarian heterogeneity as a source for creating a corporeal world various and diverse. This corporeal world became the abode of fallen minds, who took up residence there in newly fashioned bodies.[19]

Origen searched for biblical passages, especially in the opening chapters of Genesis, that directly or symbolically indicated some facet of his doctrine of preexistence.[20] As he saw it, the Edenic vestments God gave the inhabitants of paradise after their fall fortuitously symbolized bodies bestowed on previously incorporeal souls in the heavenly paradise. In book four of *Against Celsus*, he insists against his critic that the events recorded in the opening chapters of Genesis should be understood allegorically. Adam, he claims, does not have to refer exclusively to a single individual. According to its etymological sense, after all, "Adam" means "humanity" (ἄνθρωπος), and "that in what appears to be concerned with Adam Moses is speaking of the nature of man," that is, the whole, populous "human race." Moreover, it was this race that sinned in paradise and, as a result, was cast out of the garden. As the passage continues, Origen describes this dismissal by referring to the "garments of skins" (Gen 3:21) in a way that suggests he sees these as bodies. He writes:

> And the statement that the man who was cast out of the garden with the woman was clothed with "coats of skins" (Gen 3:21), which God made for those who had sinned on account of the transgression of mankind, has a certain secret and mysterious meaning, superior to the Platonic doctrine of the descent of the soul which loses its wings and is carried hither "until it finds some firm resting-place." (*Cels.* 4.40, Chadwick)

According to this passage, the whole human race was given "garments of skins" when it was cast out of paradise on account of its transgression. Since this statement in Genesis has a "certain secret and mysterious meaning," we can almost certainly eliminate the mundane, literal interpretation of these skins as actual animal hides. The implication, based upon the reference to the similar Platonic doctrine, is that these garments stand

19. Versions of this narrative can be found esp. in *Princ.* 1.6.2; 1.8.1–2; 2.1.1; 2.6.3–6; 2.8.3–4; 2.9.1–2, 5–6.

20. I have developed this argument at greater length in my article, "Origen's Doctrine of Pre-existence and the Opening Chapters of Genesis" (2013).

for bodies: in the section of the *Phaedrus* to which Origen alludes, Plato writes of the soul shedding its wings through some "foulness and ugliness" and then wandering until it lands on something solid, "where it settles and takes on an earthly body" (*Phaedr.* 246e, c, Nehamas and Woodruff). The Edenic garments, Origen says, refer to a superior version of this Platonic doctrine. They appear, then, to facilitate the soul's descent into this firm, corporeal world—by implication, they represent the bodies that envelope fallen souls, allowing them to reside in a similarly corporeal world.[21]

If this is how this paragraph from *Against Celsus* is to be read, then we see Origen allegorizing the Edenic garments of skins to advance his larger narrative of the preexistence of souls, particularly their embodiment as they are cast out into the corporeal world. It is, moreover, certainly plausible that his similar allegorization of the garments in his *Commentary on Genesis* was intended to bolster this same doctrine of preexistence. While we only have Theodoret's excerpt of his interpretation of Gen 3:21 from the *Commentary on Genesis*, we know that Origen repeatedly sought parallels between the opening chapters of Genesis and his narrative of preexistence.[22] Moreover, it is hard to see what other doctrine such an allegory about the bestowal of a body on a discarnate soul dismissed from paradise could support.

How to Interpret Corporeality Prior to Gen 3:21?

In light of the foregoing discussion, we are in a better position to revisit the exegetical objection Origen initially raised in his *Commentary on Genesis* about identifying the garments of skins with bodies. As we have already seen, the single objection to this allegory was that it seemed to propose a second, redundant bestowal of the body on Adam and Eve. After all, there were corporeal depictions of this couple in the narrative that preceded the

21. For the same reading of the garments as bodies in this passage, see Strutwolf 1993, 253 n. 263. Dechow 1988, 318, also sees Origen alluding to the body, but not to the *first* reference to the body in Genesis, but rather a "further stage of body-ness or mortality." In the notes to his critical edition, Borret says: "Origen envisions as possible the Gnostic interpretation according to which the tunics of skins represent the body" (1968, 290, n. 1). Origen makes the same allusion to Plato's *Phaedrus* again in *Cels.* 6.43. For a strikingly parallel passage, see *Comm. Jo.* 2.175–192, already discussed above, where the souls of Adam and John the Baptist are said to be given bodies as they depart from paradise to enter into this corporeal world.

22. See n. 20 above.

bestowal of garments (particular reference was made to Gen 2:23—"bone from my bones"). Origen's first response to this critique was indirect, denying the need for corporeal bodies in paradise, since it was a "divine place." But how, then, *did* he interpret passages in Genesis about the first couple's corporeality prior to the bestowal of garments? At the very end of the fragment from the *Commentary on Genesis*, he revisits this issue. But rather than offer the expected alternative to the literalist rendering of Gen 2:23, he turns to a different passage: Gen 2:7. While at first glance this move is curious, closer inspection suggests that it probably had strategic importance for Origen since this verse was the first reference in the Eden pericope to the seeming corporeality of Adam and Eve. There God was said to form "man" from the dust of the earth and animate him with the breath of life, and subsequent references to his and his companion's corporeality, such as in Gen 2:23, would inevitably be traced back to it.[23] At any rate, Origen was clearly aware that Gen 2:7 suggested that humans were already embodied in paradise, and so his response (not entirely unpredictable) was to cast doubt upon its literal interpretation. He remarks that when it says that God "breathed the breath of life" into the "nostrils" (as in the translations of Aquila and Symmachus) or "face" (as rendered in the Septuagint), this passage should not be taken literally. The reader "ought not to cling to the letter of Scripture as if it were true, but rather search for the 'hidden treasure' [see Matt 13:44] in the letter, because the letter of the divine scripture speaks untruth" (125.23–29). Unfortunately, the fragment does not convey more of Origen's thought about how this passage ought to be understood allegorically. What *is* clear is that he was calling into question a surface assessment of this episode.[24]

23. Note that Methodius (*Res.* 1.39.1–4) turned to both Gen 2:7 and 2:23 to argue for the corporeality of Adam and Eve prior to the bestowal of their garments. As for Origen's interpretation of Gen 2:23, there are only a few extant references to this verse in his corpus. None of these, however, deal explicitly with the issue of corporeality prior to the bestowal of garments (see esp. *Hom. Exod.* 1.3 and *Comm. Matt.* 14.16). Methodius, however, suggests Origen interpreted Gen 2:23 with reference to "intelligible" bones and flesh (*Res.* 1.39.2).

24. Recall the parallel passage in *Against Celsus*, where Origen rejects Celsus's "wicked" literal interpretation of Gen 2:7, as if this verse implied that God was actually inflating skins. Rather, this expression was "meant allegorically and needs an explanation which shows that God imparted a share of His incorruptible spirit to man" (4.37, Chadwick). It is likely that this is the sort of literal interpretation that Origen rejects here in the *Commentary on Genesis*.

We need to turn elsewhere in Origen's corpus to see how he allegorized references to the body in Genesis prior to the fall. It is important to acknowledge that this issue posed a difficulty not simply from the perspective of narrative sequence—the objection raised above in the *Commentary on Genesis* to the view that the garments signified bodies. Also from the perspective of Origen's own doctrine of preexistence, these references to corporeality would have presented a high obstacle: they portrayed humans as already embodied *prior* to their fall, a textual detail that explicitly contradicted his account of preexistence where it was only *after* the fall that human souls became embodied.

Origen responded to this difficult situation through allegory. While we are relatively uninformed about how he interpreted Gen 2:23 ("bone from my bones"), several passages survive in which he expounds on Gen 2:7 at length. As we will see below, the reference in Gen 2:7 to a man formed from the dust of the earth certainly referred to corporeality, yet not to corporeality in paradise *prior* to the fall, but rather to bodies given *after* the preexistent fall. In other words, the passages about a man made from the dust of the earth (Gen 2:7) and God bestowing garments on the couple (Gen 3:21) were allegorized with reference to the drama of preexistence. For Origen, both passages *symbolized the same event*, the bestowal of a body on a previously incorporeal soul leaving paradise for this earth.[25]

---

25. Simonetti 1962 and more recently Crouzel 1989 have offered a very different reading of the interpretation of Gen 2:7 and 3:21. Both acknowledge that Origen identified the garments of Gen 3:21 with the bestowal of earthly bodies. Moreover, both note that according to the narrative in Genesis, these garments came after the fall, which also coincides with Origen's allegorization of them: according to his account of preexistence, bodies were only given after the fall. What puzzles them, however, is that Origen also speaks of bodies for Adam and Eve when interpreting, e.g., Gen 2:7, a passage that occurs *prior to the fall* in the Genesis narrative ("it is difficult to understand how the creation of the earthly body could be recorded in chapter two, that is prior to the fall" [Crouzel 1989, 94]). They view this as a contradiction, since Origen only introduces bodies after the fall in his narrative of preexistence.

Simonetti and Crouzel propose a solution to this puzzle: the bodies Origen discusses when interpreting passages prior to the fall in Genesis (esp. 2:7) must have been different from the terrestrial bodies signified by Gen 3:21: they were ethereal bodies. For the evidence supporting this view, see Crouzel 1989, 90–91, 94, and 218 (see also Dechow 1988, 318–26; Tzvetkova-Glaser 2010, 104–8). For the criticisms of this view, including the difficulties with the evidence and the fact that Origen *does* associate Gen 2:7 with terrestrial bodies granted after the fall, see esp. Strutwolf 1993, 253–55; Gasparro 1978, 63–64; Beatrice 1985, 448–54.

A few passages illustrate this reading of Gen 2:7. Origen often juxtaposed Gen 1:26–27 (humans made "according to the image and likeness" of God) and 2:7 (a man formed "from the dust of the earth"), and when he did so, he identified two sequential stages in the creation of humanity.[26] The former passage signified the first phase, the creation of their preexistent minds or souls that alone were made in the image of God. The latter passage symbolized the subsequent formation of their bodies after they had fallen, first the bodies of Adam and Eve, but by extension, the bodies of all other humans. In his *Homilies on Jeremiah*, for instance, Origen wrestles with the passage spoken by God about the prophet Jeremiah: "Before I formed [πρὸ τοῦ με πλάσαι] you in the womb, I knew you" (Jer 1:5). To help him decipher this verse Origen distinguishes, as he does elsewhere, between "making" (ποιέω) and "forming" (πλάσσω). He argues that the creation of male and female in accordance with the image of God (Gen 1:26–27) was an act of "making," whereas creating a man from the dirt of the earth (Gen 2:7) was an act of "forming." As he continues, he distinguishes what is "made" (our souls which are made according to the image of God) from what is "formed" (our bodies): "For what is made [τὸ γαρ ποιούμενον] does not arise in a womb, but what is formed [τὸ πλασσόμενον] from the clay of the earth, this is created in the womb" (*Hom. Jer.* 1.10.1). Thus when God says of Jeremiah, "Before I formed [πλάσαι] you in the

In my estimation, both authors have incorrectly assumed that for Origen Gen 2 and 3 formed chronologically sequential narratives that needed their corresponding sequential phases in the drama of preexistence. In other words, if Origen spoke of bodies in conjunction with texts that preceded the account of the fall in the narrative of Genesis and then again of bodies in conjunction with passages after the fall in Genesis, then there must have been a corresponding "body-fall-body" sequence in his drama of preexistence. But this need not be the case. The presence of bodies in the narrative of Genesis prior to the fall would undoubtedly have been perceived by Origen as a problem, but this is why, as we have seen, he allegorized Gen 2:7 to refer to an episode that occurred *after* the fall, even though (or precisely because) the passage *preceded* the account of the fall in Genesis.

26. There is a significant debate in the literature about whether Gen 1:26 and 2:7 refer to *successive* creative acts (first the creation of souls, then the creation of bodies) or to *simultaneous* acts, so that souls were never without bodies. The passages provided here strongly suggest Origen could, at least on some occasions, entertain the former interpretation, which would have been integral to his drama of preexistence (so also Bürke 1950, 30–33; Crouzel 1956, 148–53; Gasparro 1978, 63–64). Yet others insist on the latter interpretation, most notably Simonetti 1962, 370–81; Harl 1985, 245; so also the later Crouzel 1989, 90–92.

womb, I knew you," Origen argues that God was referring to the preexistent soul of Jeremiah that had been made, and thus known, before Jeremiah's body would later be formed: "For he knew Jeremiah before being formed in the womb" (*Hom. Jer.* 1.10.2).[27] Origen offers a similar interpretation in book twenty of his *Commentary on John*. There he is speaking of the fall of the "first man" who descended "from the superior things and desired a life different from the superior life." As he narrates this preexistent fall, he again introduces his distinction between making and forming and how Gen 2:7 signifies the forming of bodies after the initial fall. This "first man," Origen writes,

> deserved to be a beginning neither of something created nor made [κτίσματος οὔτε ποιήματος], but "of something formed [πλάσματος] by the Lord, made to be mocked by his angels" [Job 40:19]. Now, our true substance too is in our being according to the image of the Creator [see Gen 1:26–27], but the substance resulting from guilt is in the thing formed [πλάσματι], which was received from the dust of the earth [see Gen 2:7]. (*Comm. Jo.* 20.182, Heine 1989 modified)

Our "true substance" that is "made" according to the image of the Creator is the soul or mind. But humans are also made of another, different substance "resulting from guilt." Here Origen refers to the fall and how bodies, something "formed" from "the dust of the earth" (Gen 2:7), enveloped souls after they fell from their original state of contemplation.[28]

Origen thus offered similar allegorical interpretations of Gen 2:7 and Gen 3:21. Both passages symbolized the same event: the embodiment of preexistent minds, after their fall, as they are placed in a corporeal world. In light of this interpretation of Gen 2:7, we now find ourselves in a position to revisit the objection raised in the fragment from the *Commentary on Genesis* to the interpretation of the garments of skins as bodies. Did the Genesis narrative that preceded the bestowal of garments not suggest that the first couple was already embodied before they were clothed with the garments of skins? From his interpretation of Gen 2:7, it appears that Origen had drafted a response. Rather than read the references to

---

27. Note as well the application of this verse to the Savior, of whom Origen says, he too was known before he appeared in the womb.

28. For other passages where Origen distinguishes Gen 1:26–27 from 2:7 in this manner, see *Hom. Gen.* 1.13; *Comm. Cant.* prologue; *Hom. Ezech.* 7.6; esp. *Comm. Matt.* 14.16; *Dial.* 15–16.

corporeality before Gen 3:21 literally, so that the first couple was already embodied in paradise before their fall and subsequent reception of "garments of skins," he read passages such as Gen 2:7 allegorically to signify bodies received after the fall. In concert with Gen 3:21, these passages referred to a postlapsarian corporeality first visited upon the minds that had fallen from their preexistent state of glory.[29]

In this first section of the essay, I have examined two passages from the early and late stages in Origen's literary career in which he allegorized the garments of skins in the same way, as bodies given by God. Origen considered it a viable interpretation even though, as we have seen, it was contentious in his day and required some defense. This interpretation proved central to helping him advance his doctrine of preexistence, in particular the embodiment of human souls after they fell. In short, Gen 3:21 provided Origen an opportunity to find references to the beginnings of his theological vision in the early chapters of Genesis.

Interlude: Two Rejected Interpretations

But Origen did not consider every circulating interpretation of the garments suitable. In his *Commentary on Genesis*, he addressed two additional readings that he found problematic for ultimately similar reasons. The first of these interpretations claimed that the garments signified actual animal hides. This reading contended "that after having removed the skins from certain animals (which had been either killed or died in some other way), God made a kind of dress out of skins by stitching garments together like a leather worker [δίκην σκυτοτόμου]" (124.3–6). Unfortunately, Origen does not offer any further elaboration on this literalist view. Rather, he quickly dismisses it, claiming it is "exceedingly foolish and old womanish and unworthy of God" (124.2–3).

While at first glance he gives the indication of categorically rejecting every literal view of the garments as animal hides, closer inspection suggests otherwise. It is striking, I think, that when he forwards his critique, the emphasis lies not on the garments as animal hides, so much as on how some people think God produced these garments. Origen belabors how

29. Even if we are relatively uninformed about how Origen actually interpreted Gen 2:23, Vogt has, I think, correctly argued that if he could allegorize Gen 2:7 in the manner here described, it is highly unlikely that he would have been troubled by an objection based upon a *literal* reading of Gen 2:23 (1985a, 102).

God would have first had to kill animals or find some who had already died, then skin them, and finally stitch their hides together "like a leatherworker." What animates his objection, in other words, is the crass, anthropomorphic depiction of God implied in this particular literal interpretation.[30]

We find Origen inveighing against such a popular (mis)conception of God throughout his writings, but especially when it came to the opening chapters of Genesis that he thought were vulnerable to such an interpretation. In a famous passage in *First Principles*, for instance, he objects to a literalist understanding of the planting of the garden in Eden: "And who is so silly," he asks, "as to believe that God, after the manner of a farmer [τρόπον ἀνθρώπου γεωργοῦ], 'planted a paradise eastward in Eden [Gen 2:8]'" (*Princ.* 4.3.1, Görgemanns and Karpp)? The concern to erase the God of Gen 1–3 of anthropomorphic hues strongly parallels the objection Origen raises above in the *Commentary on Genesis* regarding the garments of skins: it is just as absurd to think of God as a human farmer, as it is to portray God as a leather worker who tailors clothing for humans. The objection to this literal interpretation of the garments, then, appears to be focused on a particular version that implied, to those who embraced it, an all-too-human view of God.

The second interpretive possibility for the garments of skins was equally problematic. Origen notes that some people were desirous to avoid the "difficulties" of identifying the garments with bodies. They envisioned Adam and Eve as already embodied and the "garments" as allegorical symbols of the mortality to which they later became subject after they sinned.[31] Such interpreters "declare that the 'garments of skins' were the

30. Origen does not identify any of the proponents of this position in this fragment. However, in another passage from the *Commentary on Genesis*, he identifies Melito of Sardis who, according to him, advanced the idea that God lived in a body and thus that the anthropomorphic depictions of God in the Bible could be taken at face value (Metzler 2010, D11). According to Eusebius, Melito wrote a treatise entitled *On the Embodiment of God* (Eusebius, *Hist. Eccl.* 4.26.2). Another likely candidate for this literal reading of Gen 3:21 surfaces from Origen's immediate ecclesiastical context. He repeatedly targeted the interpretations of the "simpler" Christians (*simpliciores*) within the church who were susceptible to the sort of literalistic, anthropomorphic conceptions of God that he finds objectionable in this first view of the "garments of skins" (see esp. Hällström 1984).

31. Origen does not identify who these interpreters might be. There is perhaps a reference to Hippolytus here (Petit 1992, 282–83, frg. 437). For later Christian interpreters who pursue this interpretation, see Metzler 2010, 192 n. 261, as well as Valevi-

mortality [τὴν νέκρωσιν] with which Adam and Eve were clothed, because they had been condemned to death on account of their sin" (125.12–15). Origen immediately raises several objections to this interpretation, but does not offer any rebuttal, thereby leaving the reader with the distinct impression that he considered these objections sufficiently forceful to deny the identification of the garments with mortality. According to one objection, those who associated the garments with mortality "are not easily able to explain how God, and not sin, produces mortality [νέκρωσιν ἐμποιεῖ] in the one who has transgressed" (125.15–17). How could God have introduced the "garments"—that is, death—to the human race? This objection is phrased in such a way that Origen himself might have raised it. Earlier in his *Commentary on Genesis*, he turned to the divine prohibition in Gen 2:17 not to eat from the tree of the knowledge of good and evil, lest the man die. There Origen is quick to note that while death ensues from violating this command, "God does not effect death [οὐχὶ τοῦ θεοῦ τὸν θάνατον ποιήσαντος], but rather the man" (180.10–11, frg. 259).[32] He buttresses this assertion with Wis 1:13 ("God did not make death") and further notes that the prohibition in Gen 2 did *not* read, "On the day you eat from it, *I will kill you* [θανατώσω ὑμᾶς" (180.16–181.17). Rather, God announces the natural consequences of violating the law of justice: "On the day you eat, you will surely die" (181.17–22).[33] It is, thus, very much

---

cius 1995, 163–75. Like the allegorization of the garments as bodies, this allegorical interpretation also had appeal: since these garments came from *deceased* animals, they could stand for mortality.

32. On the close association of "death" with (i.e., as a result of) "sin" or "evil", see *Princ.* 3.6.3; *Hom. Ezech.* 1.3.8; *Hom. Lev.* 6.2.7; *Comm. Jo.* 1.121.

33. At stake for Origen in this issue was his anti-Marcionite and Valentinian agenda. Rather than posit an inferior, draconian God who harassed humanity with death, there was one God who was both just and good and who only made good things (*Princ.* pref. 4; also *Princ.* 2.5.1). Note that even the devil, in so far as he is an existing being, is good. When Paul writes that death will be destroyed, he does not mean the devil will cease to exist, but rather that his hostile intent will come to an end (*Princ.* 3.6.5; also *Hom. Ezech.* 1.3.7–9). Thus the origins of death had to be sought elsewhere. As Origen repeatedly insisted, death was the consequence of sin, and sin, in turn, was the result of choice—it was rational beings who first willingly "withdrew from good," and in so doing, became "immersed in evil" (*Princ.* 2.9.2). "The important thing," he preaches in his *Homilies on Ezekiel*, is that "'God did not make death' [Wis 1:13]. Nor did he work evil. To man and angel he conceded free choice in all things" (*Hom. Ezech.* 1.3.7–9, Scheck). It was inconceivable, then, for Origen that God would be the one who introduced death into the world. Indeed more fittingly, death was something God

Origen's own criticism that drives the rejection of the view that Adam and Eve were corporeal *and* somehow immortal, only succumbing to mortality ("garments") after they sinned.

Noteworthy about Origen's assessment of both of these interpretations, one literal and the other allegorical, is that his rejection was deeply motivated by what he thought each implied about God. The literal interpretation presented God in crude anthropomorphic terms, while the allegorical reading portrayed God as a draconian figure bent on destruction.

Position Two: The "Garments of Skins" as Animal Hides

In light of the evidence surveyed thus far, Origen endorsed the position that the "garments" of Gen 3:21 referred to the bestowal of bodies on previously incorporeal souls. He also rejected two other interpretations, one literal (they signified actual animal hides) and another allegorical (they symbolized mortality). In this last section we need to attend to a final, complicating passage. In his *Homilies on Leviticus*, delivered sometime between 239–242, Origen expounds upon the clothing with which Moses dressed his brother Aaron, the first high priest (Lev 8:1–9). Origen presses for a contrast between these "holy and faithful garments" and "those unfortunate garments [*illa infelicia indumenta*], with which the first man was clothed after he had sinned" (*Hom. Lev.* 6.2.7, Barkley modified). In light of his earlier reflections on these garments in the *Commentary on Genesis*, he makes a puzzling claim: that God *did*, in fact, bestow actual animal hides on the first couple. "Indeed, it is said that God made those. 'For God made skin tunics and clothed Adam and his wife' (Gen 3:21). Therefore, those were tunics of skins [*tunicae de pellibus*] taken from animals. For with such as these, it was necessary for the sinner to be dressed" (*Hom. Lev.* 6.2.7, Barkley). As the passage continues, Origen offers an important supplementary commentary that again seems to challenge his earlier views that these garments did not refer allegorically to mortality. The garments were made of animal skins, he says in his *Homilies on Leviticus*, but intriguingly they harbored additional significance: they were "a symbol of the mortality [*mortalitatis … indicium*] which he received because of his

sought to conquer (e.g., *Princ.* 2.3.3 and 3.6.5). By implication, then, the garments bestowed *by God* could not refer to mortality.

sin and of his frailty [*fragilitatis*] which came from the corruption of the flesh" (*Hom. Lev.* 6.2.7).[34]

This passage is striking because Origen seemingly advocates an interpretation of the garments that he earlier repudiated. While in his *Commentary on Genesis* he cast aspersion on a literal interpretation of the garments of skins, in his *Homilies on Leviticus* he matter-of-factly states that they were actual animal hides. He offers no hint of how he would respond to the charge in the *Commentary on Genesis* that a troubling anthropomorphism was implied by such an interpretation (of God as a leather worker). Moreover, he associates the garments with mortality in the *Homilies on Leviticus*, whereas he rejects it in his earlier *Commentary on Genesis*. Finally, he does not mention that the garments stand for the bodies, as he explained elsewhere.[35] How, then, do we deal with these tensions?[36]

If we accept the Origenian authorship of the material Theodoret attributed to Origen's *Commentary on Genesis*, one option is to argue for a shift in his thought between the *Commentary on Genesis* and the later *Homilies on Leviticus*. This is certainly a possibility, and such shifts have

34. There is an error in the English translation of this passage, which reads: "which are a symbol of the mortality which he received because of his *skin*" (*Hom. Lev.* 6.2.7, Barkley)—"because of his *sin* [*pro peccato*]" was intended. More importantly, note Reuling's dismissal of this passage: "In the Homilies on Leviticus, Origen states that the garments of skin are an *indicium mortalitatis et fragilitatis*; a vague remark that could mean almost anything" (2006, 74–75). As we will see below, this turns out to be a coherent comment that dovetails well with what he says elsewhere of clothing made from animal skins.

35. In his notes to the SC edition of the *Homilies on Leviticus*, Borret claims about this passage that "Origen rejects the Gnostic interpretation, according to which the garments represent the body" (1981). In fact, Origen says nothing about this allegory here, leaving the reader to wonder what he thinks about it. Borret's note tries to distance Origen from this gnostic allegory, but to do so he ignores Origen's endorsement of this interpretation in his *Commentary on Genesis* and tries to explain away the same allegory in *Cels.* 4.40 by saying that Origen was not discussing "corporeality pure and simple" but rather the ethereal body of preexistent humans (see n. 25 above).

36. Very few scholars have puzzled over these conflicts. Borret, for instance, ignores the fact that Origen mocked the literal interpretation of the garments in the *Commentary on Genesis* (SC 286, 371–72). See as well, Dechow 1988, 316–18; Strutwolf 1993, 253, esp. n. 263; Reuling 2006, 74–76. None call attention to these discrepancies, especially the most glaring one between Origen's rejection of the literal interpretation of the garments in the *Commentary on Genesis* and his endorsement of it in the *Homilies on Leviticus*.

been detected in other areas of Origen's theology.[37] But this conclusion should only come as a last resort, after relevant passages have been examined as closely as possible. Another option would be to consider whether the problem lies with the *Homilies on Leviticus*. There is certainly no need to call into question their Origenian provenance, but we *can* exercise caution about their transmission. They only survive in Rufinus's Latin translation, composed amidst the first Origenist controversy, in which Epiphanius and Jerome sharply criticized Origen's views of Genesis, including the "garments of skins."[38] Is it possible that Rufinus modified an original allegorical interpretation of these garments so as to render it more favorable to an early fifth-century Latin audience: the garments were actual animal hides?

It would be tempting to answer this question affirmatively, were it not for two other parallel passages in Origen's writings that corroborate the interpretation of the "garments of skins" as actual animal hides symbolic of mortality. Both texts focus on God's command to Moses at Mount Sinai to remove his sandals because he was standing on holy ground (Exod 3:5).[39] In his first *Homily on 1 Samuel*, Origen remarks that it is hard to believe how there is not something mysteriously hidden in these words to Moses, since God was surely not cursing "material shoes [*calciamenta … corporalia*]." Instead, Origen proposes, we ought to think of Moses, while leaving the land of Egypt, as wearing "the shoes of mortal skins [*calciamenta de pellibus mortuis*]" that were "symbols of mortality [*indicia mortalitatis*]"

37. See Heine 2010 for the most recent attempt to identify the discontinuities in Origen's career.

38. On Epiphanius's criticisms, see esp. the discussion in Dechow 1988, 315–33, as well as 391–448. This controversy raged throughout the last quarter of the fourth century, and reached into the early fifth when the homilies were translated (between 400–404 [SC 286, 52]).

39. The link between these passages about the sandals and the garments of skins would have been facilitated on two levels: not simply were both items of clothing made from animal skins, but there were also structural resemblances between the narratives of the dismissal from Eden and the approach to Sinai. Moses had been commanded to *remove* his footwear when entering the presence of God on Mount Sinai, whereas the first couple was *given* clothing as it was leaving the divine presence in the paradise of Eden. In both episodes, clothing is portrayed as irrelevant, if not a hindrance, in the presence of God. This association of Adam in Eden with Moses on Sinai extends the parallel Anderson draws (depending upon Origen) between Adam and Moses's brother, Aaron, at Sinai (2001b, 121–24).

(*Hom. 1 Reg.* 1.6). God's subsequent rejection of these shoes of skins did not concern the actual shoes, but was rather an acknowledgement that Moses had begun to make progress in virtue as he climbed Mount Sinai to become a minister of "*immortal* mysteries."

Origen interprets Moses's sandals similarly in his *Treatise on the Passover*. There he asks why the command was given to eat the first Passover with sandals *on* the feet (Exod 12:11) when this order seemed to contradict the earlier oracle delivered to Moses on Sinai to take *off* his sandals (Exod 3:5). Origen proposes that the sandals of the Passover signified the flesh and that wearing them was a mystical reference to the "resurrection of the flesh: it is that the flesh itself also goes out with us when we depart from Egypt," that is, our life in this world (*Pasch.* 37, Guéraud and Nautin; Daly 1992, 48). But later, approaching the holy ground, Moses's sandals referred to mortality. By taking them off, he signified an eschatological state subsequent to the resurrection, when "there will no longer be anything mortal [νεκρότητά τινα] to conceal," that is, when death will eventually be vanquished (*Pasch.* 37, Guéraud and Nautin; Daly 1992, 48). In both passages Origen offers very similar interpretations of Moses's sandals. He seizes upon their physical material—they were made from mortal animal skins—and on this basis concludes that their symbolic content was the corresponding mortality of humans.

Both passages corroborate the interpretation of the Edenic garments that Origen offers in his *Homilies on Leviticus*. The garments, like Moses's sandals, are made from animal skins. Moreover, both share the same symbolic value: as with the sandals, so the garments are "a symbol of the *mortality* … and the *frailty* which came from the corruption of the flesh" (see *Hom. Lev.* 6.2.7). Thus, in light of these two passages on Moses's sandals, it seems almost certain that the interpretation of the garments we find in the *Homilies on Leviticus* was legitimately Origenian.

But this interpretation, of course, compels us to revisit the problem of whether Origen's earlier comments in his *Commentary on Genesis* conflicted with his later reflections in the *Homilies on Leviticus*. Whether we see conflict between these two discussions depends in large measure on whether we think he intended in his *Commentary on Genesis* to reject *every* literal interpretation of the garments that identified them with actual animal skins. If so, then there certainly is a shift in Origen's view of this verse over his career. However, as I argued above, his objection to the literal interpretation of the garments in the *Commentary on Genesis* focused narrowly on one *particular* literal interpretation that implied an unsuitable conception of God. This targeted critique is a long way from claiming he rejected every literal interpretation of the garments.

When we turn to the *Homilies on Leviticus*, we find Origen contending for a *fitting* literal interpretation of the garments. What is striking here is that the same concern for an appropriate conception of God expressed earlier in his *Commentary on Genesis* has not disappeared: he thinks that God indeed made these garments, but did so appropriately. Origen's focus is not on the mechanics of how the garments were made. He ignores the issue, and readers are left to presume that they were not made in the crassly anthropomorphic way he described in his *Commentary on Genesis*.[40] Rather, he justifies their fabrication by highlighting what he thinks was the underlying divine rationale behind their construction. "It was necessary," he writes, for the sinner to be clothed with garments of skins, because by making them from the hides of dead animals, God symbolized the "mortality which he received because of his sin" (*Hom. Lev.* 6.3.7; Barkley 1990, 120). This interpretation forges an intertextual link between Gen 3:21 and Gen 2:17, where God had first announced that death would be a consequence of sin. The actual construction of the garments was justified, because through them God wished to instruct embodied souls about what had been prophesied earlier, that in eating of the tree of the knowledge of good and evil, they would experience death.

We see, moreover, that Origen is very careful not to slip into a contradiction with his earlier objections to the symbolism of mortality in the *Commentary on Genesis*. There he only contested the view that *God* was responsible for imposing mortality (allegorical garments) on humans. Here he asserts that God *actually* bestowed garments and that these were symbolic of a mortality derived not from God, but from humanity's own sin: again, they were "a symbol of the mortality *which he received because of his sin* and of his frailty *which came from the corruption of the flesh*"

---

40. Epiphanius responded to Origen's objection in *Commentary on Genesis* to God being a "leather worker" by contending that God's creative power was not limited to human ingenuity: "And in Adam's time too, you unbeliever, God willed, and made actual skin tunics without animals, without human craft and any of the various sorts of human work—[and] made them for Adam and Eve at the moment of his willing them, as he willed at the beginning, and the heaven, and all things, were made at that very moment" (*Pan.* 64.66.5,Williams). The impression given by Epiphanius is that Origen did not think in this way about the construction of the literal garments in *Homilies on Leviticus*, but it is entirely possible that he did. See as well the Antiochene interpretation of this verse that resembled Epiphanius's approach (Layton 2007, 19–20).

(*Hom. Lev.* 6.2.7; Barkley 1990, 120).[41] Clothing the first couple in this manner, then, was a deliberate pedagogical exercise that vindicated God's role in this seemingly haphazard activity. In short, in both the *Commentary on Genesis* and *Homilies on Leviticus*, the same concern for a fitting portrayal of God led Origen to reject one literal interpretation of Gen 3:21 and accept another.

The plausibility of this assessment of Origen's two literal interpretations of the garments is strengthened when we note how closely his exegetical strategy mirrored Philo's earlier discussion of Gen 3:21 in his *Questions and Answers on Genesis* (with which Origen was almost certainly familiar).[42] Philo noted that people might "ridicule" this verse "when they consider the cheapness of the apparel of tunics, as being unworthy of the touch of such a Creator" (Philo, *QG* 1.53, Marcus). Philo, just like Origen after him, was concerned that some literal interpretations of the garments would call into question the worthiness of God. But rather than dismiss every literal interpretation, Philo intriguingly argued, as Origen later would, that one nevertheless *could* accept a literal interpretation of Gen 3:21 without succumbing to an unfitting view of God. God did, in fact, make literal garments, and well-disposed readers should see this act as "suitable to God," who intended to teach wisdom through these lowly garments—that frugality was to be preferred to luxurious splendor (Philo, *QG* 1.53, Marcus). Philo, thus, created space for a legitimate literal interpretation of these garments by highlighting the divine pedagogical intent expressed through their construction.

As we have already seen, this was the very approach Origen adopted: God intended to convey a message through these coats of skins about the consequences of sin.[43] It seems to me, then, that what we see in Origen's *Commentary on Genesis* and *Homilies on Leviticus* are not two conflicting

---

41. Dechow 1998, 317–18 and Heine 2010, 114 suggest that Origen recycled his allegorical interpretation of mortality from the *Commentary on Genesis* for his *Homilies on Leviticus*, whereas I am contending that these interpretations were not identical.

42. See Van den Hoek 2000, esp. the references to this work (*Questions and Answers on Genesis*) in the reversed index (113–16).

43. Note that Philo also argues in this section for the inherent propriety of his figurative interpretation of the garments as bodies. "It was proper," he asserts, "that the mind and sense should be clothed in the body as in a tunic of skin, in order that [God's] handiwork might first appear worthy of the divine power. And could the apparel of the human body be better or more fittingly made by any other power than God?" (1.53, Marcus).

approaches to the literal interpretation of these garments. Rather, the same concern to preserve a fitting portrayal of God finds expression in the rejection of one literal interpretation and the endorsement of another. In so doing, Origen's exegetical strategy was parallel, if not dependent, on Philo.

Conclusion

Several of Origen's late antique critics gave the misleading impression that he only allegorized the garments of skins as bodies. Rarely did these authors mention that he openly debated several different interpretations, let alone acknowledge that he ultimately endorsed two views, not just one. As we have seen, Origen contended that the "garments" could be interpreted both literally and allegorically. This twofold interpretation of Gen 3:21 needs to be seen against the backdrop of his overarching conviction that Moses, like a "distinguished orator," composed Genesis in a twofold manner. He paid attention "to the outward form" of his text, but he also gave "opportunities for deeper study for the few who are able to read with more understanding and who are capable of searching out his meaning" (*Cels.* 1.18, Chadwick).

The literal and allegorical interpretations Origen advocated for Gen 3:21, then, mirrored the twofold manner in which he thought the text had been originally composed. But as we have seen, his twofold interpretation also reinforced his view of the double consequence of sin: that it led first to embodiment and then to mortality. According to the allegorical interpretation, the garments stood for the bodies God had bestowed on preexistent minds after their fall. According to the literal interpretation, this verse pointed to a subsequent phase in this narrative of preexistence, where God fashioned actual garments for the first embodied couple in a fitting way, with the intent of instructing them in their mortality.

Yet alongside these endorsed interpretations, Origen also rejected two other views of the garments of skins. Canvassing these rejected opinions alongside the views he ultimately supported turns out to be instructive, since a unifying theme emerges: his concern to extract a fitting portrayal of God from a passage with mythological undercurrents. He dismissed as crude any literal interpretation that envisioned God making garments as an ordinary tailor would. Moreover, he argued against the allegorical view that the garments stood for a mortality imposed by God, primarily because it implicated God too intimately with death. Yet it was this same conviction that informed the interpretations he endorsed. The defense of the allegorization of the garments as bodies rested, in part, on its portrayal of God fittingly *not* granting bodies to souls who were without need of them in the divine paradise. And when God did later provide garments for the first embodied souls, this was done with appropriate intent: to convey a pressing message about the deathly consequences of sin. What we learn from this reconstruction of Origen's approach to the "garments of skins," then, is not simply what interpretations he supported and dismissed. We also gain insight into the deeper, underlying concern that shaped his hermeneutical decision-making process. He was always concerned to talk fittingly about God.

Works Cited

Anderson, Gary. 2001a. Garments of Skin in Apocryphal Narrative and Biblical Commentary. Pages 101–43 in *Studies in Ancient Midrash*. Edited by James L. Kugel. Cambridge: Harvard University Press.

———. 2001b. *The Genesis of Perfection: Adam and Eve in Jewish and Christian Imagination*. Louisville: Westminster John Knox.

Bammel, Caroline P. 1989. Adam in Origen. Pages 62–93 in *The Making of Orthodoxy: Essays in Honour of Henry Chadwick*. Edited by Rowan Williams. Cambridge: Cambridge University Press.

Barkley, Gary W., trans. 1990. *Origen: Homilies on Leviticus 1–16*. FC 83. Washington, D.C.: Catholic University of America Press.

Beatrice, Pier Franco. 1985. Le tuniche di pelle: Antiche letture di *Gen.* 3,21. Pages 433–82 in *La tradizione dell'Enkrateia: Motivazioni ontologiche e protologiche (Atti del Colloquio Internazionale Milano, 20–23 aprile 1982)*. Edited by Ugo Bianchi. Rome: Edizioni dell'Ateneo.

Bietz, Wolfgang Karl. 1973. *Paradiesvorstellungen bei Ambrosius und seinen Vorgängern*. Giessen: Schmacht.

Bockmuehl, Markus. 2010. Locating Paradise. Pages 192–209 in *Paradise in Antiquity: Jewish and Christian Views*. Edited by Markus Bockmuehl and Guy G. Stroumsa. Cambridge: Cambridge University Press.

Borret, Marcel, ed. and trans. 1967–1976. *Origène: Contre Celse*. 5 vols. SC 132, 136, 147, 150, 227. Paris: Cerf.

———. 1981. *Origène: Homélies sur le Lévitique*. Vol. 1. SC 286. Paris: Cerf.

———. 1989. *Origène: Homélies sur Ézéchiel*. SC 352. Paris: Cerf.

Brock, Sebastian. 1982. Clothing Metaphors as a Means of Theological Expression in Syriac Tradition. Pages 11–40 in *Typus, Symbol, Allego-*

rie bei den östlichen Vätern und ihren Parallelen im Mittelalter. Edited by Margot Schmidt and Carl-Friedrich Geyer. Regensburg: Pustet.

Bürke, Georg. 1950. Des Origenes Lehre vom Urstand des Menschen. *ZKT* 72:1–39.

Chadwick, Henry, trans. 1953. *Origen: Contra Celsum*. Cambridge: Cambridge University Press.

Crouzel, Henri. 1956. *Théologie de l'Image de Dieu chez Origène*. Paris: Aubier.

———. 1989. *Origen: The Life and Thought of the First Great Theologian*. Translated by A. S. Worrall. San Francisco: Harper & Row.

Daly, Robert J., trans. 1992. *Origen: Treatise on the Passover and Dialogue of Origen with Heraclides and His Fellow Bishops on the Father, the Son, and the Soul*. ACW 54. New York: Paulist.

Daniélou, Jean. 1967. Les Tuniques de Peau chez Grégoire de Nysse. Pages 355–67 in *Glaube, Geist, Geschichte: Festschrift für Ernst Benz zum 60. Geburtstage am 17. November 1967*. Edited by Gerhard Müller and Winfried Zeller. Leiden: Brill.

Dechow, Jon F. 1988. *Dogma and Mysticism in Early Christianity: Epiphanius of Cyprus and the Legacy of Origen*. Patristic Monograph Series 13. Macon: Mercer University Press.

Doutreleau, Louis, and Pierre Nautin, eds. and trans. 1976. *Didyme l'Aveugle: Sur la Genèse*. SC 233. Paris: Cerf.

Edwards, Mark Julian. 2002. *Origen against Plato*. Ashgate Studies in Philosophy and Theology in Late Antiquity. Aldershot: Ashgate.

Gasparro, G. Sfameni. 1978. Doppia creazione e peccato di Adamo nel Peri Archon di Origene: Fondamenti biblici e presupposti Platonici dell'esegesi Origeniana. Pages 45–82 in *La "Doppia Creazione" dell'uomo negli Alessandri, nei Cappodoci e nella gnosi*. Edited by Ugo Bianchi. Rome: Edizioni dell'Ateneo & Bizzarri.

———. 1981. Restaurazione dell'immagine del celeste e abbandono dell'immagine dell terrestre nella prospettiva Origeniana della doppia creazione. Pages 231–73 in *Arché e telos: L'antropologia di Origene e di Gregorio di Nissa. Analisi storico-religiosa (Atti del Colloquio Milano, 17–19 Maggio 1979)*. Edited by Ugo Bianchi. Milan: Università Cattolica del Sacro Cuore.

Görgemanns, Herwig, and Heinrich Karpp, eds. 1992. *Origenes: Vier Bücher von den Prinzipien*. 3rd ed. Darmstadt: Wissenschaftliche Buchgesellschaft.

Guéraud, Octave, and Pierre Nautin, eds. 1979. *Origène: Sur la Pâque, traité inédit publié d'après un papyrus de Toura*. Christianisme antique 2. Paris: Beauchesne.

Harl, Marguerite. 1985. La préexistence des âmes dans l'oeuvre d'Origène. Pages 238–58 in *Origeniana Quarta: Die Referate des 4. Internationalen Origeneskongresses (Innsbruck, 2.–6. September 1985)*. Edited by Lothar Lies. Innsbrucker Theologische Studien 19. Innsbruck: Tyrolia.

Hällström, Gunnar af. 1984. *Fides Simpliciorum according to Origen of Alexandria*. Helsinki: Societas Scientiarum Fennica.

Heine, Ronald E., trans. 1989. *Origen: Commentary on the Gospel according to John. Books 1–10*. FC 80. Washington, D.C.: Catholic University of America Press.

———. 2003. Origen's Alexandrian *Commentary on Genesis*. Pages 63–73 in *Origeniana Octava: Origen and the Alexandrian Tradition*. BETL 164. Edited by Lorenzo Perrone, P. Bernardino, and D. Marchini. Leuven: Peeters.

———. 2005. The Testimonia and Fragments Related to Origen's Commentary on Genesis. *ZAC* 9:122–42.

———. 2010. *Origen: Scholarship in Service of the Church*. Oxford: Oxford University Press.

Lambden, Stephen N. 1992. From Fig Leaves to Fingernails: Some Notes on the Garments of Adam and Eve in the Hebrew Bible and Select Early Postbiblical Jewish Writings. Pages 74–90 in *A Walk in the Garden: Biblical, Iconographical and Literary Images of Eden*. JSOTSup 136. Edited by Paul Morris and Deborah Sawyer. Sheffield: JSOT Press.

Layton, Richard A. 2007. Didymus the Blind and the *Philistores*: A Contest over *Historia* in Early Christian Exegetical Argument. Paper presented at the International Symposium of the Orion Center for the Study of the Dead Sea Scrolls and Associated Literature. Hebrew University of Jerusalem, Mt. Scopus. January 9–11. Online: orion.mscc.huji.ac.il/symposiums/11th/papers/LaytonDidymus.doc.

Ledegang, F. 2001. *Mysterium Ecclesiae: Images of the Church and its Members in Origen*. Leuven: Leuven University Press.

Martens, Peter W. 2013. Origen's Doctrine of Pre-Existence and the Opening Chapters of Genesis. *ZAC* 16:516–49.

Metzler, Karin. 2005. Weitere Testimonien und Fragmente zum Genesis-Kommentar des Origenes. *ZAC* 9:143–48.

———, ed. and trans. 2010. *Die Kommentierung des Buches Genesis*. Vol. 1 of *Origenes: Werke mit deutscher Übersetzung*. Freiburg: Herder.

Nautin, Pierre, ed. 1976. *Origène: Homélie sur Jérémie*. 2 vols. SC 232. Paris: Cerf.

———. 1977. *Origène: Sa vie et son oeuvre*. Christianisme Antique 1. Paris: Beauchesne.

Nautin, Pierre, and Marie-Thérèse, eds. 1986. *Origène: Homélies sur Samuel*. SC 328. Paris: Cerf.

Nehamas, Alexander, and Paul Woodruff, trans. 1997. *Plato: Phaedrus*. Pages 506–56 in *Plato: Complete Works*. Edited by John M. Cooper and D. S. Hutchinson. Indianapolis: Hackett.

Noce, Carla. 2002. *Vestis Varia: L'immagine della veste nell'opera di Origene*. Rome: Institutum Patristicum Augustinianum.

Philo. *Questions and Answers on Genesis*. 1953. Translated by Ralph Marcus. LCL 380. Cambridge: Harvard University Press.

Perrone, Lorenzo. 1995. Perspectives sur Origène et la literature patristique des 'Quaestiones et Responsiones.' Pages 151–64 in *Origeniana Sexta: Origène et la Bible [Origen and the Bible: Actes du Colloquium Origenianum Sextum] (Chantilly, 30 août–3 septembre 1993)*. BETL 118. Edited by Giles Dorival and Alain Le Boulluec. Leuven: Peeters.

Petit, Françoise, ed. 1986. *Collectio Coisliniana in Genesim*. Vol. 2 of *Catenae Graecae in Genesim et in Exodum*. CCSG 15. Turnhout: Brepols.

———. 1992. *La chaîne sur la Genèse: Édition intégrale I*. Traditio Exegetica Graeca 1. Louvain: Peeters.

Pisi, Paola. 1987. Peccato di Adamo e Caduta dei Noes nell' Esegesi Origeniana. Pages 322–35 in *Origeniana Quarta: Die Referate des 4. Internationalen Origeneskongresses (Innsbruck, 2.–6. September 1985)*. Innsbrucker theologische Studien 19. Edited by Lothar Lies. Innsbruck: Tyrolia.

Preuschen, Erwin, ed. 1903. *Origenes Werke: Der Johanneskommentar*. GCS 4. Leipzig: Hinrichs.

Rauer, Max. 1961. Origenes über das Paradies. Pages 253–59 in *Studien zum Neuen Testament und zur Patristik*. TU 77. Berlin: Akademie.

Reuling, Hanneke. 2006. *After Eden: Church Fathers and Rabbis on Genesis 3:16–21*. Leiden: Brill.

Scheck, Thomas P., trans. 2010. *Origen: Homilies 1–14 on Ezekiel*. ACW 62. New York: Newman.

Simonetti, Manlio. 1962. Alcune osservazioni sull'interpretazione Origeniana di Genesi 2:7 e 3:21. *Aevum* 36:370–81.

Smith, Jonathan Z. 1965–66. The Garments of Shame. *HR* 5:217–38.

Stroumsa, Guy. G. 2010. The Paradise Chronotrope. Pages 1–14 in *Para-*

dise in Antiquity: Jewish and Christian Views. Edited by Markus Bockmuehl and Guy G. Stroumsa. Cambridge: Cambridge University Press.

Strutwolf, Holger. 1993. *Gnosis als System: Zur Rezeption der valentinianischen Gnosis bei Origenes*. Göttingen: Vandenhoeck & Ruprecht.

Toepel, Alexander. 2010. When Did Adam Wear the Garments of Light? *JJS* 61:62–71.

Tzvetkova-Glaser, Anna. 2010. *Pentateuchauslegung bei Origenes und den frühen Rabbinen*. Early Christianity in the Context of Antiquity 7. Frankfurt: Lang.

Valevicius, Andrius. 1995. The Greek Fathers and the "Coats of Skins." *Logos* 36:163–75.

Van den Hoek, Annewies. 2000. Philo and Origen: A Descriptive Catalogue of their Relationship. *SPhilo* 12:44–121.

Vogt, Hermann-Joseph. 1985a. Seminar I: Texte zum Hauptreferat. Pages 100–11 in *Origeniana Quarta: Die Referate des 4. Internationalen Origeneskongresses (Innsbruck, 2.–6. September 1985)*. Innsbrucker theologische Studien 19. Edited by Lothar Lies. Innsbruck: Tyrolia.

———. 1985b. Warum wurde Origenes zum Häretiker erklärt? Kirchliche Vergangenheits-Bewältigung in der Vergangenheit. Pages 78–99 in *Origeniana Quarta: Die Referata des 4. Internationalen Origeneskongresses (Innsbruck, 2.–6. September 1985)*. Innsbrucker theologishe Studien 19. Edited by Lothar Lies. Innsbruck: Tyrolia.

Williams, Frank, trans. 1994. *The Panarion of Epiphanius of Salamis, Books II and III (Sects 47–80, De Fide)*. Leiden: Brill.

Part 2
Zoharic, Kabbalistic, and Alchemical Speculations

Bifurcating the Androgyne and Engendering Sin: A Zoharic Reading of Gen 1–3

Elliot R. Wolfson

> Too early for the rainbow,
> too early for the dove.
> These are the final days:
> this is the darkness, this is the flood.
> And there is no man or woman
> who can be touched,
> but you who come between them,
> you will be judged.
> (Leonard Cohen, "The Gypsy Wife")[1]

The first three chapters of Genesis are overflowing with themes that have had a decisive impact on the formation of major theological and anthropological conceptions that have shaped Judaism and Christianity through the centuries. The kabbalistic tradition is no exception. In this essay, I will offer a modest reading that focuses on the construction of gender typologies that emerge from the narrative accounts of the creation of man and woman, the nature of sin, and the implicit sense of rectification, which may be elicited from Sefer Hazohar, the main compendium of Jewish mystical lore that began to circulate in fragmentary form in the thirteenth and fourteenth centuries, most likely in the regions of Catalonia and Castile and received a relatively stable literary form in the sixteenth century when

1. I have followed the version in Leonard Cohen's *Stranger Music* (1994, 302). The recorded version on the album *Recent Songs*, released in 1979, has some slight variations, including the title ("The Gypsy's Wife") and the critical last lines "And there is no man or woman who can't be touched/ But you who come between them will be judged." The lyrics are available at http://www.leonardcohen.com/us/music/recent-songs/gypsys-wife.

the manuscripts were prepared for the first printings in Mantua and Cremona (1558–1560).[2]

Imaginal Body: Between Literal and Figurative

Since the ensuing analysis will center principally on the matter of gender and since this cannot be understood in isolation from the larger question pertaining to the nature of embodiment, I will initiate this study with a brief observation about the nature of divine corporeality that pervaded the theosophical speculations of the kabbalists active in the time and place of the first stages of the literary and historical manifestation of the zoharic phenomenon. Despite the wide diversity of opinions expressed in kabbalistic sources, it is fair to say that the overwhelming hermeneutical principle was articulated succinctly by Moses ben Nahman, the thirteenth-century Spanish kabbalist, exegete, and talmudic commentator: Scripture, he wrote, speaks about what is below and alludes to what is above (Wolfson 1989, 110–12). As the dictum of Nahmanides demonstrates, the archaic doctrine concerning the correspondence of the upper and lower realms is applied to the twofold sense of the scriptural text, the exoteric associated with the historical and the esoteric with the symbolic. Just as the figurative meaning cannot be separated from the literal, indeed the latter is ascertained by peering through the guise of the former rather than by discarding it (Wolfson 2007, 56–110, esp. 73–74), so the supernal realm of divine potencies cannot be comprehended except through the mirror of the terrestrial realm.

Reversing the typical approach to anthropomorphism articulated by medieval philosophical exegetes, the kabbalists maintained that the spiritual entities can be described in human terms, for the tangibility of the human body is determined by the divine body to which it corresponds. Biblical anthropomorphisms, accordingly, are not to be explained simply as a concession to the limitations of human reason—"the Torah speaks in human language," according to the talmudic maxim appropriated by the philosophers to formulate the principle of accommodation; on the contrary, the anthropomorphic expressions inform us about the comport-

2. For a review of the textual problems surrounding the zoharic anthology, see Abrams 2010, 17–117, 224–428. Abrams offers a thorough review of the relevant scholarly literature.

ment of divine bodiliness, which illumines, in turn, the corporeal nature of the world and that of the human being.

Kabbalistically speaking, the notion that the limbs of the physical body signify the limbs of the spiritual body entails the supposition that the reality of both is constituted by the letters of the Hebrew alphabet. One of the more lucid formulations of the point was offered by Joseph Gikatilla, a Spanish kabbalist active in the second half of the thirteenth century, in the introduction to one of his major compositions, *Sha'arei Orah*, an expansive commentary on the ten *sefirot*, the ten luminous emanations of the divine, a passage that had a significant impact on subsequent kabbalists[3] and has also commanded the attention of a number of scholars.[4] Gikatilla begins by noting categorically that there is no similarity between divine and human with regard to either the internal essence (*etsem*) or the external form (*tavnit*), which leads him to conclude that the limbs of the human body are "made in the image of signs" (*bedimyon simanim*) that allude to the "hidden, supernal matters that the mind cannot know except in the manner of signification" (*kedimyon zikkaron*), just as the words "Reuben the son of Jacob" serve as a sign that points to the reality that is the person so named. The experiential dimension is underscored by Gikatilla's further observation that God creates the "hidden and revealed limbs" in the human body "in the image of a sign of the account of the chariot [*bedimyon siman lema'aseh merkavah*], and if a person merits to purify a limb of his limbs, that limb will be in the image of a throne for that inner, supernal matter that is called by that name" (*Sha'arei Orah* 1:49–50).

The reference to the account of the chariot is an allusion to the supernal chariot, that is, the *sefirotic* pleroma, as opposed to the angelic realm envisioned by the prophet Ezekiel, a standard distinction found in many kabbalistic sources. To say that the corporeal limbs are signs alluding to this chariot is indicative of the ontological homology between human and divine. The technical term *siman*, on this score, functions performatively as a mental icon that is similar to the material icon in Byzantine culture;[5]

---

3. Recanati, *Perush al Hatorah*, 37b–c; idem, *Perush Hatefillot* (MS Vatican ebr. 310, fols. 6b–7a); Cordovero, *Pardes Rimmonim*, 20:2; Toledot Adam, sec. 128 in Horowitz, *Shenei Luhot Haberit*. See reference to Ibn Gabbai cited below (n. 12), and compare Mottolese 2004, 204, 334.

4. Huss 1996, Wolfson 2002 (316–17). For an extensive discussion of the sign and symbol in Gikatilla's linguistic theory, see Morlok 2011 (209–75, esp. 247–66).

5. My discussion here is indebted to Pentcheva 2006, but in previous work I have

that is to say, the limbs are not merely passive surfaces upon which the *sefirotic* potencies are imprinted, but they are themselves textured surfaces by which the human agent—embodied ideally in the body politic of Israel—is conjoined to and participates in the hidden divine reality. The physical image, therefore, is the means of access to the transcendence that exceeds the very physicality of that image. The sign, like the icon, is an amalgamation of presence and absence, insofar as it makes the invisible visible within the confines of the imagination and thereby enacts the presence of what must remain absent in order to be present.

The conclusion to be drawn from Gikatilla's passage is opposite from the view advanced by exponents of a more rationalist religious philosophy, epitomized by Moses Maimonides: ascription of a body to God is not merely a rhetorical device to enunciate the inherent metaphoricity of theological language; it is rather a mode of discourse that calls into question our naturalistic and commonsensical assumptions about human and cosmic corporeality. While no kabbalist presumed that the depictions of the divine body should be construed literally as affirming that God is a fleshly being, it is also clear that no kabbalist could accept the philosophical orientation that would interpret these expressions merely as allegorical, thereby denying the ontic reality of the entity to which the expressions refer. The following statement by Charles Mopsik concerning the perspective of Abraham ben David of Posquières on anthropomorphism can be applied more broadly to other kabbalists: "Rabad, like Maimonides, does not attribute a bodily form to the supreme Being. However, biblical or rabbinic texts which appear to attribute a corporeal form to God need to be accounted for without relying on metaphor which simply neutralizes the literal meaning of the writings" (2005, 79–80).[6]

One can detect in these words an echo of Gershom Scholem's many observations on the nature of the symbol in kabbalistic literature. To cite one relevant remark from his essay, "Shi'ur Komah: The Mystical Shape of the Godhead," a study that traces the evolution of the anthropomorphic

---

independently referred to the role of the image as a mental icon in similar terms. See Wolfson 1994 (63–65, 106, 130, 167, 199–200 [in n. 43, I suggested the resemblance between the German Pietistic worship of mental icons and an approach found in a number of Greek Orthodox theologians], 201 n. 48, 275, 394–95); idem 2005 (34, 39, 122–23).

6. See also the pertinent comments of Morlok 2011, 270–71.

representations of the divine in Jewish esotericism, medieval theology was dictated by philosophers, who

> sought to push the biblical concept of monotheism to its utmost extreme, and even outdid the Bible itself in removing any vestiges therein of mythical or anthropomorphic parlance.... In the newly evolving Kabbalah, by contrast, we find the opposite tendency. Here, too, the spiritualization of the idea of God is an accepted fact, but ... the ancient images reemerged, albeit now with symbolic character. Unlike the philosophers, the Kabbalists were not ashamed of these images; on the contrary, they saw in them the repositories of divine mysteries. (1991, 38)

Elsewhere Scholem expresses this point by distinguishing between the prevalence of allegory on the part of philosophers and that of symbol on the part of kabbalists.[7] Admittedly, this distinction is too simplistic, and there are less oppositional ways to render the nature of the relationship of metaphor and symbol that can be applied more judiciously to kabbalistic texts.[8] However, with respect to the issue I discuss here, the textual evidence validates a clear-cut contrast of the philosophical and the kabbalistic approaches: kabbalists accepted the dogma of divine incorporeality but resisted interpreting anthropomorphisms as metaphorical.

An interesting example of the kabbalistic rejection of the hyperallegorization of the philosophers is found in the following comment in Menahem Recanati's *Perush Hatefillot*:

> According to the ancient and holy wisdom, everything receives the efflux from what precedes it and overflows to what is beneath it, from the First One, blessed be He, until it reaches us. Not as the reckoning of the philosophers, those of a deficient matter, who deny everything except what is comprehended by their reasoning, which is like an illusion [*ahizat einayim*]. But know in truth that with respect to everything that is in the lower world there is a matter above whence it emanates. And even though we know that there is no composition [*harkavah*] from the four elements in the angels of God, blessed be he, and they are completely intellect, they are enclothed in images [*temunot*] in accordance with the

7. The contrast between the philosophical allegory and mystical symbol is repeated in many of Scholem's writings, of which I will here mention a few examples: 1956, 26–28; 1965, 51–52, 93–94. See Schweid 1985, 43–44, 126–27; Idel 2002, 280–89.

8. See, for instance, Haskell 2005, 68–119 and 2008, 335–62.

> act that they must perform, whether merciful or judgmental. (*Perush Hatefillot*, 38a [1581])[9]

The focal point of Recanati's comments is the angels, but we can justly assume that his words can be transferred to the *sefirotic* potencies. Indeed, as he insists in the same treatise, the relationship of the Infinite—referred to both as *Ein Sof* and as the Cause of Causes (*illat haillot*, *sibbat hasibbot*)—to the *sefirot* can be compared to the relationship of the soul to the body (*Perush Hatefillot*, MS Vatican ebr. 310, fols. 3a, 4a.). This analogy is not to be interpreted just as a metaphor; rather it conveys the same sense of somatic presence implied in the depiction of the angels garbed in images that reflect either the attribute of mercy or the attribute of judgment. Although Recanati is known for viewing the *sefirot* as instruments (*kelim*) and not as the essence (*atsmut*) of the Infinite, this should not lead one to think that he considered the attributes extrinsic to God.[10] On the contrary, as he plainly states, the *sefirot* are garments (*levushim*, *malbushim*) that emanate from the essence and thus they are not ontically separate from it, a claim that he legitimates on the basis of the rabbinic pronouncement that the shell is an integral part of the snail's body (*Perush Hatefillot*, MS Vatican ebr. 310, fols. 4a–b). In my scholarship, I have employed the locution *imaginal body*, borrowed from the work of Henry Corbin on Islamic esotericism, in order to convey this sense of embodiment that is not material flesh but which is nevertheless a concrete phenomenon and not merely a figure of speech (Wolfson 1994, 108, and 2005, 38–39, 41–42, 119, 122, 246, 248–49).

I will illustrate the kabbalistic position further by referring to Meir Ibn Gabbai's criticism of Maimonides's explanation of biblical anthropomorphisms as a concession to the inability of the masses to comprehend the existence of an incorporeal being. For Ibn Gabbai, "these matters are from the class of the mysteries of the Torah, which cannot be apprehended through the way of deduction or logical syllogism, but rather through the tradition that has been received from the prophets to Moses, peace be upon him, from Sinai." Ibn Gabbai goes on to explain—based in part

---

9. I have also consulted the version in MS Vatican ebr. 310, fols. 40b–41a.

10. For a discussion of Recanati's "instrumentalist theosophy" and his attempt to combine the Maimonidean rejection of positive attribution with the kabbalistic notion of the powers of an emanated divinity, see Idel 2011, 119–21. For a more extended discussion of Recanati's view of the *sefirot* as instruments, see Idel 1998, 184–91.

on the aforementioned passage of Gikatilla—that "the lower microanthropos [*haadam haqatan hatahton*] is made and arrayed in the image of the supernal macroanthropos [*haadam hagadol haelyon*], which comprises all the potencies contained in the great name [YHWH] that is depicted figuratively as the human seated upon the throne" (*Avodat Haqodesh* 3:65). These potencies, which are "interior, subtle, and spiritual," are designated by the parts of the body even though they do not resemble the physical body either in substance or structure. The kabbalist, so to speak, wishes to burn the proverbial candle on both ends. On the one hand, there is a categorical denial of any resemblance between the human and the divine bodies, and yet, on the other hand, there is an insistence that ritual behavior on the part of Jews is endowed with theurgical significance based on the homologous relation between the two, an idea encapsulated in the motto "limb strengthens limb" (*ever mahaziq ever*)[11]: through observance of the law the limb of the human body fortifies the corresponding limb in the divine body, which is the Torah.[12]

To understand this avowal of ostensibly contradictory positions, we must bear in mind that the imaginal body in kabbalistic tradition is related to the much older belief[13] that the initial enfleshment of Adam was that of the glorious or luminous body, which was changed, as a consequence of the sin of eating of the fruit of the tree of knowledge, into the mortal body made of corruptible skin,[14] identified in some sources (e.g., Pirqe R. El.

11. Concerning this phrase, apparently first used in kabbalistic literature in the end of the thirteenth century by Joseph of Hamadan and the anonymous author of *Sefer Hayihud*, see Idel 1988, 185, and the references to other scholars cited on 367 n. 81; idem, 2002, 73 and 2005b, 138–39. See also Wolfson 1988, 231; Mopsik 1993, 217–18; Felix 2005, 95–98.

12. A cogent enunciation of this much older idea in kabbalistic theurgy, based in part on the language of Gikatilla, is found in Ibn Gabbai, *Avodat Haqodesh*, 3:65. On the isomorphic relation of the Torah and the human body, see Idel 2002, 71–74.

13. Goshen-Gottstein 1994, esp. 178–83, and see the rejoinder by Aaron 1997.

14. The idea is often expressed in kabbalistic sources on the basis of the comment in Gen. Rab. 20:12 that in the Torah of R. Meir the second word in the expression *kotnot or* (Gen 3:21) was written with an *alef* instead of an *ayin*, thereby changing the meaning from "garments of skin" to "garments of light." Concerning this motif, see Goshen-Gottstein 1994, 179–80; Kugel 1999, 132–34. Kabbalists interpreted this as an expression of the idea that the original body of Adam and Eve was a glorious and incorruptible body. See Zohar Hadash 78c (Midrash Ruth); Sefer Hazohar 1:36b; 2:229b [hereafter cited as Zohar]; Recanati, *Perush al Hatorah*, 15a; Vital, *Sefer Haliqqutim*, 28a.

46a) as the skin cast off by the serpent. The eschatological future is marked by the shedding of the garments of skin and the donning of the garments of light.[15] For some kabbalists, it was possible for the corporeal body to be transfigured proleptically in the present through ascetic practices into the ethereal or angelic body,[16] which they also viewed as the textual or linguistic body, a conception based on the widely held belief—attested in older streams of Jewish mysticism and magic—that the name of an entity is its essence or literally its body (*guf*). This perspective, which has run its course through the history of Jewish esotericism, presupposes an intrinsic connection between language and being, not simply in the mimetic sense that the former mirrors the latter but rather in the mythopoeic sense that words—both spoken and written—configure the nature of reality.

After decades of study, I have not discovered any kabbalist who would not assent to the view that what exists in the world, examined subphenomenally, are the manifold permutations of the twenty-two Hebrew letters, themselves enfolded in the Tetragrammaton, identified as the mystical essence of the Torah (Wolfson 2005, 197–202).[17] YHWH is thus the name through which the nameless is declaimed. There is no tension in the kabbalistic teaching between the view that ultimate reality is ineffable and the postulate that the nature of being is constituted by the Hebrew language. Utilizing the Heideggerian trope of ontological difference, we can describe *Ein Sof*—the infinite essence whose essence, paradoxically, is to lack any essence—as the withdrawal of being that occasions the manifestation of the myriad of beings that come to light in the concatenation of the multiple worlds. The attribute of substance, which entails both the positive demarcation of presence and the negative denotation of absence, does not apply to *Ein Sof*, the groundless ground beyond being and nonbeing, the "negation of all negation" (Scholem 1991, 38)[18] as Scholem put it in one study, reflecting, it seems, the technical term applied by Meister Eckhart to the one beyond all distinction.[19] The apophatic tendency to submerge

15. Bachrach, *Sefer Emeq Hamelekh*, 41c. See ibid., 45c, where the matter is connected to the description of the radiance of the skin of the face of Moses in Exod 34:29, 35. Concerning this theme in rabbinic texts, see Rubin and Kosman 1997.

16. For a discussion of the motif of the astral or angelic body, which is linked to the divine image, see Scholem 1991, 251–73.

17. See also the reference to other scholars cited on 422 n. 251.

18. For the original German, see Scholem 1995, 31: "der Negation aller Negationen."

19. Eckhart uses both the Latin *negatio negationis* and the Middle High German

all forms of sentient imaging in the unknowable formlessness cannot be severed from the kataphatic insistence on the possibility of apprehending that formlessness through those very forms that collectively inhere in the name that is the Torah, the linguistic measure of carnality in the divine, human, and cosmic planes (Wolfson 2005, 118–19).

Divine embodiment, accordingly, sheds light on the complex notion of body as the sign of the signified that is itself the signifier of that for which there is no correlative signification, the mystery of the plenitudinal lack—the fullness of the infinite emptiness—that is beyond symbolization. The anthropomorphic images, when viewed through the lens of this signifying network, portend that the semiotic nature of the body is such that the imaginary is real, since there is no reality apart from what is imagined to be real. The thread that binds the imaginal and the real as the antipodal forces circumscribed within this circularity is the metaphysical conjecture that the constituent element of matter is the letter.[20] This is the mystical import of the kabbalistic appropriation of the archaic belief that the human body is a microcosm of the macroanthropos (see Altmann, 1969, 19–28). The nature of that anthropos is specularized through the prism of sexual difference, a central doctrine that impacted both the theosophic understanding of the *sefirotic* emanations promulgated by the kabbalists and their understanding of the texture of the ecstatic experience of the divine.

versagen des versagennes. Many scholars have written about this Eckhartian expression and traced its sources. See, for example, Kelley 1977, 106–13; McGinn 1981, 7–8 and 2001, 84, 94, 231–32 nn. 141–42; Mojsisch, 2001, 95–97; Charles-Saget 1998, 312; Hollywood 1995, 130–31; Tobin 1986, 74–78; Dobie 2010, 138–49.

20. My thinking here is in accord with the one embraced by Mottolese 2004, 328–31. After referring positively to my Corbinian approach regarding the *mundus imaginalis*, the author adds that the emphasis on the analogical in kabbalistic symbolism has its "roots" in the "linguistic ontology" of the kabbalists, that is, "the idea that reality is basically language.… A semiotic net stands, therefore, behind both the corporeal and incorporeal layers of reality; names represent the essence of all entities, from the human to the supernal ones. In the formulas employed by Gikatilla—'analogy of signification' [*dimyon simanim*] and 'analogy of memorization' [*dimyon zikkaron*]—the term *dimyon* goes beyond any figurative or docetic orientation. These formulas allude to the fact that a linguistic-ontological relation … is given between signifier and signified, and that it links in-depth the human and the divine realms defined by the same names." It appears that Mottolese has not grasped that this is precisely my own position concerning the status of the imaginal realm.

Masculine Androgyne: From Man Woman Born

As is well-known, the accounts of the creation of man and woman in the first two chapters of Genesis—stemming respectively from the Priestly and the Yahwist strata—offer seemingly disparate perspectives on gender construction. The first account relates that God created Adam as male and female concurrently, which has been interpreted through the centuries as an affirmation of the androgynous status of the primordial human being. By contrast, the second chapter recounts that man was created first and then woman was created from his side or rib (*tsela*), an ontological dependency instantiated linguistically in the fact that woman is called *ishshah*, the feminine form derived from the masculine *ish*.[21] With good reason some contemporary feminist readers have argued that the first account has greater egalitarian potential than the second. For the medieval Jewish exegete, however, this strategy was not viable given the presumption regarding the underlying unity of the biblical text. The kabbalists were no exception to the rule, and thus, in spite of their attending to the feminine dimension of the divine, the attribute of judgment, which complements the masculine attribute of mercy, they interpreted the description of woman being fashioned from man in the second account as a midrashic explication of the androgynous nature of primal Adam implied in the first account.

Due to limitations of space, I will restrict myself in this study to interpretations of the biblical text culled from the zoharic compilation, although it should be understood that a more exhaustive examination of this material requires an exposition of other kabbalistic sources prior to and/or contemporary with the beginning of the circulation of parts of the Zohar in the last decades of the thirteenth and the first decades of the fourteenth century.

Gender Binary

Let me begin my analysis with the citation of a critical passage that has been invoked by several scholars in support of the contention that the medieval kabbalists, as opposed to the encratic tendency of other forms of mystical piety, including especially in the history of Christianity, celebrated

---

21. For a summary of the Priestly and the Yahwistic accounts in the first two chapters of Genesis, see Noort 2000.

heterosexuality as the means to bring about the rectification of the schism within the divine, which corresponds to the exilic state of the Jewish people in the world:

> R. Simeon said: Supernal mysteries were revealed in these two verses [Gen 5:1–2]. "Male and female he created them," to teach about the supernal glory, the mystery of faith, for out of this mystery Adam was created.... "Male and female he created them." From here [we learn that] any image in which there is not found male and female is not a supernal image as is appropriate, and this has been established in the mystery of our Mishnah. Come and see: in any place where male and female are not found as one, the blessed holy One does not place his dwelling there, and blessings are not found except in a place where male and female are found [b. Yebam. 62b], as it is written: "He blessed them and called them Adam in the day he created them." It is not written: "He blessed him and called his name Adam," for even the name Adam is not invoked except when male and female are one. (Zohar 1:55b)

The divine image (*tselem elohim*) with which the human being was created is interpreted in light of the gender binary, an interpretation that accords not only with the literal sense of the scriptural text but one that was hinted at in at least two rabbinic pericopae that surely influenced the kabbalists: the first, attributed to R. Jeremiah ben Eleazar, maintained that God created Adam as an androgyne (אנדרוגינס), and the second, attributed to R. Samuel ben Nahman, maintained that God created Adam two-faced (דיפרוסופון); whatever the differences between the two explanations, they both proffer a somatic and specifically gendered understanding of the image (Gen. Rab. 8:1).[22] The polarity of masculine and feminine in the pleroma of the divine emanations is alluded to in the statement ascribed to Simeon ben Yohai, the master of the imaginary fraternity, that the verses from Gen 5, which basically reiterate the Priestly account of Gen 1, instruct us about the "supernal glory" and the "mystery of faith." Just as the earthly Adam was fashioned in the image that is male and female, so the image above of which the human image is but an image (Zohar 3:10b). Moreover, it is incumbent on each Jewish male to be conjoined to a female, so that the

22. See Aaron 1995, esp. 8–10. On the somatic understanding of the divine image in rabbinic literature, see the studies of Goshen-Gottstein and Aaron cited above in n. 13, as well as the references in Wolfson 1994, 23 n. 57, and Lorberbaum 2004, 83–104.

image below will be complete. If a man is not paired with a woman, there is no appropriate vessel to receive the blessings from the supernal image.

On the face of it the text might support the view that kabbalists operated with a theory that accords equal value to both genders, since heterosexual union is affirmed as necessary to merit the divine effluence; indeed, the very name "Adam" is invoked only when masculine and feminine are united. But to adopt such a position fails to take into account the dynamics of gender construction underlying the kabbalistic symbolism. Androgyny, and the nature of the heterosexual union implied thereby, cannot be grasped by simply repeating the literal words espoused in the primary sources and listing each reference to the female who complements the male.[23] Even in the aforecited passage, if one is attuned to the subtle nuances of the gender politics, as it were, one can detect the androcentrism at play: the male must couple with the female to complete his own image by having the space—sometimes demarcated on the basis of rabbinic precedent as the house—in which to extend and overflow, characteristics that are troped as decidedly masculine in the kabbalistic axiology. By so doing, he becomes himself a container to receive the divine efflux issuing from the dwelling of the Shekhinah, and consequently, the female above is masculinized and the male below feminized.[24]

The key to comprehending the symbol of the androgyne in the kabbalistic material is to discern the manner in which the scriptural narratives

23. This is the case with the presentation of the kabbalistic discussions of the motif of the androgyne in Idel 2005a and 2005c, 94–103. The conceptual framing of Idel's analysis of gender and kabbalah is, in great measure, polemical in nature, inasmuch as it is an attempt to refute my perspective either explicitly or implicitly—indeed, Idel often attacks my views without mentioning my name, a rather questionable scholarly practice. It is impossible to engage here in a detailed refutation of Idel's relentless criticisms, but I will say that they are all based on a fundamental inability to understand the feminist appraisal of androcentrism and phallocentrism, two analytic categories that have informed my work. To engage my analyses properly, it is not sufficient either to list sources where the feminine is mentioned or even to delineate places where a seemingly more active role is assigned to the woman (see, for instance, the appendix in Idel 2005c, 247–50, which deals with some texts that allocate a theurgical role to women in the act of coitus; see Wolfson 2005, 63, where I have already alluded to such a possibility, a discussion ignored by Idel). The piling up of texts does not challenge the androcentric and phallocentric aspects of the tradition I have uncovered through the use of various interpretative strategies.

24. For more on the feminization of the masculine, see Wolfson 2005, 329–32.

are read. As I have documented in detail elsewhere, the position adopted in the first chapter of Genesis that Adam was created male and female was read by kabbalists through the prism of the description of woman being created out of man in the second chapter of Genesis.[25] Consider this section from a homily on the verse, "The Lord is my strength and might" (Exod 15:2), which begins with R. Hiyya's exposition of "You formed me from behind and in front; you lay your hand upon me" (Ps 139:5):

> R. Isaac said: Adam was created two-faced [*du partsufin*] as it has been established. "He took one of his sides" [*wa-yiqah ahat mi-tsal'otaw*] [Gen 2:21]—the blessed holy One split him and two were produced, one from the east and one from the west, as it is written "You formed me from behind and in front" [Ps 139:5]. "From behind" [*ahor*] is the west and "in front" [*qedem*] is the east. R. Hiyya said: What did the blessed holy One do? He adorned that female, perfecting her beauty above everything, and brought her to Adam, as it is written "And the Lord God fashioned the side that he had taken from the man into a woman" [Gen 2:22].[26] Come and see: What is written above? "He took one of his sides." What is "one"? As it is said, "Only one is my dove, my perfect one, the only one of her mother" [Song 6:9]. *Mi-tsal'otaw*—"from his sides," as it is said "And for the [other] side of the Tabernacle [*uletsela hamishkan*] [Exod 26:20]. (Zohar 2:55a)

Weaving together threads from various rabbinic sources, the author of the zoharic text affirms that the construction of woman from man according to Gen 2 should be understood as the severing of the original androgyne depicted in Gen 1. The sawing apart of the androgyne is what brought about the gender polarity, the masculine symbolized as the front or the east and the feminine as the back or the west. The fashioning of the side conveys that God adorned and beautified the female, ostensibly to make her an object worthy of the male gaze, a theme that

25. See my extended discussions of the symbol of the androgyne in Wolfson 2005, 67–77, 142–89.

26. Compare the interpretation of the verse "And the Lord God fashioned the side that he had taken from the man into a woman" (Gen 2:22) transmitted in the name of R. Simeon ben Yohai in Gen. Rab. 18:1: "He adorned her like a bride and brought her to him. There are places where plaiting [*qeli'ata*] is called building [*binyata*]." And see the explanation of the same verse attributed to Simeon ben Menasia in b. Ber. 61a: "This teaches that the blessed holy One plaited Eve's hair and brought her to Adam, for in the seacoast towns plaiting is called building."

bespeaks an androcentric viewpoint. The process below is paralleled by what happened above, and thus the "one" side symbolically alludes to the Shekhinah (based on the images from Song of Songs), who becomes an independent potency when she is separated from *Tiferet*.

Androgyny: Two Autonomous or One Sovereign Gender?

But what is the status of the feminine and the masculine in the state of androgyny? Does this reflect an equivalence of two autonomous genders, or is there one sovereign gender in which the distinction is not yet operative? The following passage can help to clarify the matter:

> R. Simeon began to expound, "You carefree women, attend, hear my words!" [Isa 32:9]. How much must a man [*bar nash*] contemplate the glory of his master, so that he will be found to be a perfect creature before the blessed holy One. When the blessed holy One created man, he created him perfect, as it says "God made man straight" [Eccl 7:29]. "Man" [*et haadam*]: male and female. And the female was contained in the male [*wenuqva itkelilat bidekhura*], and thus it is written "straight" [*yashar*]. (Zohar 3:18b–19a)

Significantly, the containment of the female in the male is applied here not to the union of the two sexes after they have been separated, but to the androgynous state. The perfection of Adam—his straightness or rectitude—consists, therefore, of an androcentric subjugation of the woman. This is confirmed in another zoharic homily:

> Come and see: Adam and Eve were created side by side [*da vesitra deda*]. Why were they not created face to face [*anpin beanpin*]? Because, as it is written, "for the Lord God had not sent rain upon the earth" [Gen 2:5], and the pairing [*ziwwuga*] was not found in its arrayment [*tiqquneih*] as is fitting. When the ones below were arrayed, and they turned face to face, then it was found above.... When it was established below, so it was established above. And because until now it was not arrayed above, they were not created face to face. The verse proves it, as it is written "for the Lord God had not sent rain upon the earth," and hence "there was no man," for he was not in his arrayment. When Eve was perfected, Adam was perfected, and prior to that he was not perfected. And the secret is that up to here there is no [letter] *samekh* in the portion [of the Torah] ... and the *samekh* is a helper [*ezer*]. And this is the helper above, for it turned above face to face, male and female, one supported [*iste-*

> *makh*] by the other, certainly [as it is written] "supported for all eternity, wrought of truth and equity" [Ps 111:8]. "Supported" [*semukhim*]—male and female, for they are supported as one.... From here on there is [the occurrence of the letter] *samekh*. What is it? "He closed up [*wayisgor*] the flesh at that spot" [Gen 2:21]. She was in his side, and the one was in the side of the other. The blessed holy One certainly uprooted them and transplanted them in another place, and they turned face to face for [the sake of] perdurance [*weithadderu anpin beanpin leqiyyuma*]. (Zohar 1:35a–b)

Following the earlier opinion transmitted in the name of R. Samuel ben Nahman (Gen. Rab. 8:1), the zoharic author understands the androgynous state as one in which female and male were attached on the side and then separated by God so that they could confront one another face to face, a posture that suggests the intimacy of sexual union, which is required for the sake of procreation and the elongation of what Mopsik aptly called the body of engenderment (1989).

> Male and female: the female cleaved to his side until a great sleep fell upon him and he slumbered. And he was lying on the site of Temple below, and the blessed holy One split him, and he arrayed her as a bride is arrayed,[27] and ushered her in, as it is written "He took one of his sides and closed up the flesh at that spot" [Gen 2:21]. "He took one"—precisely! (Zohar 1:34b)

The theme is reiterated in another zoharic passage:

> It is written "You formed me from behind and in front; you lay your hand upon me" [Ps 139:5]. This verse has been established, but come and see: When the blessed holy One created Adam, they were created male and female. And the two of them were bound together, the female in the back and the male in the front, until the blessed holy One split them apart. He arrayed her and brought her before Adam so that [they could] look [at each other] face to face. When they looked face to face, love increased in the world and they gave birth to offspring in the world, which did not happen previously, as we have established. (Zohar 2:231a)

27. See above, n. 26.

The arrayment or rectification (*tiqqun*) of Adam is dependent on Eve, because without Eve being separated from Adam there could not be the possibility of coitus and the reproductive extension of the chain of existence. Hence, it is correct to say that Adam was not perfected until Eve was perfected. The original androgyne—the male that comprises the face of the male in the front and the face of the female in the back—is imperfect until it yields a division of the sexes. Nevertheless, heterosexual bonding facilitates the restoration of the female to the male whence she was taken, a hyperliteral reading of the verse "Hence a man leaves his father and mother and clings to his wife, so that they become one flesh" (Gen 2:24).[28] The "one flesh" (*basar ehad*), as the contextual sense intimates, signifies the reconstitution of the state before the woman was severed from the man, the state that I surmise displays a uniform "gender" as opposed to the dual "sex" that ensues from the split of the androgyne. With this split there emerges the patriarchal hierarchy. The deferential rank accorded the female is made explicit in the following zoharic passage:

> Come and see: when a woman is conjoined to her husband, she is called by the name of her husband, man [*ish*] and woman [*ishshah*], righteous one [*ṣaddiq*] and righteousness [*ṣedeq*].... "Hence a man leaves his father and mother and clings to his wife, so that they become one flesh"—everything to draw her in love and to be conjoined to her. (Zohar 1:49a–b)

If one reads the last sentence out of context, it can be upheld as evidence for the romantic celebration of sexual equality. However, if one reads in context, then it is evident that the goal of sexual desire from the male's point of view is to restore the part of him that was amputated. This is the meaning of the comment that when the woman is conjoined to her husband, she is called by his name. It does not say that, reciprocally, the husband is called by her name. Although it is reasonable to presume that sexual union alters

28. For discussion of various kabbalistic commentaries on this verse, see Mopsik 2005, 115–27. While I respect Mopsik's textual mastery and the civil tone of his rhetoric, his analysis of the sources does not demonstrate a sensitivity to the feminist understanding of gender dynamics. For instance, he does not even take note of how the "theme of the fundamental unity of the human being, or more precisely the unity of man who regains his original bodily unity by uniting with his wife," which serves as "a model for the destiny of the soul" (119), might be problematic from a woman's standpoint.

the male as much as the female, the passage gives voice to the belief that coitus ontologically, and not just functionally, is a masculinization of the female—they will be one flesh (Wolfson 1995, 92–98 and 2005, 147–49).

The effort to discredit the androcentric import of the kabbalistic symbolism by reiterating comments about the female body misses the point. Nor is it sufficient to cite passages like the one I have translated above, which clearly presume that the perfection of the human being turns on the coupling of the masculine and the feminine. That the male-female dimorphism is a prevalent motif in zoharic literature is incontestable, but the issue is how it is to be interpreted, what framework is most suitable to explain the construction of gender identity. To affirm this binary on behalf of the kabbalists is an obvious platitude that proves nothing about the values assigned respectively to femininity and masculinity in the overall semiotic register that informed their worldview.[29]

Similarly, the appeal to a feminine erotics in zoharic homilies is not sufficient to undermine the androcentric vantage point (see Hellner-Eshed 2009, 169–70). That women yearn erotically for men and men reciprocally for women goes without saying; from that standpoint heterosexuality is understood dynamically as a mutual commingling of opposites: the female can become male and the male female, a process that I have referred to as the crossing of gender boundaries. However, this crossing is not ambivalent in the kabbalistic symbolism; there is fluidity, but there is no ambiguity: the female that overflows is masculinized, and the male that delimits is feminized (Wolfson 1995, 110–12; 2005, 94–95).

Masculine Androgyny

The deep structure undergirding the kabbalistic construction of gender—and this includes the possible subversions of that structure—is that of a masculine androgyny. Thus, while the pairing of male and female

29. This is the methodological flaw in the criticism of my views mounted by Abrams 2004, 3–7, and in his more recent discussion of sexual coupling, arousal, and the motif of the androgyne in Abrams 2011, 23–30. Abrams has incorporated my work (without citing me directly) in the statement, "In Kabbalah there is one form of being and it is masculine," but he goes on to argue that "there are masculine and feminine forms of arousal" (26). I never denied that this is the case, but I have tried to show that both forms of arousal are an expression of phallomorphism. A similar misrepresentation of my work is found in Gamlieli 2006, 61–64, 248–52.

undoubtedly impacts both—in the language of one zoharic passage describing the relationship of *Yesod* and *Malkhut*, "two gradations that are one, encompassing male and female" (*terein dargin deinun had kelala dekhar wenuqva*; Zohar 2:70a)—kabbalistic texts repeatedly emphasize that the result of the union is an amelioration of judgment by mercy, which translates in gender terms as a taming of woman by man (Wolfson 1995, 80–85; 2005, 169–70). I am not unaware of the principle that every attribute is contained in and interacts with its opposite, and hence we can speak of the containment of the left in the right or of the containment of the right in the left. Notwithstanding the validity of this tenet, there is a qualitative difference: the conjunction of the feminine left and the masculine right brings about a fundamental alteration of the former and not of the latter, judgment is ameliorated by mercy and not mercy by judgment (Wolfson 1995, 200 n. 18).

For all the criticism of my position, not one person has cited a kabbalistic text that describes the consequence of heterosexual intercourse as mercy becoming judgmental. This imbalance ratifies the suitability of the term "male androgyne" to describe the zoharic orientation, which is inspired, as I noted above, by reading the second account of Adam's creation as an exposition of the first. The kabbalistic exegesis, in my opinion, is based on presuming one gender (the male that is both male and female) with two sexuated manifestations (the female constructed from the male). The partition of the androgyne gives rise to two sexes, which establishes the very heterogeneity that is effaced in the reinstallation of the originary state. It behooves me to note that even when kabbalists emphasize that in the androgynous Adam male and female were "equal in power" and "one in actuality,"[30] this does not necessarily measure up to the criterion of egalitarianism amenable to our contemporary sensibility; the equality and oneness may denote a unifying gender without sexual differentiation. Alternatively expressed, the androgynous nature of Adam—human and divine—is one in which there is neither male nor female as discrete constellations but only the male that comprises male and female. The equality of power and oneness of actuality defuse a sense of genuine difference (Wolfson 2005, 56–59).

One of the most striking articulations of the point is the zoharic adaptation of the aggadic motif of the diminution of the moon attributed to

30. See the text of Isaac of Acre cited and analyzed in Wolfson 2005, 61–62.

Simeon ben Pazzi (b. H ul. 60b). Noting the discrepancy in the reference to the sun and the moon first as "two great lights" and then respectively as the "greater light" and the "lesser light" (Gen 1:16), the rabbinic sage reportedly taught that the initial intention was that the luminosity of the sun and the moon would be equal, but the moon complained to God, "Can two kings make use of one crown?" As punishment she was instructed to diminish herself. Kabbalists considered this talmudic legend to be one of the profound mysteries of the tradition.

For my purposes I wish to focus only on one aspect that emerges from the zoharic revision of this theme. Prior to the lessening of the lunar light, there was no difference in stature between the sun and the moon, even though day and night were still discriminated. After the moon decreased her size, her only illumination was the light reflected from the sun, a commonplace idea in medieval astronomy. The symbolic import of the legend instructs us about the feminine potency of *Malkhut* in relation to the masculine potency of *Tiferet*: once the former separates from the latter, she is inferior and submissive (Zohar 1:20a; 2:219b; Tiqqunei Zohar, sec. 36, 78a).[31] It is noteworthy that in one zoharic context, the insinuation that the moon was originally the same stature of the sun is questioned. The ascription of the word "great" to the moon denotes that when the moon is united with the sun, literally "stands with the sun in one mystery," she is called "great" on account of him (Zohar Hadash, 70d–71a [Shir Hashirim]), a reading that accentuates the androcentricism. Be that as it may, based on the theory that everything below is parallel to what is above, this can be applied as well to the lower anthropos. In the original androgynous state, there was no gender differentiation; after the division into male and female, the latter is relegated to a compliant position vis-à-vis the former.

To offer another example in a somewhat less negative register: in a zoharic homily on Gen 2:22, it is emphasized that just as in the divine realm the feminine potency, the Oral Torah, is derived from the masculine, the Written Torah, so in the human realm woman is constructed from man. And just as above the Oral Torah must be united with and contained in the Written Torah, so below the goal is for the woman to be conjoined to the man whence she receives her sustenance (Zohar 1:48b). In a typical androcentric reversal, the power of nourishment and the bestowal of

31. See also Zohar 1:181a, where the blemish of the moon is linked directly to the "side of the evil serpent," that is, the demonic force. See, however, Zohar 2:144b, where this explanation is questioned.

life are apportioned to the male rather than to the female. The respective values assigned to each gender are brought into clearer focus in another zoharic text, interpreting the verse "The Lord God formed man" [*wayyitser YHWH elohim et haadam*] (Gen 2:7):

> Here everything was perfected in the right and in the left. We have thus established [the import of the words] "The Lord God formed"—the good inclination and the evil inclination. Why? The good inclination for himself, the evil inclination to be aroused for his female, and it is aroused always from the left side. The mystery of the matter that we learn from here is that the north is aroused always vis-à-vis the female and it is bound to her, and thus she is called *ishshah.* (Zohar 1:49a)[32]

The zoharic exegesis is based on the earlier rabbinic interpretation of the orthographic doubling of the letter *yod* in the word *wayyitser* as signifying the creation of the two impulses (Gen. Rab. 14:4).[33] What is crucial in the kabbalistic exposition is the theosophic and gender overlay of the rabbinic taxonomy. First, the two psychic inclinations emanate from the two potencies in the divine realm, which are symbolized by the names of God—together they constitute the "complete name" (*shem male*)—YHWH corresponds to the masculine and Elohim to the feminine. Second, the evil impulse is correlated with the female and the good impulse with the male. Since Adam was created androgynous, he comprised both impulses. The good impulse on the right side is his natural deportment; the evil impulse on the left side is the female aspect, which is labeled as the means by which the male is sexually aroused toward the female. Rather than representing the adulation of the female, as some scholars of the kabbalah have naively insisted, this is another facet of the androcentric—and here I would add phallomorphic—pigeonholing: the woman is responsible for stimulating the man's erotic drive.

32. I have translated the version of this passage as it appears in *Sefer ha-Zohar* (Cremona: Vicenzo Conti, 1559–1560), Bere'shit, 137.

33. The bibliography on the rabbinic notion of the two inclinations is vast. For a relatively recent study that provides an innovative approach and addresses much of the previous scholarship, see Rosen-Zvi 2008. The passage from Genesis Rabbah is discussed on 533–34. See also Rosen-Zvi 2011, 65–96, esp. 72–73.

Transgression and the Demonization of the Feminine

In the biblical narrative, immediately after the creation of woman from man, the serpent enters the scene and serves as the causal agency to occasion the act of disobedience. Consider the zoharic treatment of this narratological shift:

> "Hence a man leaves his father and mother and clings to his wife, so that they become one flesh" [Gen 2:24]. Everything was to draw her in love and to cleave to her. When all of these matters were aroused what is written? "And the serpent was the shrewdest [of all the wild beasts]" [Gen 3:1]. The evil impulse was aroused to seize her, in order to be bound to her in carnal desire, and arousing in her other matters in which the evil impulse delights. And as a consequence, what is written? "When the woman saw that the tree was good for eating and a delight to the eyes, and that the tree was desirable as a source of wisdom, she took of its fruit and ate" [Gen 3:6]—she received it voluntarily, "and also gave some to her husband who was with her." For now she was aroused in desire toward him, to bestow passion and love on him. This matter shows human beings how the act corresponds to what is above. Rabbi Eleazar said: If so, how can we establish that above the evil impulse seizes the female? He [R. Simeon bar Yohai] replied: We have already conferred about the good impulse and the evil impulse above and below. The good impulse is from the right and the evil impulse is from the left, and the left above seizes the female to be bound to her as one in her body, as it says "His left hand was under my head" [Song 2:6]. (Zohar 1:49b)

Again we see that the split of the male androgyne into male and female results in the need for heterosexual union. Copulation between a man and his spouse repairs that split by restoring the one flesh that is simultaneously male and female and therefore neither male nor female in any recognizable sexualized sense. The state of liminality between the fissure of exile and the unity of redemption is precarious, affording the possibility for the demonic to intrude into the space of the feminine and forge an illicit cohabitation. This is precisely the zoharic explanation of the scriptural tale: the serpent is the demonic force, which attaches itself primarily to the woman, since she is aligned with the evil impulse in contrast to the man, who is aligned with the good impulse. What is particularly noteworthy is that the carnal desire of the feminine is problematized, a theme that is well attested in the patriarchal stereotype of the wanton woman. I do not say that this is the only view of feminine sexuality in the zoharic compilation.

There are plenty of passages that relate to women's eroticism as an integral part of the *hieros gamos* above and the sacralization of sexuality below.

As I have already noted, the erotic arousal is always instigated from the left side of judgment, which rendered psychologically endows the woman's capacity to contain with the power to stimulate the man's potency to overflow. In this respect the feminine attribute of judgment is hardly passive; to contain or to delimit is an energetic force that is vital for the creative ebb and flow of being. But one cannot ignore the leitmotif of the passage explaining the sin in the garden of Eden. Right after Scripture announces the need for man to cleave to his wife to be one flesh, the woman is allured by and cohabits with the serpent, an illicit union that leads to the sin of eating from the tree of knowledge. What is ostensibly an act of fusion morphs into a divisive gesture that induces further division by activating the duality of good and evil and bringing death to humankind (Zohar 2:144b).

The disobedience of Adam and Eve serves as a prototype that sheds light on the nature of sin in general. Needless to say, this is a vast topic that cannot be easily simplified, but one can elicit from many zoharic passages, not to mention other kabbalistic sources, that transgression is understood concurrently as the cause and the effect of the severance of the male and the female, the sixth and tenth emanations, leading especially to the reification of the latter as an object of veneration. The division of the sexes is detrimental for both male and female, and often we encounter in zoharic homilies the admonition that every Jewish man must be paired with a woman to strengthen the faith and to ensure that the blessings of the divine presence will not depart from him (Zohar 1:49b, 50a, 228b). In spite of this emphasis, the separation of the female from the male is treated in a far more deleterious way than the separation of the male from the female; indeed, it is portrayed as heresy or idolatry—linked to many of the major acts of impertinence recorded in the biblical narrative, including the erection of the tower of Babel and the worshipping of the golden calf—and referred to metaphorically as the cutting of the shoots or the plucking of the fruit of the tree (Wolfson 2005, 374, 505 n. 200).

As we have seen, the primordial insurrection was set into motion by the collusion of the demonic serpent and Eve, which is perfectly logical given that the feminine is located on the left side of judgment whence the demonic emanates. An even more pernicious expression of this alliance is found in the zoharic reworking of the rabbinic motif (b. Šabb. 145b–146a; Pirqe R. El. 21, 48a) regarding the insemination of the serpent's filth into

Eve, which resulted in the birth of Cain (Zohar 1:54a; 2:231a),[34] or in the more attenuated version, Cain and Abel were both born from Adam, but the former inherited the slime of the serpent that had entered into Eve (Zohar 1:54a). Some kabbalists even went as far as connecting the sin of Eve with the fable about the moon's impudence, which I discussed above.[35] I have not found this in zoharic material, but the intent of that explanation is consistent with the view disseminated therein: transgression comes about through the woman usurping power for herself and seeking to control man. The punishment, accordingly, was the allocation of man's dominance over the woman.

Neither Male nor Female: Redemption and Overcoming Gender Dimorphism

In the concluding section, I would like to consider Mopsik's more extensive analysis of different kabbalistic interpretations of Gen 1:26–27 (2005, 75–114), which on the face of it challenges my notion of the male androgyne.[36] Mopsik distinguishes two exegetical approaches, one that views the account of the creation of woman from man in Gen 2 as an explication of the account of Adam being created simultaneously as male and female in Gen 1 and the second that views the account of Gen 2 as a sequel to Gen 1. According to the second possibility, championed especially by Solomon ben Isaac (Rashi), the primordial bisexual man is separated into two halves,

34. See also Zohar 1:37a, where Cain is said to have been born from the filth of Samael with which Eve was inseminated.

35. See the references above, n. 31.

36. For an explicit criticism of my explanatory model, see Mopsik 2005, 27. Mopsik's rejection of my position is part of a long study on the "masculine woman," which is predicated on the idea that each gender is contained in and expressed through the other. I obviously accept this to be the case, and I have written on the phenomenon, but this does not disprove my claims, and none of the sources that Mopsik cites refute my perspective, since they all deal with the dynamic of gender after the division into male and female. The question for me is whether the standpoint from which the gender dimorphism is to be evaluated is truly egalitarian, as Mopsik claims, or another facet of the androcentricism, as I have claimed. See my comments in Wolfson 2005, 447–48 n. 122. At the end of that note, I cite a number of feminist studies that have disclosed the androcentric underpinnings of the image of the androgyne as a privileging of male subjectivity. This is the hermeneutical lens through which I have read the kabbalistic sources, and it can be easily applied to the texts cited and analyzed by Mopsik.

whereas according to the first possibility, articulated most forcefully by Abraham ben David of Posquières (Rabad), the second story provides the ultimate meaning of the first such that androgyny implies that the female was originally part of the male (2005, 94–95). Mopsik admits that according to the Rabad, and other figures who follow his path, the creation narratives provide a textual rationale for the woman being subservient to man.[37] However, he qualifies this view by noting that only in the anthropological sphere such an imbalance prevails; by contrast, on the theosophical plane, that is, in the world of divine unity, gender divergence exists without the subordination of the feminine judgment to the masculine mercy; on the contrary, the interplay between attributes presumes that each is contained in the other (2005, 86–87).[38]

I am not convinced of the viability of Mopsik's position, since it rests on the distinction between two ways of reading the scriptural narratives that is in my mind questionable. Medieval exegetes presumed the unity of the biblical text, and thus viewing the second story as the sequel of the first would perforce be understood as a form of amplification rather than modification. To maintain that the rib or side of the man whence the woman was fashioned was, in fact, the removed "feminine side" of the primordial man so that the sides could face each other does not minimize, let alone eradicate, the androcentric subordination of the feminine. According to Mopsik, some kabbalists, including the zoharic authorship, followed in the footsteps of Rashi, leading them to conclude that the

> concept of a higher level with its dual and egalitarian structure thus could override the strictly patriarchal portrayal, although there was, however, a caveat: this equality could only be achieved on the human and societal levels at the end of time. Prior to this, male dominance corresponds to a necessity on the divine level, in which the Attribute of Judgment, which is feminine, must be subjected to the Attribute of Mercy, which is masculine. (2005, 96)

Mopsik supports his argument by citing a lengthy passage from the *Otsar Hakavod*, a commentary on the talmudic aggadot written in the second half of the thirteenth century by the Castilian kabbalist, Todros

37. See my own analysis in Wolfson 2005, 167–68.

38. On the intertwining of genders, see Mopsik 2005, 33–35, and compare Wolfson 2005, 60.

ben Joseph Abulafia, in which he asserts that the tradition (transmitted in the name of R. Jeremiah ben Eleazar) that Adam was created two-faced (*du partsufim*) (Gen. Rab. 8:1; b. ʿErub. 18a), anchored exegetically in the verse (Ps 139:5) that God formed man with a front (*qedem*) and a back (*ahor*), alludes to the mystery of the male and female potencies in the sefirotic pleroma, *Tiferet* and *Malkhut*. R. Jeremiah's adage is followed in the talmudic context by two interpretations—attributed to Rab and Samuel—of the verse that God formed woman from the side or rib of man (Gen 2:22), which ostensibly contradicts the notion that Adam was created bisexual. According to one interpretation, the side or rib refers to the face and according to the other, to the tail. Abulafia reads the rabbinic disputation as an attempt to undermine the second view. The construction of woman from man, accordingly, means that the feminine was separated from the masculine so that they could face one another in a sexual embrace. Mopsik draws the following conclusion from his detailed textual analysis: "By eliminating the presumption that woman was formed after man, secondarily to him and deriving from him, our author implies a duality on the level of the divine essence" (2005, 112).

The bipolarity of the human, which reflects the androgyny in the divine, thus implies the "recognition of an equality and a relationship of non-subservience between man and woman." Yet, as Mopsik is quick to point out, it is obvious that the kabbalists "did not want to overturn the existing social order" (2005, 113). Indeed, apart from the challenge to this order in the seventeenth-century Sabbatian movement,[39] he acknowledges

39. Mopsik refers to the evidence adduced by Scholem 1973 (403) that a sign of the messianic transformation could be seen in the attempts of Sabbatai Tsevi to change the status of women by including them in ritual deeds from which they were traditionally excluded, such as his allegedly calling women to the synagogue lectern in order to recite the blessings that precede and follow the public reading of the Torah. On the role of women in the Sabbatian movement, see also Goldish 2004, 46–47, 100, 106–7, 111; Halperin 2007, 39, 41, 76, 172; and the copious documentation provided by Rapoport-Albert 2011, 15–156. I accept that Sabbatai Tsevi sought to subvert the nomian framework of rabbinic authority by breaking down distinctions between men and women both in terms of ritual practice and study of esoteric texts, especially the Zohar. However, I would still maintain that the "egalitarian agenda" did not prevent the prevalence of the traditional phallomorphic symbolism on the part of the leading theologians of the movement. See Wolfson 1998, and my brief comment in 2005, 62. If I am correct, then we have an interesting discrepancy between the elitist and popular segments of the movement, a matter that demands further research.

that kabbalists have not only not implemented changes in the social realm to reflect the implications of the gender equality, they also have advanced "complicated formulations to support a certain form of domination of male over female, starting from the reflections on the position of *Malkhut* with its male partner *Tiferet*." Mopsik goes on to say that the

> inequality, rooted in the divine world, is considered to be temporary, and destined to disappear in the eschatological future.... It is clear that this inequality, although minimal, between the masculine and feminine attributes of Divinity, serves to justify the social and religious inequality between man and woman.... But because this inequality is not considered to be permanent, a breakthrough or anticipation of this future equality was also envisaged. (2005, 114)

How was it envisaged? According to Mopsik, while the kabbalists could not translate their "radically heterogeneous concepts" into a social reality, the harmony attained in the intimate sexual relations with their wives—difference without division—prefigured the reestablishment of the original truth to be realized in the messianic era (ibid).

The question that needs to be pondered is if the logic of the kabbalistic myth of redemption entails the equalization of gender, as proposed by Mopsik, or a restoration of the female to the male, as I have argued in many of my writings. I give credit to Mopsik for having the integrity to note that the egalitarianism in the divine would have to be implemented in a parallel fashion in Jewish liturgical communities. The example he offers from the Sabbatian movement is telling: the effort to rectify the gender inequality by acts, such as calling women to the Torah, in some measure reinforces the very hierarchical structure that is being subverted. While clearly breaking with the rabbinic norm of his day, the alleged act of Sabbatai Tsevi should be called hypernomian rather than antinomian, since the intent is not to abrogate the law but to fulfill it by extending beyond its limits.[40] Translated symbolically, the female becomes equal to the male when she rises from the status of one who receives to assume the posture of one who bestows, an idea that can be found in the depiction of the end-time in other kabbalistic and Hasidic sources (see Wolfson 1995, 120–21; 2009, 205–6). A bona fide overcoming of the patriarchal hierarchy, how-

---

40. For the use of the hypernomian to depict the Sabbatian phenomenon, see Wolfson 2006, 277–84.

ever, would require the apophatic erasure of difference to the point that the dyad of giving and receiving is transcended. It is not sufficient for the (feminine) receiver to become the (masculine) giver, as impressive as this may seem; the ideal unity would be one in which there is no more giver or receiver, only the giving that is receiving and the receiving that is giving.

Those who focus on the heterosexual pairing as the sign of redemption are, in my judgment, articulating what is appropriate for the first stage, which is the mending of the rupture of the male and the female. Beyond that stage, however, there is a second stage, one in which the division within the divine is surmounted in the place where opposites are indistinguishable. The eschatological overcoming is predicated, therefore, on the elevation of the feminine and her return to the masculine, a metamorphosis that is depicted figuratively as the diadem ascending to the head of the divine anthropos or in the biblical image of the woman of valor being the crown of her husband (Prov 12:4). To be sure, this dynamic is a transposition of gender—the female encircling the male (Jer 31:21)[41]—but it remains inscribed within the phallogocentrism, inasmuch as the female is redeemed by becoming male.[42] For there to be a true transvaluation and surpassing of patriarchy, the presumption of there being both male and female would have to give way to the discernment that there is neither male nor female, not because the female has been reintegrated into the male but because, to paraphrase the language of Derrida, we are beyond the binary opposition feminine/masculine (Derrida and McDonald 1982, 76).

The emphasis on heterosexual unity, which was the focus of Mopsik's work and that of many other kabbalah scholars, fails to take note of an even higher unity on the *scala contemplativa* that may be extracted from the sources. Ultimate redemption would consist of attaining the state of consciousness—or perhaps metaconsciousness—that entails incorporation of all differentiation in the indifferent oneness that is ascribed to *Ein Sof* or to *Keter*, the divine nothingness marked by the paradoxical coincidence of opposites such that night is day, left is right, white is black, Jew is non-Jew, male is female, and so on. Within the collapse of difference, which is characteristic of this indifference, there is no longer any mean-

41. See my discussion of these themes in Wolfson 2009, 200–23, esp. 201.

42. In this regard, there is an obvious affinity between the traditional kabbalistic system and what is expressed in some ancient gnostic texts. For a more elaborate analysis, see Wolfson 2005, 25–55.

ingful distinction between antinomies and hence no ontological basis to preserve the alterity of the feminine vis-à-vis the masculine or that of the masculine vis-à-vis the feminine. To enter this "matrixial borderspace," the "im-pure zone of *neither* day *nor* night, of *both* light *and* darkness" (Ettinger 2006, 109), what is required is not only an apophasis of gender, a resignification of the phallic law of desire, but an apophasis of the apophasis, a venturing beyond to the precipice, the chasm of the excluded middle, where opposites are identical in the opposition of their identity.[43]

While it is not at all clear to me that such an ideal can be implemented sociologically without dispelling the very path that leads to it, this may very well be the most daring implication of the messianic potential of the kabbalah: man and woman would be truly equal in the indifference of infinity where there is neither male nor female. Egalitarianism is not secured by the affirmation of dual sexuality, as Mopsik argued, but by the overcoming of the phallocentric system of signification that invariably engenders the potential for otherness as feminine. The delineation of the female as the site of alterity problematizes the hegemony of the masculine, and thus essentializing the feminine as the inessential, the essence that defies essentialization, has been a necessary step along the way of critical thinking. The apophasis of apophasis, however, demands taking the next step toward an unadulterated alterity, which would preclude not only the reduction of the other to the same but the reduction of the same to the other. This can take root within that borderspace where there is no other, because there is nothing but the other that in the absence of the same is not marked as the presence of an other. In taking that step, perhaps we commence to trespass the sign of both patriarchy and matriarchy.

Works Cited

Aaron, David H. 1995. Imagery of the Divine and the Human: On the Mythology of Genesis Rabba 8 §1. *JJTP* 5:1–62.

———. 1997. Shedding Light on God's Body in Rabbinic Midrashim: Reflections on the Theory of a Luminous Adam. *HTR* 90:299–314.

Abrams, Daniel. 2004. *The Female Body of God in Kabbalistic Literature: Embodied Forms of Love and Sexuality in the Divine Feminine* [Hebrew]. Jerusalem: Magnes.

43. See the nuanced discussion in Keller 2008.

———. 2010. *Kabbalistic Manuscripts and Textual Theory: Methodologies of Textual Scholarship and Editorial Practice in the Study of Jewish Mysticism.* Los Angeles: Cherub.

———. 2011. *Ten Psychoanalytic Aphorisms on the Kabbalah.* Los Angeles: Cherub.

Altmann, Alexander. 1969. *Studies in Religious Philosophy and Mysticism.* Ithaca, N.Y.: Cornell University Press.

Azulai, Abraham. 1685. *Sefer Hesed le-Avraham.* Amsterdam: n.p.

Bachrach, Naftali. 1648. *Sefer Emeq Hamelekh.* Amsterdam: n.p.

Charles-Saget, Annick. 1998. Non-être et néant chez Maître Eckhart. Pages 301–18 in *Voici Maître Eckhart: Textes et études réunis par Emilie Zum Brunn.* Grenoble: Million.

Cohen, Leonard. 1994. *Stranger Music: Selected Poems and Songs.* New York: Vintage.

Cordovero, Moses. 2000. *Pardes Rimmonim.* Jerusalem: Yerid Hasefarim.

Derrida, Jacques, and Christie V. McDonald. 1982. Choreographies. *Diacritics* 12:66–76.

Dobie, Robert J. 2010. *Logos and Revelation: Ibn 'Arabi, Meister Eckhart, and Mystical Hermeneutics.* Washington, D.C.: Catholic University of America Press.

Ettinger, Bracha L. 2006. *The Matrixial Borderspace.* Edited with an afterword by Brian Massumi. Minneapolis: University of Minnesota Press.

Felix, Iris. 2005. "Theurgy, Magic and Mysticism in the Kabbalah of R. Joseph of Shushan" [Hebrew]. Ph.D. diss., Hebrew University.

Gamlieli, Dvorah Bat-David. 2006. *Psychoanalysis and Kabbalah: The Masculine and Feminine in Lurianic Kabbalah* [Hebrew]. Los Angeles: Cherub.

Genesis Rabbah. 1965. Edited by Julius Theodor and Chanoch Albeck. Jerusalem: Wahrmann.

Gikatilla, Joseph. 1981. *Sha'arei Orah.* Edited by Joseph Ben-Shlomo. 2 vols. Jerusalem: Mosad Bialik.

Goldish, Matt. 2004. *The Sabbatean Prophets.* Cambridge: Harvard University Press.

Goshen-Gottstein, Alon. 1994. The Body as Image of God in Rabbinic Literature. *HTR* 87:171–95.

Halperin, David J. 2007. *Sabbatai Zevi: Testimonies to a Fallen Messiah.* Oxford: Littman Library of Jewish Civilization.

Haskell, Ellen. 2005. "Metaphor and Symbolic Representation: The Image of God as Suckling Mother in Thirteenth Century Kabbalah." Ph.D. diss., University of Chicago.

———. 2008. Metaphor, Transformation, and Transcendence: Toward an Understanding of Kabbalistic Imagery in *Sefer Hazohar*. *Proof* 28:335–62.

Hellner-Eshed, Melila. 2009. *A River Flows from Eden: The Language of Mystical Experience in the Zohar*. Stanford: Stanford University Press.

Hollywood, Amy. 1995. *The Soul as Virgin Wife: Mechthild of Magdeburg, Marguerite Porete, and Meister Eckhart*. Notre Dame, Ind.: University of Notre Dame Press.

Horowitz, Isaiah. 1997. *Shenei Luhot Haberit*. Vol. 1. Haifa: Yad Ramah Institute.

Huss, Boaz. 1996. R. Joseph Gikatilla's Definition of Symbolism and Its Versions in Kabbalistic Literature [Hebrew]. *JSJT* 12:160–64.

Ibn Gabbai, Meir. 2010. *Avodat Haqodesh*. Jerusalem: n.p.

Idel, Moshe. 1988. *Kabbalah: New Perspectives*. New Haven: Yale University Press.

———. 1998. *R. Menahem Recanati: The Kabbalist* [Hebrew]. Vol. 1. Tel Aviv: Schocken.

———. 2002. *Absorbing Perfections: Kabbalah and Interpretation*. New Haven: Yale University Press.

———. 2005a. Androgyny and Equality in the Theosophico-Theurgical Kabbalah. *Diogenes* 52:27–38.

———. 2005b. *Enchanted Chains: Techniques and Rituals in Jewish Mysticism*. Los Angeles: Cherub.

———. 2005c. *Kabbalah and Eros*. New Haven: Yale University Press.

———. 2011. *Kabbalah in Italy 1280–1510: A Survey*. New Haven: Yale University Press.

Keller, Catherine. 2008. The Apophasis of Gender: A Fourfold Unsaying of Feminist Theology. *JAAR* 76:905–33.

Kelley, Carl F. 1977. *Meister Eckhart on Divine Knowledge*. New Haven: Yale University Press.

Kugel, James L. 1999. *Traditions of the Bible: A Guide to the Bible as It Was at the Start of the Common Era*. Cambridge: Harvard University Press.

Lorberbaum, Yair. 2004. *Image of God: Halakhah and Aggadah* [Hebrew]. Tel Aviv: Schocken.

McGinn, Bernard. 1981. The God beyond God: Theology and Mysticism in the Thought of Meister Eckhart. *JR* 61:1–19.

———. 2001. *The Mystical Thought of Meister Eckhart: The Man from Whom God Hid Nothing*. New York: Crossroad.

Mojsisch, Burkhard. 2001. *Meister Eckhart: Analogy, Univocity, and Unity*. Translated with a preface and an appendix by Orrin F. Summerell. Amsterdam: Grüner.

Mopsik, Charles. 1989. The Body of Engenderment in the Hebrew Bible, the Rabbinic Tradition and the Kabbalah. Pages 49–73 in *Fragments for a History of the Human Body*. Edited by Michel Feher with Ramona Naddaff and Nadia Tazi. New York: Zone.

———. 1993. *Les grands textes de la cabale: Les rites qui font Dieu*. Paris: Verdier.

———. 2005. *Sex of the Soul: The Vicissitudes of Sexual Difference in Kabbalah*. Edited with a foreword by Daniel Abrams. Los Angeles: Cherub.

Morlok, Elke. 2011. *Rabbi Joseph Gikatilla's Hermeneutics*. Tübingen: Mohr Siebeck.

Mottolese, Maurizio. 2004. *Analogy in Midrash and Kabbalah: Interpretive Projections of the Sanctuary and Ritual*. Los Angeles: Cherub.

Noort, Edward. 2000. The Creation of Man and Woman in Biblical and Ancient Near Eastern Traditions. Pages 1–18 in *The Creation of Man and Woman: Interpretations of the Biblical Narratives in Jewish and Christian Traditions*. Edited by Gerard P. Luttikhuizen. Leiden: Brill.

Pentcheva, Bissera V. 2006. The Performative Icon. *Art Bulletin* 88:631–55.

Pirqei Rabbi Eliezer. 1852. Warsaw: n.p.

Rapoport-Albert, Ada. 2011. *Women and the Messianic Heresy of Sabbatai Zevi 1666–1816*. Oxford: Littman Library of Jewish Civilization.

Recanati, Menahem. *Perush Hatefillot*. MS Vatican ebr. 310.

———. 1581. *Perush Hatefillot*. Published in *Sefer Ta'amei Hamitzvot*. Basel: n.p.

———. 1961. *Perush al Hatorah*. Jerusalem: n.p.

Rosen-Zvi, Ishay. 2008. Two Rabbinic Inclinations? Rethinking a Scholarly Dogma. *JSJ* 39:513–39.

———. 2011. *Demonic Desires: Yetzer Hara and the Problem of Evil in Late Antiquity*. Philadelphia: University of Pennsylvania Press.

Rubin, Nissan, and Admiel Kosman. 1997. The Clothing of the Primordial Adam as a Symbol of Apocalyptic Time in Midrashic Sources. *HTR* 90:155–74.

Scholem, Gershom. 1956. *Major Trends in Jewish Mysticism*. New York: Schocken.

———. 1965. *On the Kabbalah and Its Symbolism*. Translated by Ralph Manheim. New York: Schocken.

———. 1973. *Sabbatai Ṣevi: The Mystical Messiah 1626–1676*. Princeton: Princeton University Press.

———. 1991. *On the Mystical Shape of the Godhead: Basic Concepts in the Kabbalah*. Edited and revised by Jonathan Chipman. Translated by Joachim Neugroschel. New York: Schocken.

———. 1995. *Von der mystischen Gestalt der Gottheit: Studien zu Grundbegriffen der Kabbala*. Frankfurt: Suhrkamp.

Schweid, Eliezer. 1985. *Judaism and Mysticism according to Gershom Scholem: A Critical Analysis and Programmatic Discussion*. Translated by David Avraham Weiner. Atlanta: Scholars Press.

Sefer ha-Zohar. 1559–1560. Cremona: Vicenzo Conti.

———. 1984. Edited by Reuven Margaliot. 3 vols. Jerusalem: Mosad Harav Kook.

Tiqqunei Zohar. 1978. Edited by Reuven Margaliot. Jerusalem: Mosad Harav Kook.

Tobin, Frank. 1986. *Meister Eckhart: Thought and Language*. Philadelphia: University of Pennsylvania Press.

Vital, Hayyim. 1913. *Sefer Haliqqutim*. Jerusalem: n.p.

———. 1988. *Sefer Etz Hayyim*. Jerusalem: Meqor.

Wolfson, Elliot R. 1988. Mystical Rationalization of the Commandments in *Sefer ha-Rimmon*. *HUCA* 59:217–51.

———. 1989. By Way of Truth: Aspects of Nahmanides' Kabbalistic Hermeneutic. *AJSR* 14:103–78.

———. 1994. *Through a Speculum That Shines: Vision and Imagination in Medieval Jewish Mysticism*. Princeton: Princeton University Press.

———. 1995. *Circle in the Square: Studies in the Use of Gender in Kabbalistic Symbolism*. Albany: State University of New York Press.

———. 1998. The Engenderment of Messianic Politics: Symbolic Significance of Sabbatai Ṣevi's Coronation. Pages 203–58 in *Toward the Millennium: Messianic Expectations from the Bible to Waco*. Edited by Peter Schäfer and Mark Cohen. Leiden: Brill.

———. 2002. Mirror of Nature Reflected in the Symbolism of Medieval Kabbalah. Pages 305–31 in *Judaism and Ecology: Created World and Revealed Word*. Edited by Hava Tirosh-Samuelson. Cambridge: Harvard University Press.

———. 2005. *Language, Eros, Being: Kabbalistic Hermeneutics and Poetic Imagination*. New York: Fordham University Press.

———. 2006. *Venturing Beyond: Law and Morality in Kabbalistic Mysticism*. Oxford: Oxford University Press.
———. 2007. *Luminal Darkness: Imaginal Gleanings from Zoharic Literature*. Oxford: Oneworld.
———. 2009. *Open Secret: Postmessianic Mysticism and the Mystical Revision of Menaḥem Mendel Schneerson*. New York: Columbia University Press.
Zohar Hadash. 1978. Edited by Reuven Margaliot. Jerusalem: Mosad Harav Kook.

The Genesis of Christian Kabbalah: Early Modern Speculations on the Work of Creation

Peter J. Forshaw

At the dawn of the European renaissance in the late fifteenth century, the Italian aristocrat and philosopher Giovanni Pico della Mirandola (1463–1494) became the first Christian by birth known to have studied authentic kabbalistic texts. Inspired by what he found, Pico propounded his own Christian form of kabbalah and provided material for generations of thinkers drawn to occult and esoteric philosophy. This essay discusses some continuities and differences between Jewish and Christian *kabbalah iyyunit* or "speculative kabbalah," inspired by the Jewish exegetical techniques of gematria, notariqon, and temura. This essay first introduces Jewish uses of these techniques on the opening words of Genesis 1:1, "In the beginning God created heaven and earth" (*Bere'shit bara Elohim et ha-shamayim we-et ha-ares*).[1] It then concludes with Christian appropriations of these techniques in the works of Pico and several of his Christian commentators.

Characteristics of Jewish Kabbalah

In the Jewish kabbalah the absolute perfect essence of God "lies beyond any speculative or even ecstatic comprehension" (Scholem 1978, 88). The only way to attain religious knowledge of the Godhead is through

1. This transliteration of the Hebrew is taken from Wolfson 2005, 517 n. 89. For the discussion of manifold interpretations of the first verses of Genesis by Christians and Jews, see Vignaux, *In Principio* 1973. My thanks to Dr Yossi Chajes, University of Haifa, for advice on transliterating some of the Hebrew.

contemplation of the relation between God and God's creation, as well as through speculation on the "mechanics of creation and the origins of the universe" (Giller 2001, 69). Kabbalah is generally presented as having two main preoccupations: *ma'aseh bereshit* (work of creation), based on the exegesis of Gen 1 and 2, and *ma'aseh merkavah* (work of the chariot), visions and speculations concerned with the throne on its chariot described in Ezek 1, respectively the disciplines of cosmogony and theosophy (Scholem 1978, 10–21). These two streams of speculation should be seen as complementary in the belief that "to know the stages of the creative process is also to know the stages of one's own return to the root of all existence" (Scholem 1967, 20).

Reflection on the *ma'aseh bereshit* was given a unique form in the pre-kabbalistic Sefer Yetzirah (Book of Creation), the earliest extant Hebrew text of speculative thought on cosmology and cosmogony, dating from around the third or fourth century C.E., its authorship attributed to either the patriarch Abraham or a founding figure of rabbinic thought, Rabbi Akiva.[2] The most representative themes of the Sefer Yetzirah are its declarations concerning the fundamentals of all existence: the letters of the Hebrew alphabet and the *sefirot*. The creative powers of God are embodied in the characters of the alphabet with which the Creator engraved the divine names and created the universe, each letter corresponding to a different principle of creation and having its own distinctive power. The book also introduces the notion of ten "utterances" of God, the metaphysical principles called *sefirot* (singular *sefirah*), generally translated as "enumerations" or "measures" (Wolfson 1994, 72; Herrera 2002, 407). In the Sefer Yetzirah, the *sefirot* are presented as ten principles that mediate between God and the universe, expressing ten extremities or polarities in a three-dimensional world (the dimensions of space, time, and morality): the six spatial directions (north, south, east, west, above, below), the two directions of time (beginning and end), and the two ultimate moral directions (good and evil).[3] The twenty-two Hebrew letters plus the ten *sefirot* constitute what the Sefer Yetzirah calls the "thirty-two wondrous paths of wisdom," by which Yah, the Lord of hosts "created his universe with three

2. See Scholem 1987, 24–35; Dan 1993, 198–211; Idel 2002, 113. For a scholarly edition, see Hayman 2004.

3. See the entry on the "Ten Sephirot" in van der Toorn, Becking, and van der Horst 1999, 839–43.

types of things: with writing and numbers and speech" (Sefer Yetzirah §1, Hayman 2004, 59).

The Creator's combination of writing and numbers leads not just to a plethora of created beings in nature, but also to a multiplicity of biblical interpretations. Traditional rabbinic exegesis of the Torah used a four-fold system resembling the Christian *quadriga* of literal, moral, allegorical, and mystical levels of reading scripture (Idel 1989, ch. 3). Though similar to Christian exegesis, the Jewish kabbalistic method held one fundamental difference: the Christian exegete unraveled meaning while leaving the text itself intact. The kabbalist, however, made use of interpretative techniques that reshaped and transformed the written text, reducing it to its constitutive elements, the Hebrew letters, indeed even to parts of individual letters. These textual elements were combined and permuted according to three main hermeneutical techniques, most memorably recalled by Joseph Gikatilla's (1248–ca.1305) acronym in his *Ginnat 'Egoz* (Nut Garden). The three letters of the Hebrew word for "garden" (גנת, *gnt/ginnat*) denote the techniques of gematria (arithmetical computations), notariqon (manipulation of letters into acronyms and acrostics), and temurah (permutation, commutation, or transposition of letters) (Morlok 2011, 72, 225; Reuchlin 1993, 299).

Because every Hebrew letter possesses an inherent numerical value, every letter, word, and phrase in the Torah has a mathematical significance by which correspondences are found with other words. This procedure reveals internal resonances within seemingly disparate sources. Even the most literal and mundane sounding text could, for instance, by means of the isopsephic equations in the technique of gematria, be reinterpreted in novel ways giving it a symbolic transvaluation with new depth (Dan and Kiener 1986, 11). The number thirty-two with which the Sefer Yetzirah opens, for example, is formed of the letters ל (*lamed*, with the value thirty) and ב (*bet*, with the value two), which unite to form the Hebrew word לב (*leb*, meaning "heart" (Bahir §§63, 98, Kaplan 1979, 23, 36). These letters are also the first and last letters of the Torah, the *bet* of בראשית (*bereshit*), the first word of Gen 1:1 and the *lamed* of ישראל (Israel), the last word of Deut 34:12. Thus the five books of Moses constitute the "heart" of the kabbalah (Idel 1990, 67; Secret 1964, 198; see also Kircher 1652–1654, 260). This use of gematria enabled the exegete to link not just words but scriptural passages. The thirteenth-century Spanish kabbalist Abraham Abulafia (1240–ca.1291), father of ecstatic or prophetic kabbalah, for instance, provides support for the traditional claim that the world was created with ten utterances. He demonstrated that the phrases the "work of creation" (מעשׂה בראשית, *ma'aseh bereshit*) and "with ten names" (בעשׂרה השמות, *ba'asarah hashemot*) both add up to the same total of 1,328 (Abraham Abulafia, *Sitrei Torah*, Black 2006, 143).

Numerical Interpretation in the Sefer Habahir

Strictly speaking, the term *kabbalah* refers to the particular esoteric teaching which emerged in the twelfth and thirteenth centuries in Provence and Northern Spain. The earliest extant text of kabbalah proper is the Sefer Habahir (Book of Illumination or Brilliance), initially appearing around the end of the twelfth century.[4] It is in the Bahir that we first find the image of the totality of the *sefirot* described as a "tree of emanation." Since the fourteenth century, it was depicted with a detailed diagram, the Tree of Life, listing the symbols appropriate to each *sefirah*. These ten hierarchical emanations of divine power, mediating between the God and the created universe, were to become one of the central features of kabbalah. They are typically presented, from highest to lowest, as *Keter* (Crown), *Hokhmah* (Wisdom), *Binah* (Intelligence), *Chesed* (Love), *Gevurah* (Power), *Tiferet* (Beauty), *Nezah* (Endurance), *Hod* (Majesty), *Yesod* (Foundation) and *Malkhut* (Kingdom) (Scholem 1978, 106).

The opening section of the Bahir engages with the Genesis narrative and quickly focuses on its first word, *bereshit*, with a question, "Why does the Torah begin with the letter *Beth*?" The response illustrates an approach familiar to readers and writers of kabbalistic texts. It introduces a word beginning with the same letter: "In order that it begin with a blessing [*berakah*]," and concludes: "Wherever we find the letter *Beth* it indicates a blessing. It is thus written, 'In the beginning [*bereshit*].'" *Bereshit*, we are told, is *bet-reshit* —the letter *bet*, plus the word *reshit* ("beginning"). Then, another verse from scripture is adduced in order to amplify the implications of this word. We are told, "The word 'beginning' [*reshit*] is nothing other than Wisdom. It is thus written (Ps 111:10), 'The beginning is wisdom, the fear of God' " (Bahir §3, Kaplan 1979, 1–2). We must remember here that just as the Torah begins with the letter *bet*, having the value two, so Wisdom (*Hokhmah*) is the second *sefirah* on the Tree of Life (Scholem 1987, 276). This notion is reinforced with another ques-

4. On the concept of the *sefirot* in the Bahir, see Scholem 1987, ch. 2.

tion, "Why is the letter *Beth* closed on all sides and open in the front?" The response plays on the pronunciation of the letter *bet* by introducing the homophonous word *bayit*, meaning "house." It states: "This teaches us that it is the House [*bayit*] of the world.... Do not read *Beth*, but *Bayit* (House)." The rabbi supports this idea by reminding the querent that in Prov 24:3 it is written, "With Wisdom the *House* is built, with Understanding it is established." The aspiring kabbalist is expected to grasp that this verse includes references to both the second *sefirah* (*Hokhmah*/Wisdom) and the third (*Binah*/Intelligence) (Bahir §14, Kaplan 1979, 6). We also discover in the Bahir that because the first word of the Torah begins with a capital *bet*, which has the numeric value of two thousand, it symbolizes that God contemplated Creation for two thousand years before putting it into effect (Bahir §55, Kaplan 1979, 20; Dan and Kiener 1986, 80).

Numerical Interpretation in the Sefer Hazohar

From the end of the thirteenth century, the Sefer Hazohar (Book of Splendour) became the authoritative text of Jewish mysticism. Like the Sefer Yetzirah and Bahir, it expounds the notions of the *sefirot*, but it is much longer than its predecessors. It develops a wider range of themes, beginning with the exegesis of Genesis. The Zohar does not provide one authoritative interpretation of Scripture but instead emphasizes that there are "seventy alternative explanations of the Torah" (Zohar 1:47b, Sperling and Simon 1984, 149; Matt 2004, 257), in fact "all the words of the Torah ... can all bear several meanings, and all good, and the whole Torah can be expounded in seventy ways, corresponding to seventy sides and seventy wings" (Zohar 1:54a, Sperling and Simon 1984, 171; Matt 2004, 301).

Some of the Zohar's "alternative explanations" relate to what we have already found in the Bahir. Rabbi Hamnuna the Venerable, for instance, returns to the issue of the Torah starting with the letter *bet* and points out:

> We find here a reversal of the order of the letters of the alphabet, the first two words *bereshith bara*—"in the beginning He created"—commencing with *beth*, whereas the two words following, *Elohim eth*—"God the"—commence with *aleph*. (Zohar 1:2b, Sperling and Simon 1984, 9; Matt 2004, 11)

The ensuing explanation includes both the Sefer Yetzirah's image of God, engraving the cosmos with the alphabet, and the Bahir's account of God's two thousand year anticipation of creation. When God came to create the world, all the letters presented themselves in reverse order, each pleading their case and receiving reasons why they were not quite suited for the start of creation. Eventually, the letter *bet* entered and used as argument the very same reason given at the start of the Bahir:

> O Lord of the world, may it please Thee to put me first in the creation of the world, since I represent the benedictions [*berakhot*] offered to Thee on high and below. (Zohar 1:3a, Sperling and Simon 1984, 12; Matt 2004, 16)

This, evidently, was the clinching argument. Creation begins with the alphabet's second letter, *bet*, and the first letter, *aleph*, receives the consolation that it alone expresses God's unity (Zohar 1:3a, Sperling and Simon 1984, 13; Matt 2004, 16).

The gendered relation between these two letters is developed in a later passage:

> Afterwards the letters were distinguished and inscribed in the Scripture—*Beth* in *bereshith bara*, and *aleph* in *Elohim eth*. *Beth* is female, *aleph* male. As *beth* created, so *aleph* produced letters. "The heavens" are the totality of twenty-two letters. (Zohar 1:30a, Sperling and Simon 1984, 114; Matt 2004, 177–78)

Moving from the first *letter* of Genesis to the first *word*, the Zohar explains that *bereshit* consists of six letters and that the rest of the first verse, "*bara* [created] *Elohim* [God] *et hashamaim* [the heaven] *veet* [and] *haarets* [earth]" also consists of six words (Zohar 1:9a, Sperling and Simon 1984, 37; Matt 2004, 59). The explanation refers to the six primordial days of creation, a notion supported by the fact that the letters forming *bereshit* can also be divided into the two words *bara shit*, that is, "he created six." This reading has been variously interpreted in the Zohar as concerning the "six chief supernal directions" from which issues the totality of existence, the "six sources of rivers, which flow into the Great Sea" (Zohar 1:3b, 1:15b, Sperling and Simon 1984, 13, 65; Matt 2004, 17, 114), the component parts of the "house" built by Wisdom, namely, the world, and even the six colors that enter into the "edifice" (Zohar 1:39b, Sperling and Simon 1984, 141; Tishby 1994, 277, 313).

We should not imagine, however, that the book of Genesis should be read solely for knowledge of the drama of creation. The Zohar also informs us that all the precepts of the Torah that God has given to Israel are "laid down in the first chapter of Genesis in summary." The opening words relate to the very first precept of all, namely, to "the fear of the Lord" as the beginning of wisdom (Ps 111:10) (Zohar 1:11b, Sperling and Simon 1984, 47; Matt 2004, 77). This interpretation is reinforced early on in the Zohar, when Rabbi Yudai rhetorically asks for the meaning of *bereshit*, also providing the answer. He says it means "'with Wisdom,' the Wisdom on which the world is based" (Zohar 1:3b, Sperling and Simon 1984, 13; Matt 2004, 17; see also Liebes 1993, 233). He explains that by beginning with the letter *bet*, *bereshit* indicates that there are two *reshits*, that is to say, *two* starting points, an upper and a lower wisdom, "one shrouded in mystery" and "one capable of being revealed" (Zohar 1:7b, 1:15a, 1:31a, Sperling and Simon 1984, 32, 63, 119; Matt 2004, 50, 109, 190).

The Christian Kabbalah according to Giovanni Pico della Mirandola

Such ruminations on Wisdom and Genesis were of equal importance in the Christian tradition, especially in relation to the issue of whether Christ was actively present at the creation. The discovery of these novel Jewish approaches to biblical interpretation undoubtedly impressed the Italian syncretic philosopher Giovanni Pico della Mirandola (1463–1494), the first to introduce the term kabbalah into Christian circles and thereby earning the title of "father of Christian kabbalah" (Secret 1964, 40).[5] Pico was devoted to developing his *philosophia nova*, and his synthesis of Aristotelian and Platonic thought along with esoteric doctrines gleaned from *prisci theologi* like Zoroaster, Orpheus, Hermes Trismegistus, and Pythagoras. The kabbalah provided him with a rich source of inspiration. Pico's conviction that the Jews possessed a secret, mystical interpretation of Scripture was unheard of in the Christian world of his time. Its effect must have been overwhelming when it first burst upon an unsuspecting public, "marking a watershed in the history of Hebrew studies in Europe" (Wirszubski 1989, 3, 132).

Pico was a prolific kabbalistic writer. The twenty-three year old introduced the kabbalah into the mainstream of renaissance thought in forty-

5. On Pico, see Wirszubski 1989; Farmer 1998; Copenhaver 1999; Black 2006; Allen 2008; Dougherty 2008. On this quasi-mythical account of the birth of Christian kabbalah, see McGinn 1993; Reichert 1995.

seven "Kabbalistic Conclusions according to the Secret Teaching of the Wise Hebrew Kabbalists" and seventy-two "Kabbalistic Conclusions according to My Own Opinion, Providing Powerful Confirmation of the Christian Religion from the Very Principles of the Hebrew Sages," together with further references to kabbalah in other groups of conclusions, including those on magic, the teachings of Zoroaster, and the Orphic hymns. The best known fruit of Pico's kabbalistic studies is found in his nine hundred *Conclusiones Philosophicae Cabalisticae et Theologicae*, submitted to the papacy for debate on religious and philosophical matters in 1486. His famous *Oration*, generally known as "On the Dignity of Man" and serving as the preface to his philosophical, kabbalistic, and theological conclusions, includes an alternative creation story to that found in Genesis. It details how human beings were created according to no pattern and assigned no fixed place in the universe, as such being given greater freedom to shape their fate, intimating, perhaps, the wider latitude the new Christian kabbalist believes he has to plumb the depths of Scripture:

> We have given to thee, Adam, no fixed seat, no form of thy very own, no gift peculiarly thine, that thou mayest feel as thine own, have as thine own, possess as thine own the seat, the form, the gifts which thou thyself shalt desire. A limited nature in other creatures is confined within the laws written down by Us. In conformity with thy free judgment, in whose hands I have placed thee, though art confined by no bounds.... Thou, like a judge appointed for being honorable, art the molder and maker of thyself. (Pico della Mirandola 1998, 4–5; Copenhaver 2002, 59)

In his *Oration* Pico elaborates on his interest in using the Jewish kabbalah for Christian purposes. He adopts kabbalistic techniques primarily for evangelical purposes against the Jews. He uses the "ancient mysteries of the Hebrews ... in order to confirm the holy and Catholic faith" and to defend religion "against the rude slanders of the Hebrews." "In short," he asserts, "there is hardly any dispute between us and the Hebrews" on the mystery of the Trinity, "wherein they cannot be so disproved and refuted from the books of the Cabalists" (Pico della Mirandola 1998, 29, 32).

In the Beginning: Pico on the First Word of Genesis

Although Pico's theses are terse and frequently enigmatic, they demonstrate knowledge of the *sefirot*, *shemot*, and "new" techniques of exegesis.

Pico touches on Genesis several times in his kabbalistic conclusions and some of his references look familiar in light of the previous discussion on the Jewish kabbalistic tradition. He writes: "Bresith—that is, in the beginning he created—is the same as if it had said, he created in wisdom" (Pico della Mirandola, *Conclusiones* 28.5).[6] This reference to "Wisdom" (*Hokhmah*) should be understood as the second *sefirah* of the kabbalistic Tree of Life. In the translations, prepared for him by the Jewish convert Flavius Mithridates, Pico found many examples of *sefirotic* symbolism related to the creation narrative. One of the most concise appears in the *Mysterium Operis Geneseos*, which discusses how "the work of Genesis" reveals in both a universal and a particular way the "being of the world" and the "procession of the *sefirot*." The kabbalistic author interprets the opening phrase of Genesis as "expressing the entire coming into being, in general terms, of the divine attributes," the ten *sefirotic* emanations that provide the basis for creation:

> *In the beginning*/Wisdom [second *sefirah, Hokhmah*]; *God*/Intelligence [third *sefirah, Binah*] … ; *created*/the Ancient of Days [first *sefirah, Keter*]; *eth* contains right and left, piety [fourth *sefirah, Chesed*] and power [fifth *sefirah, Gevurah*]; *hascamaim* [*the heavens*]/clemency [sixth *sefirah, Tifere*t]; *vieth* contains right and left, eternity [seventh *sefirah, Nezah*] and grace [eighth *sefirah, Hod*]; and the foundation [ninth *sefirah, Yesod*] of the ages is designated by the letters *waw* [*and*]; *haares* [*the earth*] is the assembly of Israel [tenth *sefirah, Malkhut*], and thus you have everything in a universal way (Pico della Mirandola, *Mysterium operis Geneseos*, Black 2006, 141 modified).

Another of the sources of kabbalah, translated for Pico by Mithridates, is the anonymous medieval Liber Combinationum, where we find various divisions of the word *bereshit* that suggest alternative interpretations (Wirszubski 1989, 220–221). Among them are the above-mentioned "*bara shit*, that is that "he created six," namely, the six directions. Pico mentions this interpretation in this conclusion: "By the six days of Genesis we should understand the six extremities of the edifice coming forth from Bresith, just as cedars come from Lebanon" (Pico della Mirandola, *Conclusiones* 28.9). In this conclusion, the word *edifice* denotes the lower seven

6. My translation of this and subsequent conclusions varies slightly from those given in Farmer's edition, influenced by the forthcoming edition of Pico della Mirandola, *Oration and Conclusions*.

sefirot of the Tree of Life, while the *six extremities*, an expression found in medieval Jewish Kabbalistic sources, refer to the fourth to the ninth *sefirot* on the Tree of Life. Egidio da Viterbo (1469–1532), who had discussed kabbalah with Pico, explains that the highest three *sefirot* form the upper world and are in God; the lower seven form the middle world from which our sensible world was formed. As such, for a Christian kabbalist, Pico's conclusion can be read as the opening statement for a discussion of the six intermediary emanations coming between the three supernal hypostases of the Holy Trinity and the earthly manifestation of God's creation (Wilkinson 2007, 30, 43).

In another of his kabbalistic conclusions, Pico refers to the authoritative *Targum Onqelos*, the Aramaic translation of the Torah attributed to the second-century proselyte Onkelos: "Because Onkelos the Chaldaean said *becadmin*—that is, in the eternals or through eternal things—he understood the thirty-two paths of wisdom" (Pico della Mirandola, *Conclusiones* 28.26; see also Borgonuovo, *Cabalistarum Selectiora* 118^{v}–119^{v}, 120^{v}).[7]

One of Pico's favorite kabbalistic authorities, the Italian rabbi Menahem Recanati (1250–1310) remarks that the Aramaic *beqadmin* is plural, while the corresponding Hebrew word in Genesis *bereshit* is singular (Wirszubski 1989, 41). Presumably this plurality indicates the multiple paths of wisdom to Pico.

In the "Conclusions according to His Own Opinion," Pico seems to have a change of heart: he does not completely reject his previous interpretation but does state that he prefers to interpret the plural word *beqadmin* as referring to the Platonic or Philonic ideas, over the notion of the thirty-two paths of wisdom from the Sefer Yetzirah: "It would be more correct to explain the *Becadmin* that the Chaldean gloss applies to the term *Bresit* from the sapiential ideas than from the thirty-two paths, as other Cabalists say, though both are correct in Cabala" (Pico della Mirandola, *Conclusiones* 11.58). Following the spirit of the Zohar, Pico is open to multiple interpretations. Given his avowed aim of "providing powerful confirmation of the Christian religion," however, he apparently feels that an interpretation of the plurality implied by the word *beqadmin* best serves Christian doctrine if it is taken as referring to the plurality of the "sapiential ideas" rather than the plurality of the thirty-two paths. By this he appears to be reinforcing the Christian kabbalist notion of the

7. On Arcangelo da Borgonuovo, see Fornaciari 1994.

second *sefirah*, *Hokhmah* or Wisdom, as Christ, emphasizing him as the ultimate storehouse, the source of all Platonic ideas, instead of distributing these ideas through all the thirty-two paths, that is, the ten *sefirot* and the twenty-two letters of the alphabet as described in the Sefer Yetzirah (Wirszubski 1989, 179).

The example above is not the only instance of Pico's tendency to employ Jewish exegetical approaches in support of Christian theology. A rather convoluted example occurs in the following discussion of the fourfold status of being:

> Anyone who thinks deeply about the fourfold constitution of things—first the unity and stability of remaining, second procession, third reversion, fourth beatific reunion—will see that the letter *beth* works first with the first letter, medially with the middle letter and last with the last letters. (Pico della Mirandola, *Conclusiones* 11.59; see Idel 2005b, 186)

Chaim Wirszubski offers a convincing interpretation of this passage. He explains that use of this kabbalistic technique requires the inclusion of initial and terminal forms of Hebrew letters in the alphabet, so that their total comes to twenty-seven. This then makes the first letter *aleph*, the middle *nun*, and the "final letters" *shin* and *tav*. Following Pico's suggestions for combinations, the procedure generates the words *ab* (father), *ben* (son), and *Shabbat* (Sabbath), neatly corresponding with Pico's "unity," "procession," and "reversion/reunion" (Wirszubski 1989, 164–65). Idel points out that at least three of the four states mentioned in this conclusion resemble stages that Pico describes in the *Oration*: "*processio* is the ascent, *reversio* is the descent, and *reunio* is the state of peace and perfection in the bosom of the Father" (Idel 2005b, 186). For Pico, intent on encouraging Christians to utilize the techniques of kabbalah, the fact that the word *ben* ("son") is formed by the inclusion of the medial letter in the Hebrew alphabet, must have seemed a perfectly appropriate symbol for Christ as the mediator between God and humankind. Once again, then, we have Jewish exegetical techniques employed in confirmation of a Christian message.

Continuing with our examination of Pico's Christian kabbalist exegesis of the first verse of Genesis, in his "Kabalistic Conclusions according to My Own Opinion," Pico takes up a theme also discussed in the Bahir and Zohar, namely, the two appearances of the Hebrew particle *et* in the first verse of Genesis:

> Through the term *eth* that appears twice in the text, *In the beginning God created the heavens and the earth*, I believe that Moses means the creation of an intellectual nature and an animal nature, which in the natural order came before the creation of heaven and earth. (Pico della Mirandola, *Conclusiones* 11.28)

Pico's interpretation expands on an idea from the Zohar. According to the Zohar, the particle *et* is formed of the first and last letters of the Hebrew alphabet, and so it "embraces the twenty-two letters;" the first *et* in "the [*et*] heavens," then, refers to something in the upper world, while the second "and [*veet*] the earth" intimates that the earth absorbed the twenty-two letters and this symbolizes the union of male and female (Zohar 1:29b, Sperling and Simon 1984, 113; Matt 2004, 175–76). Pico does not adhere completely to this idea and exercises his right to read the text on a different level. He thus offers a more dualistic interpretation of the two particles, which he considers as denoting the intellectual and animal natures, that is, the heavenly spiritual or angelic condition of the soul and the earthly corporeal state of being. Moreover, he chronologically places the creation of these two natures before the creation of the material cosmos.

The most ambitious example of Pico's promotion of a specifically Christian kabbalah appears in the *Heptaplus* (1489) that was published three years after the *Conclusiones*. Pico explains that in his *Heptaplus*, subtitled *On the Sevenfold Narration of the Six Days of Creation*, he did not intend to recycle the interpretations of the book of Genesis by church fathers like Ambrose and Augustine or to refer to the Greek commentaries of Philo, Origen, Basil, and others. He also does not pay attention to the interpretations found in Chaldaean or Hebrew sources. Instead, "beyond all these," he wants to contribute seven other expositions, the product of his own "invention and reflection" (Black 2006, 70).

Although Pico believes in the literal truth of God's creation of the cosmos in six days (an event he dates to 3,508 B.C.E.) (Black 2006, 224), in the *Heptaplus* he does not engage with the narrative on a literal level. Rather, in this work written at the same time as his Jewish teacher Yohannan Alemanno composed a detailed commentary on Genesis, entitled *Eineiha Eidah* (The Eyes of the Community) (Novak 1982, 132), Pico proposes a "programme of esoteric hermeneutics." It argues for the "existence of an esoteric philosophical dimension to the biblical text," that is, based on the conviction that "the secrets of the whole of nature" (*totius naturae secreta*) are contained in the Genesis account (Black 2006, 96).

In the *Heptaplus*, Pico provides a "multiple-level exegesis" (Novak 1982, 136) that contains seven main expositions, each of seven chapters and all dealing with the first day of creation from various perspectives. The first three expositions cover Pico's justification for an esoteric reading of scripture, his theory of allegory, his description of the macrocosm as being composed of three worlds (sublunary, celestial, and angelic or intellectual). The next three expositions concern a fourth world, human, the microcosm, and links between the microcosm and the other three.

Pico relied on many variations in his expositions. For instance, in the first exposition, Pico interprets the "heaven and earth" of Gen 1:1 as respectively the efficient and material cause, that is, the relationship between form and matter as discussed in Aristotelian physics. In the second exposition, Pico deals with astronomy. In the third exposition, he moves to the realm of metaphysics, in which "earth" is taken to refer to the "rough and unformed" angelic essence, "deprived of life and being," whereas "heaven" refers to the "acting of its essence and the participation of unity in multiplicity" (Black 2006, 37). In the fourth exposition he turns to the microcosm and presents a more psychological reading of Genesis. Here he suggests that "heaven" and "earth" mean the individual's rational soul and body (echoing *Conclusiones* 11.28), whereas the light of creation is the *spiritus* that connects the two extremes (Black 2006, 39–40). The following exposition focuses on the vertical hierarchy of the cosmos, moving from the angelic world to the celestial, thence to the sublunary world and then concluding with the dignity and duties of the human microcosm. In the sixth exposition Pico provides two readings of the Genesis narrative (respectively dealing with chapters 1–4 and 5–7) and presents a "universal taxonomy of logical and formal relationships between entities," for example, between heaven and earth, earth and the void, darkness and the abyss, the spirit of God and the waters, and so forth (Black 2006, 47–50). These first six expositions embrace "the orders of things proceeding from God, their distribution, the explanation of their union and their difference, their bonds and their conditions" (Black 2006, 211). Pico presents the ideal aim of this knowledge in the seventh exposition. He classifies it as an anagogical intellectual ascent up the hierarchy of being to the attainment of *felicitas*, perfection and union with God (Novak 1982, 137).

However, the *Heptaplus* offers more. Despite the fact that Pico avoids using the term kabbalah throughout the work (Blum 2008, 55), he includes an epilogue that contains a detailed Christian kabbalist exegesis or "exposition of the first phrase: *In the beginning*." If Pico showed in the initial forty-nine chapters that knowledge of all things in the universe can be derived from varied interpretations of the first twenty-seven verses of Genesis, the epilogue demonstrates that kabbalistic techniques help in extracting all of this knowledge from the Pentateuch's very first word. To make this point, Pico turns to "another system of interpretation, to give my readers a taste of Mosaic profundity," one that draws its inspiration directly from his reading of Jewish kabbalistic texts (Pico della Mirandola 1998, 170; see also Thumfart 1999, 87). The motivation behind this is undoubtedly Christian, but the method is completely Jewish.

As an indication of this, bear in mind that one of the most memorable of Pico's kabbalistic *Conclusiones* relates to the secrets discovered by an exegete with a thorough understanding of the Hebrew alphabet: "There are no letters in the whole Law which in their forms, conjunctions, separations, crookedness, straightness, defect, excess, smallness, largeness, crowning, closure, openness, and order, do not reveal the secrets of the ten numerations" (Pico della Mirandola, *Conclusiones* 28.33). In order to provide his reader with an example of the potential utility of Jewish exegetical techniques for discovering truths confirming the Christian religion, Pico carries out a series of separations and conjunctions of Hebrew letters in the *Heptaplus* and thereby generates a series of words from the term *bereshit*:

> Among the Hebrews, this phrase is written thus: בראשית [*bereshit*]. From this, if we join the third letter to the first, comes the word אב [*ab*]. If we add the second to the doubled first, we get בבר [*bebar*]. If we read all except the first, we get ראשית [*reshit*]. If we connect the fourth to the first and last, we get שבת [*shiabat*]. If we take the first three in the order in which they come, we get ברא [*bara*]. If, leaving out the first, we take the next three, we get ראש [*rosh*]. If, leaving out the first and second, we take the two following, we get אש [*esh*], etc. (Pico della Mirandola 1998, 171–72)[8]

Following these "death-defying permutational and anagrammatical leaps" (Eco 1995, 121), he then proceeds to explain the meanings of these individual words:

> *Ab* means "the father;" *bebar,* "in the son" and "through the son" (for the prefix *beth* means both); *resit*, "the beginning;" *sabath*, "the rest and end;" *bara* "created;" *rosc*, "head;" *es*, "fire;" *seth*, "foundation;" *rab*, "of

8. This passage is quoted in full in Sixtus of Siena 1566, 224–25.

the great;" *hisc*, "of the man;" *berit*, "with a pact;" *thob*, "with good." (Pico della Mirandola 1998, 172)[9]

Having separated the original word *bereshit* into its individual letters, Pico then recombines them into these twelve separate words. He then reassembles these words to produce one exceptionally Christian kabbalist message: "The father, in the Son and through the Son, the beginning and end or rest, created the head, the fire, and the foundation of the great man with a good pact" (Pico della Mirandola 1998, 172). Pico summarizes all preceding expositions in his *Heptaplus*. He writes: The "great man" refers to the macrocosm, the "head," "fire," and "foundation" refer to the three worlds, the "pact" to their interrelationship, "good" because it unites all with God (Pico della Mirandola 1998, 173; Black 2006, 215–16). This interpretation enables Pico to show how "the whole plan, relationship, and felicity ... of the four worlds" is "uncovered and explained in this one word," *bereshit*. From his kabbalistic analysis of the opening word of the Jewish Old Testament, Pico has extracted confirmation of the Christian message of the New Testament. The implication is that if so much material can be extracted out of just one word, how much is lying concealed in the whole of Scripture? This knowledge of kabbalistic exegetical techniques and, consequently of "all things," is necessary for humanity's ascent to the divine. As should be clear from Pico's expositions in both the *Conclusiones* and the *Heptaplus*, the goal of this intellectual ascent is the triune Godhead of Christianity. This goal is central to Pico despite the influence of Jewish hermeneutical methods and the quasi-decaune structure of the kabbalistic Tree of Life.[10]

The multiplicity of interpretations that look like "absolute contradictions," for instance, in the Zohar (Tishby 1994, 279) provide the space for Pico to combine letters and speculate about their meanings in considerable difference to the interpretations of his Jewish counterparts. His Christianizing efforts of the kabbalah result, on the one hand, in a Christian "supercommentary" on extant Jewish midrashic and kabbalistic texts. On the other hand, his appropriation of exegetical techniques and symbols for

9. Pico's text can also be found in Kircher 1636, 263–64. See also Vigenère, *Traicté des chiffres* 135^{v}–136^{r}, which provides a similar selection of combinations from "Mnahem Rachanat sur le commancement de Genese." On Pico's slight manipulation of the Hebrew text, see Black 2006, 216 n. 11.

10. On the notion of the *sefirot* as representation of a decaune God, see Goshen-Gottstein 2004.

apologetic and polemical purposes and the development of Christian kabbalah as a discipline in its own right finds parallels in the convert, Rici. It also becomes explicit in later scholars like Reuchlin, Giorgio, Borgonuovo, and Kircher (Wirszubski 1974, 151). For them, Jewish kabbalah confirms Christianity from the very first word of the Torah.

Later Christian Kabbalist Commentators Inspired by Pico

As cryptic as most of Pico's kabbalistic writings were, they nevertheless generated interest among a number of kindred spirits, both in Italy and abroad. One of the earliest Italian responses was by an Italian commentator on Pico's kabbalistic theses, Arcangelo da Borgonuovo (d. 1571). In his *Cabalistarum selectiora, obscurioraque dogmata* (1569), Borgonuovo informs his readers that the *senarius* (number six) is the first "perfect" number (1 + 2 + 3 = 1 x 2 x 3). After explicitly identifying *bereshit* as Wisdom and relating it to the second *sefirah Hokhmah*, Borgonuovo refers to the underlying allusion of *Conclusiones* 28.9 to the lower *sefirot*. He explains: "Just as cedars come from the mountain, so the dimensions or six lower *sefiroth* [*chesed* to *yesod*] proceed from the first three dimensions [*Kether* to *Binah*]. And these six lower dimensions are called the days of making [*dies fabricate*]" (Borgonuovo, *Cabalistarum selectiora* 44^{r}–45^{v}). Hence we are to understand that when Christian kabbalists like Giovanni Pico, Egidio, and Borgonuovo speak of "Lebanon" or the "mountain" they can also be referring to the highest three *sefirot* of the Tree of Life, which for them represent the Holy Trinity. The cedars of Lebanon, the finest earthly materials used by Solomon for the construction of the temple in Jerusalem (1 Kgs 5), here represent the emanations of the godhead invested in the days of creation.

In another work, *Dechiaratione sopra il nome di Giesu* (1557), Borgonuovo states that all three persons of the Trinity are represented by the first three letters of *bereshit*: the initials of the Hebrew words *ben* (son), *ruah* (spirit), and *ab* (father), as if it wanted to say "All the Trinity created the world [*Tutta la Trinitá hà creato il mondo*]" (*Dechiaratione* 177^{r}). With this, Borgonuovo is following his master, the Franciscan friar Francesco Giorgio (1466–1540), famous for his combination of kabbalah, neoplatonic philosophy, Pythagorean musical theory, and alchemy in *De harmonia mundi* (1525). Borgonuovo drew much of his own interpretation of kabbalah from Giorgio's commentaries on Pico's kabbalistic work. In his discussion of Borgonuovo's plagiarism of Giorgio's unpublished writings, Wirszubski elaborates on the latter's homophonous play on the very first letter of the book of Genesis, *bet*, which when pronounced sounds like the Hebrew word *bayit* (house). Giorgio repeats an idea found in the Bahir, stating that the letter *bet* "is the seal of that son who is the house of all ideas that are in divine things." This son is the "wisdom of the father and the foundation of all creatures." The *aleph*, that is, the father, is the one who "produces the creatures in real being" (Wirszubski 1974, 146, 150–51; see also Galatino 1550, 63).

As Wirszubski remarks, Giorgio took the Christianization of the kabbalah far beyond Pico's theses (1974, 154). In a similar vein, two later readers, Blaise de Vigenère (1523–1596) and Claude Duret (1565–1611) both dwell on the six Hebrew letters of *bereshit* as denoting the six days of creation (Vigenère, *Traicté des chiffres* 134^{v}; Duret, 1619, 155).[11] Both agree on the Christological argument that the first letter of Genesis is *bet*, because it represents the second person of the Trinity and places Christ at the start of everything. The alchemist and kabbalist Vigenère then followed Giorgio on the homophonous play between the letter *bet* and the word *bayit* as symbol of the "house" of the "ideas of the archetype" (Vigenère, *Traicté des chiffres* 175^{v}). For at least some Christian kabbalists, then, Christ seems to represent the Platonic storehouse of ideas from which God the Father draws the blueprints for his creation.

In his *Opus de arcanis catholicae veritatis* (first edition 1518), Pico's fellow Italian Christian kabbalist, Pietro Galatino (1460–1540), is another scholar familiar with Targum Onqelos's substitution of *beqadmita*, glossed as "in wisdom," for *bereshit* (1550, 832). In his alchemical and kabbalistic *Coelum Sephiroticum Hebraeorum* (1679), the German physician Johann Christoph Steeb (d. 1668) takes this identification a stage further by clarifying that by "wisdom" is meant the "Son of God, the fount and origin of all wisdom" (1679, 15–16). Steeb's contemporary, the Jesuit Athanasius Kircher (ca. 1601–1680), adds an extra dimension to the thirty-two paths of wisdom with the observation that the first chapter of Genesis uses the divine name Elohim thirty-two times, symbolizing the ways that God proceeded into the world by means of the *sefirot* (Kircher 1652–54, 310–311).[12] Kircher indeed reveals himself to be far more aware of the numerical possibilities of kabbalah than most of his peers, noting, for example, that the term *bereshit* is numerically equivalent to the phrase "He created in the

11. Both also remark that the capital B of *bet* symbolizes two thousand years. On Vigenère, see Secret 1973, 236.

12. On Kircher in relation to kabbalah, see Stolzenberg 2004.

Law," that is, in the Torah, both having the total 913 (Kircher 1652–54, 218). That Pico was not alone in recognizing the utility of Jewish combinatorial techniques for the purposes of Christian exegesis is demonstrated by the Jewish convert to Christianity, Paolo Ricci (ca. 1480–1541), who was arguably far more familiar with the technique than Pico. In *De Coelesti Agricultura* (1541), he supports Pico's approach with the assertion that the apex of the letter *bet*, the first "element in the book of Genesis ... designates the paternal principle, which they call the supreme crown" (that is, the first *sefirah Keter*), while the whole term *bereshit* refers to the filial hypostasis, which they call Wisdom (the second *sefirah Hokhmah*). The second term *bara* signifies "procession or emanation," and the third, *Elohim*, indicates the spirit of God, to which they give the name Prudence (the third *sefirah*, *Binah*) in the sephirotic order (Ricci, *De Coelesti Agricultura* LXXIX^{r}).

The first three words of Genesis, then, according to this Jewish convert to Christianity, support the Christian doctrine of the Trinity.[13] Similar to Pico, Ricci associates Christ specifically with procession or emanation, a notion that presumably ties in with his mediating status as God and human.

The strongest contender for Pico's Christian kabbalist crown, however, is the German humanist Johann Reuchlin (1455–1522), whose *De verbo mirifico* (1494) promoted a kabbalistic name for Christ, the Pentagrammaton YHSVH, with the claim that it superseded the Jewish Tetragrammaton YHWH.[14] In his more mature work *De arte cabalistica* (1517), Reuchlin considers the first verses of Genesis at some length, during a discussion of the kabbalists' notion of two worlds (visible/invisible; matter/ideas; lower/higher). Reuchlin then addresses the same issue found in Pico's thesis:

> Furthermore he twice employs, contrary to normal usage, the two particles *et* and *ha-*, prefixing the two things that were created. The *ha-* designates; the other can be understood in many ways. It is composed of the first letter of the alphabet, *aleph*, and the last, *tau* (in Greek, *alpha* and *omega*: the Roman "bow" and "stern"). So, in "heaven" everything spiritual is seen to be included, everything from *aleph* to *tau*, from beginning to end, and in the same way, in "earth" is contained everything physical from top to toe; and nonetheless, each individual thing was created in that beginning as if it were the only one. Just as Ezekiel has a wheel

13. On Ricci, see Roling 2003; Black 2007.

14. On Reuchlin, see Zika 1976; Schmidt-Biggemann 2003.

within a wheel, rolled into each other.... In this way the first, the intelligible world is bound round the second, in such a way that all its strength is governed from there. (Reuchlin 1993, 101)

In Conclusion

In this essay I have discussed how exegetical techniques found in such foundational Jewish kabbalist texts as the Bahir and Zohar came to be introduced into Christian circles through the pioneering work of Giovanni Pico della Mirandola towards the end of the fifteenth century. I have examined some instances of his employment of these techniques for particularly Christian interpretations of the first word of the book of Genesis. Following this, I have provided various examples of later Christian commentators who were inspired by Pico's endeavor, be that with an eye to evangelical conversion of the Jews or the search for fresh insights into familiar texts with the hope of discovering a deeper, more profound understanding of scripture. This is only part of the story, however, and I would like to conclude this excursus into *kabbalah iyyunit* or "speculative kabbalah" with at least one instance of *kabbalah ma'asit* or "practical kabbalah." There the permutations of the very letters by which heaven and earth were made suggested the possibility of influencing created things or indeed of producing creatures like the famous artificial being, the Golem. In his letter combinations the master of practical kabbalah, the *ba'al shem* or "master of the divine name," could fashion amulets for various purposes, invoking angels or devils and exorcising evil spirits who had taken possession of a human body (Scholem 1978, 310).

One amulet in particular seems to have caught the imagination of Christian readers, for it is passed on from Johann Reuchlin's *De arte cabalistica* (1517), through Heinrich Cornelius Agrippa's *De occulta philosophia* (1533), to Athanasius Kircher's *Oedipus Aegyptiacus* (1652–1654): One should take a very thin piece of virgin parchment and then, employing the method of notariqon, write the Hebrew letters בוווו (*bvvvv*) on the front and the letters צמרכה (*tsmrkh*) on the reverse. These groups of characters are the initial and final letters from the first five verses of Genesis, and as Agrippa states "a representation of the creation of the world" by which one shall be free from all mischiefs of humans and evil spirits.[15] Apparently,

15. Reuchlin 1993, 349; Agrippa 1992, 433; Kircher 1652–1654, 343. Strictly

then, for at least some Christian kabbalists (with apologies to Saint Paul), sometimes it is important to pay attention to the letters and *not* the spirits.

Works Cited

Agrippa, Cornelius. 1992. *De Occulta Philosophia Libri Tres*. Edited by V. Perrone Compagni. Leiden: Brill.

Allen, Michael J. B. 2008. The Birth Day of Venus: Pico as Platonic Exegete in the Commento and the Heptaplus. Pages 81–113 in *Pico della Mirandola: New Essays*. Edited by Michael V. Dougherty. Cambridge: Cambridge University Press.

Augustine. 2000. *Confessions: Books IX–XIII*. Translated by William Watts. LCL. Cambridge: Harvard University Press.

Black, Crofton. 2006. *Pico's* Heptaplus *and Biblical Hermeneutics*. Leiden: Brill.

———. 2007. From Kabbalah to Psychology: The Allegorizing Isagoge of Paulus Ricius, 1509–1541. *Magic, Ritual, and Witchcraft* 2:136–73.

Blau, Joseph. 1944. *The Christian Interpretation of the Cabala in the Renaissance*. New York: Columbia University Press.

Blum, Paul Richard. 2008. Pico, Theology, and the Church. Pages 37–60 in *Pico della Mirandola: New Essays*. Edited by Michael V. Dougherty. Cambridge: Cambridge University Press.

Borgonuovo, Arcangelo da. 1557. *Dechiaratione sopra il Nome di Giesu*. Ferrara: Rossi.

———. 1569. *Cabalistarum selectiora, obscurioraque dogmata, a Ioanne Pico ex eorum commentationibus pridem excerpta*. Venice: Franciscus Franciscius.

Copenhaver, Brian P. 1999. Number, Shape, and Meaning in Pico's Christian Cabala: The Upright *Tsade*, the Closed *Mem*, and the Gaping Jaws of Azazel. Pages 25–76 in *Natural Particulars: Nature and the Disciplines in Renaissance Europe*. Edited by Anthony Grafton and Nancy Siraisi. Cambridge: MIT Press.

———. 2002. The Secret of Pico's *Oration*: Cabala and Renaissance Philosophy. *Midwest Studies in Philosophy* 26:56–81.

Dan, Joseph. 1993. *The Ancient Jewish Mysticism*. Tel Aviv: MOD Books.

speaking, as Kircher makes clear, the final letter of צמרכה (*tsmrkh*) is from the word לילה ("night"), the conclusion of the first part of verse 5.

Dan, Joseph, and Ronald C. Kiener. 1986. *The Early Kabbalah*. New York: Paulist Press.

Dougherty, Michael V., ed. 2008. *Pico della Mirandola: New Essays*. Cambridge: Cambridge University Press.

Duret, Claude. 1619. *Thresor de l'Histoire des Langues de cest Univers*. Yverdon: L'Imprimerie de la Societé Helvetiale Caldoresque.

Eco, Umberto. 1995. *The Search for the Perfect Language*. Oxford: Blackwell.

Farmer, Steven A. 1998. *Syncretism in the West: Pico's 900 Theses (1486): The Evolution of Traditional Religious and Philosophical Systems*. Tempe, Ariz.: Medieval & Renaissance Texts & Studies.

Fornaciari, Paolo Edoardo. 1994. L'*Apologia* di Arcangelo da Borgonuovo in difesa delle *Conclusiones cabalisticae* di Giovanni Pico della Mirandola. *Vivens homo* 5:575–91.

Galatino, Pietro. 1550. *Opus de Arcanis Catholicae Veritatis*. Basel: Hervagius.

Giller, Pinchas. 2001. *Reading the Zohar: The Sacred Text of the Kabbalah*. Oxford: Oxford University Press.

Goshen-Gottstein, Alon. 2004. The Triune and the Decaune God: Christianity and Kabbalah as Objects of Jewish Polemics with Special Reference to Meir ben Simeon of Narbonne's *Nfilhemet Mitzva*. Pages 165–97 in *Religious Polemics in Context*. Edited by Theo L. Hettema and Arie van der Kooij. Assen: Van Gorcum.

Hayman, A. Peter. 2004. *Sefer Yesira: Edition, Translation and Text-Critical Commentary*. Tübingen: Mohr Siebeck.

Herrera, Abraham Cohen de. 2002. *Gate of Heaven*. Translated with Introduction and Notes by Kenneth Krabbenhoft. Leiden: Brill.

Idel, Moshe. 1989. *Language, Torah, and Hermeneutics in Abraham Abulafia*. New York: State University of New York Press.

———. 1990. *Golem: Jewish Magical and Mystical Traditions on the Artificial Anthropoid*. Albany, N.Y.: State University of New York Press.

———. 2002. *Absorbing Perfections: Kabbalah and Interpretation*. New Haven: Yale University Press.

———. 2005a. *Enchanted Chains: Techniques and Rituals in Jewish Mysticism*. Los Angeles: Cherub.

———. 2005b. *Ascensions on High in Jewish Mysticism: Pillars, Lines, Ladders*. Budapest: Central European University Press.

Kaplan, Aryeh. 1979. *The Bahir Illumination: Translation, Introduction, and Commentary*. York Beach, Maine: Weiser.

Kircher, Athanasius. 1636. *Prodromus Coptus sive Aegyptiacus*. Rome: Sacra Congregatio de Propaganda Fide.

———. 1652–1654. *Oedipus Aegyptiacus*. Rome: Vitalis Mascardi.

Liebes, Yehuda. 1993. *Studies in the Zohar*. Translated by Arnold Schwartz, Stephanie Nakache, and Penina Peli. Albany, N.Y.: State University of New York Press.

Matt, Daniel C. 2004. *The Zohar: Pritzker Edition, Translation and Commentary*. Vol. 1. Stanford: Stanford University Press.

McGinn, Bernard. 1993. Cabalists and Christians: Reflections on Cabala in Medieval and Renaissance Thought. Pages 11–34 in *Jewish Christians and Christian Jews: From the Renaissance to the Enlightenment*. Edited by Richard H. Popkin and Gordon M. Weiner. Dordrecht: Kluwer.

Morlok, Elke. 2011. *Rabbi Joseph Gikatilla's Hermeneutics*. Tübingen: Mohr Siebeck.

Novak, B. C. 1982. Giovanni Pico della Mirandola and Jochanan Alemanno. *Journal of the Warburg and Courtauld Institutes* 45:125–47.

Pico della Mirandola, Giovanni. 1998. *On the Dignity of Man, On Being and the One, Heptaplus*. Translated by Charles Glenn Wallis, Paul J. W. Miller, and Douglas Carmichael. Indianapolis: Hackett.

———. Forthcoming. *Oration and Conclusions*. Edited and translated by Brian P. Copenhaver, Michael Allen, and Calvin Normore. Cambridge: Harvard University Press.

Reichert, Klaus. 1995. Pico della Mirandola and the Beginnings of Christian Kabbala. Pages 195–207 in *Mysticism, Magic and Kabbalah in Ashkenazi Judaism*. Edited by Karl Erich Grözinger and Joseph Dan. Berlin: de Gruyter.

Reuchlin, Johann. 1993. *On the Art of the Kabbalah*. Translated by Martin and Sarah Goodman. Lincoln: University of Nebraska Press.

Ricci, Paolo. 1541. *De Coelesti Agricultura*. Augsburg: Stayner.

Roling, Bernd. 2003. Prinzip, Intellekt und Allegorese im Werk des christlichen Kabbalisten Paolo Ricci (gest. 1541). Pages 155–87 in *An der Schwelle zur Moderne: Juden in der Renaissance*. Edited by Giuseppe Veltri and Annette Winkelmann. Leiden: Brill.

Schmidt-Biggemann, Wilhelm. 2003. Einleitung: Johannes Reuchlin und die Anfänge der christlichen Kabbala. Pages 9–48 in *Christliche Kabbala*. Edited by Wilhelm Schmidt-Biggemann. Ostfildern: Thorbecke.

Scholem, Gershom. 1967. *Major Trends in Jewish Mysticism*. New York: Schocken.

———. 1978. *Kabbalah*. New York: Meridian.

——. 1987. *Origins of the Kabbalah*. Edited by Raphael J. Zwi Werblowsky. Translated by Allan Arkush. Princeton: Princeton University Press.

Secret, François. 1964. *Les Kabbalistes chrétiens de la Renaissance*. Paris: Dunod.

——. 1973. Beresithias ou l'interprétation du premier mot de la Genèse chez les Kabbalistes chrétiens. Pages 235–43 in *In Principio: Interprétations des premiers versets de la Genèse*. Paris: Études Augustiniennes.

Sixtus of Siena. 1566. *Bibliotheca sancta*. Venice: Franciscus Franciscius.

Sperling, Harry, and Maurice Simon, trans. 1984. *The Zohar*. London: Soncino.

Steeb, Johann Christoph. 1679. *Coelum Sephiroticum Hebraeorum*. Mainz: Bourgeat.

Stolzenberg, Daniel. 2004. Four Trees, Some Amulets, and the Seventy-Two Names of God: Kircher Reveals the Kabbalah. Pages 149–69 in *Athanasius Kircher: The Last Man Who Knew Everything*. Edited by Paula Findlen. New York: Routledge.

Thumfart, Alexander. 1999. Readings on Cabbala: Giovanni Pico della Mirandola. Pages 83–90 in *Judaism from the Renaissance to Modern Times*. Vol. 2 of *Jewish Studies at the Turn of the 20th Century*. Edited by Judit Targarona Borrás and Angel Sáenz-Badillos. Leiden: Brill.

Tishby, Isaiah. 1994. *The Wisdom of the Zohar: An Anthology of Texts*. Vol. 1. Translated by David Goldstein. London: Littman Library of Jewish Civilization.

Toorn, Karel van der, Bob Becking, and Pieter W. van der Horst, eds. 1999. *Dictionary of Deities and Demons in the Bible*. Leiden: Brill.

Vigenère, Blaise de. 1587. *Traicté des chiffres, ou secretes manieres d'escrire*. Paris: L'Angelier.

Vignaux, Paul, ed. 1973. *In Principio: Interprétations des premiers versets de la Genèse*. Collection des Études Augustiniennes: Antiquité 51. Paris: Études Augustiniennes.

Wilkinson, Robert J. 2007. *Orientalism, Aramaic and Kabbalah in the Catholic Reformation: The First Printing of the Syriac New Testament*. Leiden: Brill.

Wirszubski, Chaim. 1974. Francesco Giorgio's Commentary on Giovanni Pico's Kabbalistic Theses. *Journal of the Warburg and Courtauld Institutes* 37:145–56.

——. 1989. *Pico della Mirandola's Encounter with Jewish Mysticism*. Cambridge: Harvard University Press.

Wolfson, Elliot R. 1994. *Through a Speculum that Shines: Vision and Imagination in Medieval Jewish Mysticism*. Princeton: Princeton University Press.

———. 2005. *Language, Eros, Being: Kabbalistic Hermeneutics and Poetic Imagination*. New York: Fordham University Press.

Zika, Charles. 1976. Reuchlin's *De Verbo Mirifico* and the Magic Debate of the Late Fifteenth Century. *Journal of the Warburg and Courtauld Institutes* 39:104–38.

The Mystery of *Mysterium Magnum*: Paracelsus's Alchemical Interpretation of Creation in *Philosophia ad Atheniensis* and Its Early Modern Commentators

Georgiana Hedesan

In his highly influential book *The Chemical Philosophy* (1977), Allen G. Debus drew attention to the significance of the alchemical interpretation of creation, which had been a popular topic amongst the Paracelsian followers of the sixteenth and seventeenth centuries. Debus traced this trope back to Paracelsus's treatise *Philosophia ad Atheniensis* ("Philosophy Addressed to the Athenians"), which presented creation "as an essentially chemical process of separation" (Debus 1977, 56). Debus's analysis generated a moderate interest in the subject of Paracelsian Genesis commentaries amongst scholars, being followed up by such articles as Michael T. Walton's "Genesis and Chemistry in the Sixteenth Century" (1988), Norma Emerton's "Creation in the Thought of J. B. Van Helmont and Robert Fludd" (1994), Peter J. Forshaw's "Vitriolic Reactions: Orthodox Responses to the Alchemical Exegesis of Genesis" (2007), Didier Kahn's "L'interprétation alchimique de la Genèse chez Joseph Du Chesne dans le contexte de ses doctrines alchimiques et cosmologiques" (2004), and most recently, Michael T. Walton's book, *Genesis and the Chemical Philosophy: True Christian Science in the Sixteenth and Seventeenth Centuries* (2011).

This paper seeks to contribute to the wider scholarly discussion of the topic of Paracelsian hermeneutics of Genesis. In the first section, it takes an in-depth look at the work that inspired the flurry of early modern alchemical interpretations of creation, the possibly spurious Paracelsus treatise *Philosophia ad Atheniensis* (henceforth *Ad Atheniensis*).[1] This treatise is an

1. I use the English translation provided by Edward Arthur Waite in *The Hermetic*

abstruse work which generated controversy, admiration, and emulation during the flourishing period of Paracelsian philosophy (roughly 1560–1650). Although the treatise does not lend itself to easy interpretation, this article reviews its themes, ideas, and intentions as far as they transpire from the text itself.

In the second section, the paper investigates some of the most significant responses to *Ad Atheniensis* to explain how Paracelsian followers and opponents read and made sense of this ambiguous text. I hence refer to Thomas Erastus's antagonistic interpretation before delving into the commentaries of Gerhard Dorn (1602), Richard Bostocke (1585), and Jacob Böhme (1623). In the final section, I will discuss the comments of modern historian Walter Pagel on Paracelsus's "prime matter" before summarizing the common themes of the *Ad Atheniensis* commentaries and drawing conclusions on the nature and influence of the treatise.

An In-Depth Look at *Philosophia ad Atheniensis*

First published in 1564 in Cologne in German, *Ad Atheniensis* was included in Johannes Huser's edition of Paracelsus's works (Paracelsus 1590) and appeared in Latin in *Operum medico-chemicorum sive paradoxorum* (Paracelsus 1603) and in the *Opera omnia* (Paracelsus 1658). As with many of Paracelsus's works, we do not know if the treatise is genuine. Karl Sudhoff, whose German edition of Paracelsus's medical works is still definitive, has disputed the attribution of this text to Paracelsus (Paracelsus 1931, xi), but Kurt Goldammer (1953, 33) argued on behalf of its authenticity. Needless to say, no early modern reader doubted its attribution to Paracelsus. On the contrary, everyone considered the treatise as one of the chief exponents of his thought (Pagel 1958, 91). Consequently, the question whether *Ad Atheniensis* is an authentic work of Paracelsus or not will be of less concern here, because this article is mainly concerned with this text's internal content and reception. I hence refer to the author as "Paracelsus" with the understanding that the work may very well be by "pseudo-Paracelsus."

The treatise itself is divided into three books, comprising twenty-four, twenty-three, and six texts respectively. The editor considered that the

---

and Alchemical Writings of Paracelsus (see Paracelsus 1894). However, in some cases the translation is not clear, and I rely on the Latin (Paracelsus 1658) or German (Paracelsus 1590) versions.

work was either unfinished or the rest of the treatise was lost, since both the German and the Latin versions end with a note in Latin stating: "The rest (for without a doubt the author progressed further) we do not have" (Paracelsus 1590, 47; 1658, 252).[2] The title of the treatise clearly refers to the New Testament, specifically Paul's famous address to the Athenians on the Areopagus (Acts 17:22–34).[3] Paul's brief address was intended to convert philosophical nonbelievers to a Christian view of the world by employing philosophical arguments. In this sense, he made reference to Epicurean and Stoic doctrines, including the Stoic view of the *logos*, the principle of all things (Bruce 1951, 332–39). Indeed, Paul insisted on the "oneness" of God, his omnipresence, and his role as universal cause.

Paracelsus's insistence that all things come from one principle recalls Paul's main argument in his speech. Yet an intention of conversion is much harder to detect in this treatise than in the New Testament address. There is a statement in book 2, text 16 that can be surmised to refer to the Christian faith: "There is only one way and one religion, nor should others be rashly adopted." This subtly alludes to John 14:6 ("I am the way, the truth and the life"), but the author avoids making this connection overtly.[4]

Beyond its indebtedness to Paul's speech to the Athenians, *Ad Atheniensis* offers an elaborate interpretation of creation through the lens of natural philosophy. The key to *Ad Atheniensis*'s understanding of creation lies in the uncreated *mysterium magnum* ("great mystery") used by God to make the world:

> As children come forth from the mother, so from the Great Mystery are generated all created things.... The Great Mystery is uncreated, and was prepared by the Great Artificer Himself.... For the supreme arcanum, that is, the goodness of the Creator, created or brought together all things into the uncreated, not, indeed, formally, not essentially, not qualitatively; but each one was latent in the uncreated, as an image or a statue in a block of wood. (Paracelsus 1894, 249–52)

---

2. In Latin, "Reliqua (sine dubio enim ulterius progressus est auctor) non habentur." Interestingly, the first edition of *Ad Atheniensis* (1564) seemed much less certain there was a continuation: "Reliqua, si quae deerant, desiderabantur."

3. There is a wide literature on Paul's speech on the Areopagus, including Bruce 1951, Stonehouse 1957, Barrett 1974.

4. Perhaps the author consciously follows the example of Paul's address, where the Christian faith is implied, but not stated clearly either.

In this perspective, God's creation is equivalent to a separation of each individual out of the *mysterium magnum*. First, we are told, God divided the *mysterium* (first separation), then the elements (second separation), and then the elements were themselves separated into individual beings (third separation) (Paracelsus 1894, 253).

What is this *mysterium magnum*? Paracelsus defines it as a principle (*principium*), and "common matter of all things" (Paracelsus 1894, 249). It is "the mother of all the elements" but also of "all the stars, trees and carnal creatures" (1894, 249). More suggestively, he also refers to it by the philosophical term *die erste Matern* ("the first matter"; Paracelsus 1590, 1) or *prima materia* ("prime matter"; Paracelsus 1658, 239). This concept was associated in the epoch with ancient Greek philosophy, particularly with Aristotle, though modern scholarship has pointed out that the Stagirite may not have actually believed in an underlying substrate at all (King 1956, 370–71, Charlton 1983, 197). Nevertheless, by the sixteenth century the concept of *prima materia* was part of mainstream Aristotelian Scholastic speculation, being upheld by such Scholastic authorities as Thomas Aquinas (1225–1274), Duns Scotus (1266–1308), or William of Ockham (1288–1347). The Scholastics generally agreed that *prima materia* was an underlying but potential substratum that could not exist without a substantial form. Aquinas defined it as pure potency without actuality, although the late Scholastic Francisco Suarez (1548–1617) was willing to grant it some actuality and independence (Kronen, Menssen and Sullivan 2000, 870–71).

Yet no Scholastic would dare state that the prime matter, despite its name, was actually "material," else the orthodox Christian doctrine of *creatio ex nihilo* would be denied.[5] To avoid accusations of heresy, a Christian thinker that made reference to *prima materia* had to clearly distance himself from the Aristotelian tenet that the universe was uncreated. If he failed to be absolutely clear on that, he risked being attacked by suspicious theologians. In the sixteenth century, with its heightened theological controversies, this was almost certain to happen. For instance, the learned attempt of Agostino Steuco (1497–1548) to propose the concordance between the chaos of Genesis and the prime matter of Greek philosophy was immediately attacked by Jean Calvin (1509–1564) as advocating pagan ideas (Walton 2011, 23–25).

---

5. For the formation of the *creatio ex nihilo* dogma in Christian thought, see May 1994; an alternative view is given by Copan 1996.

It is tempting to see Paracelsus's *mysterium magnum* as a version of the Scholastic *prima materia*, keeping in mind that *Ad Atheniensis* is far from being a Scholastic treatise. There is a definite emphasis on potentiality in a manner that recalls Thomist arguments. Thus, Paracelsus maintains that "its comprehension could not be prefigured or shaped by any certain essence or idea, neither could it incline to any properties, seeing that it was free at once from colour or elementary nature" (Paracelsus 1894, 249). In addition, Paracelsus points out that "the Great Mystery was not elementary, though the elements themselves were latent therein. Nor was it carnal.... Neither was it wood or stone" (1894, 252). Substantial matter (*materia substantialis*) only appeared following the initial separation, when the *mysterium magnum* became a kind of "smoke" that was diffused everywhere (Paracelsus 1894, 252). From this one can conclude that the *mysterium magnum* was something before matter and substance, a type of formless potentiality that is more in line with Thomist than Aristotelian arguments. Yet, as we shall see further on, Paracelsus's concept of the *mysterium* will clearly depart from Scholastic antecedents in its elaboration and historical view.

The fact that *mysterium magnum* is not matter is further clarified later on, when Paracelsus affirms that the *prima materia* of the elements "is invisible and impalpable, but present in all," and that "the first matter of the elements is nothing else than life" (Paracelsus 1894, 264). It is also inappropriate to define the *mysterium magnum* as having physical dimensions, since "neither growing things, nor animals, nor the like, were created therein" (1894, 250). Instead, it could be defined as the source of being, imprinting the generative principle within all things: the *mysterium magnum* "gave the mystery of self-propagation according to their own form, to each its essence" (1894, 250).

If the *mysterium magnum* is pure potentiality, completely immaterial, it can be easily deemed as "nothing" rather than "something." Indeed, in a passage that is rather abstruse, Paracelsus (1894, 259) maintains that all creatures originate from nothing and hence must return to nothing:

> A figure painted into a picture, when it is there, has been certainly made of something.... If the figure be blotted out with a sponge, it leaves nothing behind it, and the picture returns to its former shape. So, assuredly, all creatures will be reduced to their primeval state, that is, to nothingness.[6]

6. The English translation is not ideal here. The Latin reads: "Effigies, in tabulam depicta, cum adest, ex aliquo certe facta est.... Et imago si spongia abstergatur, dum

From this imagery one can surmise that Paracelsus is supporting the Christian doctrine of *creatio ex nihilo*. Yet decoding the passage is much more complex than it looks. Contrary to an ordinary reading, what Paracelsus appears to set forth here is that the "figure" (*das Bildt, imago*, or *effigies*) is in fact the matter of each being; once the image is erased, the only thing that remains behind is the frame or canvas, which is not physical matter at all, but what he calls the eternal arcanum, or eternal spirit. This reading is supported in the subsequent text, where we read: "Hence it should be realised that all creatures are a picture of the supreme Arcanum, and so nothing more than, as it were, the colouring spread over a wall" (1894, 259).[7] Thus, the *mysterium magnum* in a sense is "nothing": once it is wiped out, the only thing that remains is the eternal arcanum.

Thus, Paracelsus postulates that prior to the *mysterium magnum* there is something else, the uncreated "eternal" arcanum.[8] This is the "supreme principle," the "eternal essence," the "goodness of the Creator," or the "supreme Arcanum" (1894, 258, 260, 270–71). Paracelsus explains the arcanum thus: "We do not say that the Arcanum is an essence like the immortal, but that it is this in its perfection" (1894, 271). This "eternal" does not seem to be God *per se*, who is the "Author of creation and the Ruler of the eternal" (1894, 272), but the text sometimes switches ambiguously between the two.

The work posits a dualism between the element, the offspring of the *mysterium magnum*, and the arcanum, or eternal essence: "There is a difference between an element and an Arcanum. The one is mortal or perishable from the elements, the other permanent" (1894, 271). Thus, each existing being is comprised of two things, one mortal and the other immortal: the

---

nihil sui post relinquit, tabula ad priorem suam formam redit. Sic nimirum creaturae universae ad statum suum primaevum, hoc est, ad nihilum redigentur" (Paracelsus 1658, 243). The German version (Paracelsus 1590, 6) reads: "Ein Bildt, dass auff ein Taffeln gemahlet wirdt, das ist da, ist auch auss Etwas gemachet ... das Bild, das wieder abgewischet wirdt, und ist nichts mer da; so ist also die Taffeln wieder in ihrer ersten Gestalt. Also werden alle Creaturen sommen an ihr ersten Statt, das ist, zu Nichts."

7. Latin: "Unde statui debet, creaturas omnes picturam esse summi arcani, adeoque: nihil quicqua aliud, qua illitum parieti colorem" (Paracelsus 1658, 243). German (Paracelsus, 1590, 6–7): "Darumb also zuverstehen ist, dass alle Creaturen ein Mahlung ist des höchsten Arcanen und ein angeworffen Farb an der Wand, nicht anderst ist."

8. Waite translates both *supremus* ("Höchsten," "highest") and *aeternum* ("Ewige") as the "eternal"; indeed, by these names, Paracelsus seems to refer to the same subject.

first (the "element," by which Paracelsus likely refers to the mortal body made up of the four elements) is bound to die, while the second (the arcanum) remains in eternity. At first glance this distinction seems to warrant a gnostic understanding of the world: the arcanum is somehow trapped in matter by creation and is only freed when the elements are destroyed. Yet a closer reading shows that Paracelsus does not draw any such conclusions in the treatise. The text does not convey that this world is evil, but that it is "frail," and in order to achieve eternity, all things must first be destroyed (1894, 261). There is an implication that the entire creation must undertake a journey which ends in the acquisition of eternity.

The entity that governs this journey is God, described as the "Great Artificer" (*artifex*) or "Supreme Architect" (*supremus architectus*) (Paracelsus 1894, 250, 280; 1658, 239, 252) in a manner recalling Plato's demiurge (*Tim.* 28c, 30a, 50d). Yet, again, this traditional terminology can be deceiving. While Paracelsus compares God with a sculptor that chops away matter to reveal the perfect form within, elsewhere he expresses the view that God is not an external force. Instead, "when the Mystery was filled with such essence and deity and with addition of eternal power, before all creatures were made, the work of separation began" (1894, 253). Hence God, or perhaps the uncreated arcanum, fills the *mysterium magnum* from within, and this energy breaks the *mysterium* apart by division. This separation is sudden and final: the *mysterium magnum* is transformed into a single mass (a thin smoke), and then the four elements arise from it (1894, 255). Neither the smoke nor the elements are yet material: Paracelsus affirms that the elements are mortal "souls" (Paracelsus 1894, 266).[9]

The initial "filling" of the *mysterium magnum* with divinity results in a sequence of transformations, defined as separations, taking place throughout time. Thus, Paracelsus posits that the *mysterium* has so far undergone three separations, but the fourth is yet to happen. Hence the "uncreated" *mysterium magnum* is not eternal: the act of creation alters it in an irreversible manner, and it will be destroyed in a fourth, and "final separation," which will return all things to nothing (1894, 258–60). The apocalyptic destruction of the universe will unravel the *mysterium magnum* as well: "Then all the others will perish, not even the Mystery will remain.…

---

9. Paracelsus maintains: "An element is really neither more nor less than a soul." For a discussion of the spiritual nature of the elements in Paracelsian speculation, see also Daniel 2006.

By that separation all things are reduced to their supreme principle, and that only remains which existed before the Great Mystery, and is eternal" (1894, 258–59). Paracelsus concludes, "As a picture is liable to destruction or conflagration, so is the Great Mystery, and we with it" (1894, 259).

Even though the present *mysterium magnum* is slated for destruction, a new one will appear on the ruins of this one. Thus, Paracelsus posits the existence of two *mysteria magna*, the current, frail *mysterium magnum*, and the ultimate, indestructible one (1894, 261, 271). Paracelsus elsewhere is very guarded about this subject: "It is reasonable to think, perhaps, that after the destruction of the four elements spoken of, certain others will come into existence essentially unlike those before mentioned; or, that after the passing away of the present creation a new *Mysterium Magnum* may supervene" (1894, 269–70). At the same time he also surprisingly states that "a new *Mysterium Magnum* is not possible. That would be a greater miracle than we are able even to speculate about" (1.24). It can be surmised that by this he is trying to affirm that the *mysterium magnum* cannot repeat itself in the current form, so essentially the ultimate *mysterium* will be something of a very different substance than the present one.

Thus, the "eternal" arcanum will be fully revealed after the fourth separation, or the destruction of the present world: "By that separation all things are reduced to their supreme principle, and that only remains which existed before the Great Mystery, and is eternal" (1894, 258–59). The arcanum, or the eternal essence, then renders the "ultimate matter" (1894, 259). Here again Paracelsus uses the term "matter," but just as in the case of the *mysterium magnum*, it is obvious that the eternal matter will not be material. The arcanum will be incorporated into a new *mysterium magnum* and remain "permanent in the ultimate *Mysterium Magnum*, wherein all things will be renewed, yet no other things will be produced save what have been" (1894, 271).

Essentially, *Ad Atheniensis* posits the existence of three divine entities: an "uncreated" eternal (the arcanum), an "uncreated" mortal (the *mysterium magnum*), and God the Maker and Architect, the "Author of creation" (1894, 272, 280). The problem in interpreting *Ad Atheniensis* arises from the fact that, apart from God the Creator, the other two entities are hard to comprehend through the perspective of established theology or philosophy. Although the *mysterium magnum*'s origins probably lie in Scholastic *prima materia* and the arcanum appears somewhat similar to the philosophical concept of "form," ultimately they represent Paracelsus's idiosyncratic ideas.

Furthermore, intertextual analysis within Pararcelsus's huge opus is of limited usefulness in clarifying the two terms. While the arcanum appears in other treatises and one can talk about a theory of the arcanum in the early Paracelsian treatise *Archidoxis* (ca. 1525),[10] the *mysterium magnum* never occurs as a syntagma again. It is possible that a relationship may exist between the *mysterium magnum* and the "mystery" that Paracelsus refers to in the *Archidoxis*, which denotes an occult essence that can be extracted from bodies (1660, 46, 108, 113). The Paracelsian follower Martin Ruland explains the term *mystery* as

> the Essence of the Interior Nature, the sum of the whole substance in the subtle and withdrawn part of the given matter. Hence it differs greatly from sap, as much indeed as sap differs from the body. And because it is concealed in the most retired recesses of corporeal matter, and has an exceeding subtle nature, it is called a Mystery and an Arcanum. (1964, 235; 1612, 342–43)

Yet it is only a matter of presumption that the *Ad Atheniensis* uses the term *mysterium magnum* in the sense of an exalted *Archidoxis* mystery.

Moreover, *Ad Atheniensis* avoids clear definitions, leaving relationships ambiguous. For instance, the treatise postulates that God divides the *mysterium magnum*, an action that establishes an active-passive relationship between the two entities. Yet no other interaction is mentioned in the treatise, and the subsequent separations seem to take place on their own, without any intervention from God: "When this [the primordial separation] had commenced, afterwards every creature emerged and shone forth with its free will.... A second separation ensued upon the first, and this emanated from the elements themselves" (1894, 253–54). Similarly, *Ad Atheniensis* does not always make a clear-cut difference between the *mysterium magnum* and the arcanum. Both the *mysterium* and the arcanum are sometimes called essences or principles (1894, 252, 280).[11] This ambiguity mirrors the one in *Archidoxis*, where arcana and mysteries sometimes refer to the same thing (1660, 46). Moreover, at the end of time, both the new *mysterium magnum* and the arcanum will be eternal, rendering the difference between the two meaningless.

---

10. As Daniel 2006 (129) has noted, the arcanum in the *Archidoxis* is similar to the alchemical quintessence.

11. Paracelsus: "Everything had its essence in the Great Mystery" (1894, 280); "it embraced every mortal thing in its undivided essence" (1894, 280).

There is also no doubt that the vision of *Ad Atheniensis* is fraught with paradoxes. How can an uncreated being such as the *mysterium magnum* be destroyable? How can a mortal *mysterium* become an immortal one? How can Paracelsus affirm that an uncreated being (the *mysterium magnum*) comes after another uncreated one (the arcanum)? It is clear that Paracelsus did not expect such paradoxes to be solved through rational inquiry. The text is not meant to be philosophical in the modern sense of the word, but revelatory: it seeks to postulate certain "truths" about the universe that cannot be verified or examined logically.

The revelatory quality of the treatise reflects the Genesis account, which purports to state, rather than argue, the way the world came to be. There are other elements that identify it as an interpretation of the Genesis, including a temporal beginning of the universe manifested as a creative act and the presence of God as Creator (albeit interpreted as separation). Another important detail that Paracelsus takes from Gen 1:1 is the description of heaven as being the first created element (this "universal element," he considers, is the same as fire) (1894, 254). Yet *Ad Atheniensis* soon deviates from a literal interpretation of Genesis. Although this is not clearly stated, the treatise could be read as unfolding an esoteric, metaphysical meaning of the Bible that fundamentally alters its literal sense. The assumption that *Ad Atheniensis* sought to unveil an invisible Genesis lying within the written one was made by many later Paracelsian commentators.

Ad Atheniensis also contains elements that connect it to Christianity, such as the apocalyptic theme of the final destruction of the *mysterium magnum*, the resurrection of all "frail" things as eternal bodies, the creation of things out of nothing, and the existence of a Trinity, albeit formed by God, the supreme arcanum and the *mysterium magnum*. God is also described in familiar Christian terms as Author of creation and Judge of all creatures (1894, 272). Furthermore, there is a vague allusion to the Johannine doctrine of the Word, when Paracelsus affirms: "All things were created from the Great Primal Mystery.... This is nothing more than saying that a house has been built by a word [or from a word, *ex verbo*]. This is an attribute of the eternal" (1894, 261).[12]

If the Christian themes are not always easy to make out, the same

12. In Latin: "Hoc nihil est aliud, quam, si ex verbo domus aliqua exstrueretur. Ubi res ita intelligenda venit, quod soli supremo illud adiaceat" (Paracelsus 1658, 244). In German (Paracelsus 1590, 7): "Wiewol es nichts ist sondern gleich als wen auss eim Wort ein Haus würde: So ist das also zuverstehen, solchs dem höchsten allein."

cannot be said about the strong alchemical tone, which is much more overt. Creation, as many scholars have pointed out, is made by separation, not composition (for instance, Debus 1977, 56; Bianchi 1994, 20). In this sense the process whereby God created the world resembles an alchemical procedure, and Paracelsus indeed suggests that one could gather a glimpse of the creation by separating vinegar in milk or macerating tincture of silver (1894, 252). Moreover, Paracelsus states that the divine process of separation was not supernatural, but could be achieved by "natural magic" or alchemy, which involves "the intensest penetration and most rapid separation" (1894, 252). In essence, the *mysterium magnum* behaves like an alchemical ferment or an acid: "Like macerated tincture of silver, so the Great Mystery, by penetrating, reduced every single thing to its own special essence" (1894, 252). Moreover, alchemy culminates with the dramatic regeneration of matter into the supreme philosophers' stone, a process that is similar to the final fourth separation of the *mysterium magnum*. The entire destiny of the universe seems to be the manifestation of the concealed spiritual force (the arcanum), a journey from inner to outer that reflects traditional alchemical ideas (Bianchi 1994, 24–25). Underneath the corporeal form there is a spiritual essence which seeks to become manifest. Paracelsus affirms:

> If, therefore, whatsoever things are created return to that unto which they were predestinated from the beginning, in that place an arcanum will be produced.... And thus, the eternal is a sign of the dissolution of Nature, and not the beginning of created things, and the end in all things which no nature is without (1894, 272–73).

The implication is that, by isolating the arcanum in the laboratory, the alchemist is able to glance at and understand the entire history of matter, including the "ultimate *mysterium magnum*." The method of achieving dissolution of matter is through putrefaction. This is a process whereby "that which is eternal is taken back again into the eternal" (1894, 260). It is achieved through the decay of the elements,

> for decay is terrestrial, aerial, igneous, and aqueous. Each of these, with those created with it, is turned and led downwards to decay with the eternal which is left. Nevertheless, these four decays will reduce their eternal portion to one similitude, notably and visibly, not with their works, but with their essence (1894, 273).

The insistence on dissolution and complete destruction reminds one of the basic tenet of alchemy that physical matter has to be destroyed in order for transmutation to occur. Nothing less than a complete dissolution of matter is required, the so-called *nigredo* stage of the work. Yet death is only that of the body; the essence of the matter, the elusive mercury, survives and is extracted through the alchemical process into a new, regenerated body, the philosophers' stone. The new, exalted body bears a connection with the old one, but it is also something completely new and powerful. Paracelsus projects this laboratory drama on a macrocosmic scale, unveiling the grand image of universal destruction, wherefrom the new world is generated. The new world is likewise an image of the old, but its form is now perfect.

From this brief review of *Ad Atheniensis*, it is clear that the treatise sought to explain the nature and destiny of the universe by referring to its creation. In a manner mirroring the biblical Genesis, it posits that the world came about at a definite point in time, being "created" or "separated" by God. However, *Ad Atheniensis* departs from a literal reading of Genesis, seeking to explain creation in terms of a spiritual principle called *mysterium magnum*, which is filled from within and successively separated by God or the inner arcanum. This *mysterium magnum* is somewhat comparable to the Scholastic view of *prima materia*; however, it becomes a much more elaborate and abstruse concept in the mind of Paracelsus. Thus, he posits the continuous transformation of the *mysterium magnum* and foresees its eventual destruction and rebirth. Embedded in this grand vision of the universe is the idea that the process of creation and destruction is similar to that of alchemical separation and can be reproduced or understood at a small scale in the alchemical laboratory. *Ad Atheniensis* hence offered the promise of comprehending the nature of the universe and the divine within it by means of both alchemical theory and practice. This novel concept would make *Ad Atheniensis* a particularly meaningful treatise for later alchemists to pore over.

Early Modern Interpretations of *Ad Atheniensis*

Given the ambiguousness of *Ad Atheniensis*, readers projected dramatically different interpretations on it. The opacity of the text invited widely differing accounts, as commentators attempted to "interpret" its tenets in a manner intelligible to them. It is equally noteworthy that almost all commentators focused on the *mysterium magnum* and ignored other topics found in the *Ad Atheniensis* treatise.

One of the most influential exegetes of *Ad Atheniensis* was also the most antagonistic one. He was Thomas Erastus (1524–1583), a Heidelberg theologian who had also acquired a physician's degree (Gunnoe 1994). Erastus singled Paracelsus out as a magician possessed by the devil and as a charlatan who killed rather than cured his patients (1572, 16). Even worse, the writings of Paracelsus betrayed a heretic who denied the dogma of *creatio ex nihilo*, upheld by the fathers of the church. This impiety Erastus uncovered in the *Ad Atheniensis* treatise, where he took the increate *mysterium magnum* to be nothing else than the discredited prime matter of Aristotle. To Erastus, Paracelsus maintained the eternity of matter and relegated God to the inferior status of a craftsman or demiurge. The German theologian was shocked by Paracelsus's suggestion that the *mysterium magnum* was alchemically separated from what Erastus understood to be a preexisting chaos. To him, this statement was a crass denial of creation.

Despite its strident anti-Paracelsian rhetoric, Erastus's interpretation of the *mysterium magnum* proved influential, surprisingly, even among the supporters of Paracelsus. Many Paracelsians accepted the theory that the *mysterium* was *prima materia* or a dark chaos. For instance, Martin Ruland's *Lexicon Alchemiae* (1612, 342; 1964, 235) explained that *mysterium magnum* is "the First Matter of all Things, the Principle and Mother of all the Corruptible Creatures of God, the Chaos, dark and rude." Thomas Vaughan (1621–1666) similarly associated the *mysterium magnum* with the Chaos as the "Center of all Sciences" (1651, 18).

Despite their tendency to associate the *mysterium magnum* with the Aristotelian *prima materia* or the Platonic chaos, Paracelsian supporters were keen to prove that the work of Paracelsus was based on the Scriptures and represented a true Christian philosophy. For the proponents of Paracelsian ideas, *Ad Atheniensis* provided a novel understanding of Genesis that was based on alchemical concepts. Paracelsian supporters were hence eager to show that *Ad Athenienses* was grounded in a thorough understanding of the scriptural account.

The foremost early Paracelsian commentator of *Ad Atheniensis* was Gerhard Dorn, an elusive Flemish alchemist who acted as the editor of many of Paracelsus's works and translated them into Latin.[13] He produced

13. On Dorn, see Kahn 1994 and Marquet 1993.

a treatise called *Tractatus de naturae luce physica ex Genesi desumpta (Iuxta sapientiam Theophrasti Paracelsi)*, published first in Frankfurt in 1583 and subsequently in the first volume of the *Theatrum Chemicum* of Lazarus Zetzner (1602). In this work, Dorn attempts to defend the ideas advanced by Paracelsus in *Ad Atheniensis*. Thus, he claims that Paracelsus's *mysterium magnum* represents the first principle of creation, or the first word of the Scripture, *in principio* ("in the beginning").[14] Dorn denies the ordinary or "vulgar interpretation" of *in principio* as a reference to time and instead proposes that in fact the first principle was a primordial space or locus where creation could take place (338–40). He affirms that "the principle is the foundation of the world's creation" and that within this principle the word of God created heaven and earth (338). Dorn's conviction that the *mysterium magnum* is an uncreated spatial framework makes him rephrase the first sentence of Genesis to read: "In the uncreated *Mysterium magnum* God created heaven and earth" (338). He further asserts that "Moses does not say that the principle of creation was created, but that in it the entire creation was undertaken" (338). By this first creative act of God, the spatial principle of *mysterium magnum* was transformed into the prime matter, or the chaos. Out of this physical chaos, God then separated heaven and earth.

Ironically, rather than accomplishing its task of mitigating Paracelsus's orthodoxy, Dorn's argument regarding the *mysterium magnum* could in turn be criticized as a denial of *creatio ex nihilo*. Dorn was aware of this danger and mitigated this potential accusation by arguing that God actualized the *mysterium magnum* from a potential and immaterial existence into prime matter. Hence, he affirms that this interpretation does not in fact contradict *creatio ex nihilo* (1602, 338–39) and that the *mysterium magnum* is essentially "nothing" before God's creative act. To clarify his views, Dorn compares the *mysterium magnum* to a point, the "center of nature," which has no dimension and no end (339). The *mysterium* only becomes "something" when it is "excited" by the word of God (340).

Dorn supports Paracelsus's view that the universe appeared by alchemical separation, but qualifies this to say that separation occurred only after

14. "Paracelsus autem ex narratione Geneseos a Deo per Moysen tradita fidelibus, sua deducit primorum principiorum Physices fundamenta, a primo rerum omnium principio faciens exordium: quod quidem alio nomine mysterium magnum appellare voluit: ac si Moysen pro viribus a Deo sibi concessis, imitaretur ac hunc modum: In mysterio magno increato creavit Deus coelum et terram" (Dorn 1602, 338).

the physical *prima materia*, or chaos, was created within the *mysterium magnum*. This chaos God divided into two parts, namely, heaven and earth, upper and lower waters, light and darkness, man and woman, and so on (1602, 342). To Dorn, the act of creation becomes one of sundering of the one into two, an archetypal division which is the source of all existence. This separation is also viewed in alchemical terms, as similar to the division of pure and impure in alchemy (1602, 344).

Less famous than Dorn's treatise, but intriguing in its arguments is Richard Bostocke's apology for the *mysterium magnum*, published in his 1585 work *The Difference between the Auncient Phisicke ... and the Latter Phisicke*. While it is possible that Bostocke may have already perused Dorn's arguments at this point, it is certain that he read and was outraged by Erastus's censure some ten years earlier. Similarly to Dorn, Bostocke maintains that *Ad Atheniensis* advocates a spiritual *mysterium magnum*. He emphasizes that Paracelsus did not mean that the *mysterium* was physically present before the beginning of time, but that it existed spiritually with God at the time of creation. Bostocke argues that the *mysterium magnum* was a source in which the virtues of God were concentrated and were then sent to do their offices into creation. He articulates this idea in the following statement:

> In the beginning the vertues of visible thynges were united in their fountaine, neither were they separated in diversity and multitude of offices: but after that by the vertue of the spirite, whiche was caryed upon the waters, they were commaunded to do their offices in the worldly ministration.... We neede not here to imagine that these did proceede of Chaos, but out of the treasures of the divine wisdom. (Bostocke 1585, ch. 21)

Hence he maintains that the divine virtues were at first concentrated in a spiritual source and upon creation they dispersed throughout the universe.

This center of virtue Bostocke identifies with the divine Wisdom and the Word. Indeed, the English physician sought to ground his interpretation of *Ad Atheniensis* in orthodox Logos theology, which postulated that the Word as Jesus Christ had participated in the creation of the world.[15] Hence, Bostocke interprets Paracelsus's *mysterium magnum* to actually mean Jesus Christ as Wisdom and the Word. He supports his interpreta-

15. For a review of the interpretations of the Word as cocreator, see Nautin 1973.

tion by reproducing the statement that Paracelsus made in another work, *Opus Paramirum*, namely, "the first matter of the world was fiat [let it be]" (Paracelsus 2007, 323). *Fiat*, the first word of God, Bostocke explains, is the divine Will and the divine Word and refers implicitly to Christ (1585, ch. 21). He hence concludes that "Christ that great mystery was the beginning of all things" (1585, ch. 21). Thus, Bostocke takes the view not only that Christ as the Word created the world, but that Christ himself was the prime matter of all things and that the world was borne out of his body. Since in Bostocke's interpretation, Paracelsus's *mysterium magnum* is Christ and Christ was with God at the beginning, the English thinker concludes that there was nothing unorthodox about Paracelsus's treatise. In short, Bostocke presents *Ad Atheniensis* as a treatise inspired by and encompassed within orthodox Johannine theology.

This Christian interpretation of *Ad Atheniensis* was also supported by the famed work of Jacob Böhme entitled *Mysterium Magnum*. Originally published in 1623, *Mysterium Magnum* is the last great writing of the Silesian mystic and is undoubtedly influenced by *Ad Atheniensis*, although Böhme does not name the source of his speculations. In his interpretation, Böhme masterfully combines Johannine mysticism, apophatic theology, Paracelsian thought, and alchemical themes to create a grand vision of creation and the universe. To Böhme, God is the Abyss itself, the Chaos, or the *Ungrund*. God is profoundly unknown, since "nothing comprehends him save the True understanding; which is God himself" (Böhme 1656, 2).[16] As in the Christian Logos tradition, Böhme's Creator is the Word as the manifest form of the Abyss. From the Word derives the *mysterium magnum*, which is called "the Centre of the Eternall Nature." This *mysterium* is spiritual and lies deeply hidden within the corporeal body of the universe (4–5). Böhme also refers to *mysterium magnum* as a "spirituall essence" and as a fundamental element, which is the origin of the other four. Although he does not state so directly, he clearly draws on the concept of the quintessence, which was deeply embedded within alchemical thought.[17] Hence, he maintains that the world is made of this "Eternall Mystery," the kernel of the "inward Spirituall world," which had assumed corporeal form (5).

16. See also Koyré 1929 (320–21); Deghaye 1992.

17. For the alchemical concept of the quintessence, see Sherwood Taylor 1953.

In further alignment with Paracelsus, Böhme describes the process whereby God the Abyss creates the world. To him, no being exists but God, who is in his purest form, nothing. Consequently, creation can only be produced out of himself as a *creatio ex Deo*.[18] Still, as Böhme is eager to point out, this is not to say that God is the world, a statement that would have drawn Böhme into the pantheistic heresy. Rather he affirms that the world is ultimately a "manifestation of God," without itself being divine (1656, 23). Böhme unfolds the process of creation in the following terms: the Abyss conceives a desire to be, or the word *Fiat*, which by conjunction with the "Power of God" becomes the "Eternal Word." The Word then sets in motion a complex process involving, just as in *Ad Atheniensis*, separation. God eventually creates a "Spiritual Essence," which consists of one element, the spiritual water or "Heaven." This "Essence" is the *mysterium magnum*, which gives birth to the four physical elements (1656, 26).

Böhme understands the *mysterium magnum* to be a ground of the corporeal world without ever becoming corporeal itself. It is a quintessence, a fifth element from which all the others spring. The *mysterium magnum* is not, as in Paracelsus, something that is either increate or changeable; instead, it is engendered by the Word and remains within physical matter as long as the world endures. The *mysterium magnum* is the very principle of life, since "the reall Element dwelleth in the Essence.... Otherwise the Earth could bring forth no fruit" (1656, 43). In this sense, then, Böhme's *mysterium* resembles Bostocke's virtues that emanate from God without being God themselves.

Like Dorn and Bostocke, Böhme avoids the controversy of *creatio ex nihilo* surrounding Paracelsus's *mysterium magnum* by insisting on the spiritual character of the *mysterium*. In fact, to Böhme, a prior spiritual creation precedes the Genesis account of Moses: the birth of the Word, the creation of the spiritual worlds of good and evil and the making of the "Eternal Nature." They are then integrated in the account of Genesis in accordance with the Scriptures, but interpreted in a Paracelsian-kabbalistic way (1656, 42–45).

Thus, Böhme's vision in *Mysterium Magnum* is much more intricate than in Paracelsus's treatise, seeking to answer fundamental theological questions such as the appearance of evil from God and the relationship between the spiritual and corporeal worlds. Böhme's treatise goes beyond

18. For the *creatio ex Deo* concept, see Adamson 1962.

a simple interpretation of *Ad Atheniensis* to build a complex and masterful vision of the human and divine destiny.

Final Remarks

In 1961, respected scholar Walter Pagel wrote an article entitled "Prime Matter of Paracelsus," which was part of his extended studies on the Swiss physician and alchemist. Pagel purported that the *prima materia* of Paracelsus was in fact the Logos or the Word: "The Prime Matter of the world is not matter, but spirit; in fact it is the Word Fiat, the Logos of the Fourth Gospel, the Platonic archetype and ideal pattern of the world that is to become a material creation" (1961, 122). To support his point, Pagel adduced examples from Paracelsus's *Opus Paramirum*, *Liber Azoth*, and *De Pestilitate*, but also brought into his discussion *Philosophia ad Atheniensis*. He maintained that *Ad Atheniensis* provided a "pantheistic interpretation" of creation, which was fundamentally compatible with the view of prime matter as the word of God (Pagel 1961, 125). He further supported his argument regarding *prima materia* as being the Logos by appealing to Bostocke's interpretation of the *mysterium magnum* as the Word.

Although not directly focused on *Ad Atheniensis*, Pagel's modern perspective of the *mysterium magnum* as the Word can be described as yet another interpretation of *Ad Atheniensis* in the tradition of Logos theology. However, as I have pointed out, *Ad Atheniensis* is an abstruse work, which does not lend itself to a straightforward interpretation of the *mysterium magnum* as the Christian Logos. Although the *mysterium magnum* is increate and spiritual like the Word, it is mortal and destructible, hence incompatible with the Christian notion of divinity as being eternal. Moreover, the *mysterium* is different from the arcanum, whose permanence could more easily be associated to the Logos. Despite the Christian connotations of the treatise, Paracelsus never refers directly to theological doctrines, leaving his commentators to speculate on such association.

It is fascinating in itself that most of the commentators of *Ad Atheniensis*, including Dorn, Bostocke, and Böhme, attempted to clarify its meaning by making recourse to Genesis and orthodox Christian thought. They recognized the text as an interpretation of Genesis, even though Paracelsus never overtly assumes the position of biblical commentator. Instead, one can make the argument that he intended to be cryptic and that the text was supposed to have a mysterious and even a prophetic-apocalyptic quality to it. Paracelsus's fascination with prophecy is well recorded (Webster

1980, 17–27), and in the epoch there were quite a few Paracelsian followers that were ready to bestow the status of a seer or even religious reformer to Theophrastus (Gilly 1998). If *Ad Atheniensis* was not composed by Paracelsus himself, it was surely the product of an environment that saw him as a wise or even divine man rather than an ordinary philosopher and physician. For such persons, *Ad Atheniensis* could be read as a proof of Paracelsus's divine inspiration from the Holy Spirit.

Ad Atheniensis can also be seen as a riddle and a mystery in the wisdom tradition of alchemy, which reveled in enigmas, ambiguity, and unclear symbols (Crossland 1962). This is not to mean that one should dismiss *Ad Atheniensis* as delightful nonsense; its point is not to be untruthful, but poetic. It can thus be compared to a work of art: its meaning is well hidden within the outer material form, and no matter how many interpretations are provided, none of them exhausts its inner truth. It is clear that *Ad Atheniensis* is attempting to convey something about the universe, how it came into being, and how it will disappear: yet it does so in a way that can only be half comprehended in light of traditional philosophy or theology. The rest is left in darkness purposefully. The reader is invited to explore its hidden meanings, but must do so with the understanding that its inner truth cannot be fully illuminated, but remains mysterious.

Works Cited

Adamson, Jack H. 1962. Milton and the Creation. *The Journal of English and Germanic Philology* 61:756–78.

Barrett, Charles K. 1974. Paul's Speech on the Areopagus. Pages 69–77 in *New Testament Christianity for Africa and the World: Essays in Honour of Harry Sawyer*. Edited by Mark E. Glasswell and Edward W. Fashole-Luke. London: SPCK.

Bianchi, Massimo Luigi. 1994. The Invisible and the Visible: From Alchemy to Paracelsus. Pages 17–50 in *Alchemy and Chemistry in the 16th and 17th centuries*. Edited by Piyo Rattansi and Antonio Clericuzio. Dordrecht: Kluwer.

Böhme, Jacob. 1656. *Mysterium Magnum, or an Exposition of the First Book of Moses called Genesis*. London: Lloyd.

Bostocke, Richard. 1585. *The Difference between the Auncient Phisicke … and the Latter Phisicke*. London: Walley.

Bruce, Frederick F. 1951. *The Acts of the Apostles*. Grand Rapids: Eerdmans.

Charlton, William. 1983. Prime Matter: A Rejoinder. *Phronesis* 28:197–211.

Copan, Paul. 1996. Is Creatio Ex Nihilo a Post-Biblical Invention? An Examination of Gerhard May's Proposal. *TJ* 17:77–93.

Crossland, Maurice P. 1962. *Historical Studies in the Language of Chemistry*. London: Heinemann.

Daniel, Dane T. 2006. Invisible Wombs: Rethinking Paracelsus's Concept of Body and Matter. *Ambix* 53:129–42.

Debus, Allen G. 1977. *The Chemical Philosophy*. Mineola, N.Y.: Dover.

Deghaye, Pierre. 1992. Jacob Boehme and His Followers. Pages 210–48 in *Modern Esoteric Spirituality*. Edited by Antoine Faivre and Jacob Needleman. New York: Crossroad.

Dorn, Gerhard. 1602. Tractatus de naturae luce physica ex Genesi desumpta (Iuxta sapientiam Theophrasti Paracelsi). Pages 326–32 in *Theatrum chemicum*. Vol. 1. Strasbourg: Zetzner.

Emerton, Norma. 1994. Creation in the Thought of J.B. Van Helmont and Robert Fludd. Pages 85–101 in *Alchemy and Chemistry in the 16th and 17th Centuries*. Edited by Piyo Rattansi and Antonio Clericuzio. Dordrecht: Kluwer.

Erastus, Thomas. 1572. *Disputationem de medicini nova Philippi Paracelsi*. Part 1. Basel: Perna.

Forshaw, Peter J. 2007. Vitriolic Reactions: Orthodox Responses to the Alchemical Exegesis of Genesis. Pages 111–36 in *The Word and the World: Biblical Exegesis and Early Modern Science*. Edited by Kevin Killeen and Peter J. Forshaw. Basingstoke: Macmillan.

Gilly, Carlos. 1998. Theophrastia Sancta: Paracelsianism as a Religion in Conflict with the Established Churches. Pages 151–87 in *Paracelsus: The Man and His Reputation: His Ideas and Their Transformation*. Edited by Ole Peter Grell. Leiden: Brill.

Goldammer, Kurt. 1953. *Paracelsus: Natur und Offenbarung*. Hannover: Oppermann.

Gunnoe, Charles, Jr. 1994. Thomas Erastus and His Circle of Anti-Paracelsians. Pages 127–48 in *Annalecta Paracelsica*. Edited by Joachim Telle. Stuttgart: Steiner.

Kahn, Didier. 1994. Les débuts de Gérard Dorn d'après le manuscript autographe de sa *Clavis totius Philosophiae Chymisticae* (1565). Pages 59–126 in *Analecta Paracelsica*. Edited by Joachim Telle. Stuttgart: Steiner.

———. 2004. L'interprétation alchimique de la Genèse chez Joseph

Du Chesne dans le contexte de ses doctrines alchimiques et cosmologiques. Pages 641–92 in *Scientiae et artes: Die Vermittlung alten und neuen Wissens in Literatur, Kunst und Musik*. Edited by Barbara Mahlmann-Bauer. Wiesbaden: Harrassowitz.

King, Hugh R. 1956. Aristotle without Prima Materia. *JHI* 17:370–89.

Koyré, Alexandre. 1929. *La Philosophie de Jacob Boehme*. Paris: Vrin.

Kronen, John D, Sandra Menssen, and Thomas D. Sullivan. 2000. The Problem of the Continuant: Aquinas and Suarez on Prime Matter and Substantial Generation. *The Review of Metaphysics* 53:863–85.

Marquet, Jean-Francois. 1993. Philosophie et alchimie chez Gérard Dorn. Pages 215–21 in *Alchimie et philosophie à la Renaissance*. Edited by Jean-Claude Margolin and Sylvain Matton. Paris: Vrin.

May, Gerhard. 1994. *Creatio ex nihilo*. Edinburgh: T&T Clark.

Nautin, P. 1973. Genèse 1, 1–2, de Justin à Origène. Pages 61–94 in *In principio: Interprétations des premiers versets de la Genèse*. Edited by C. Mayer. Paris: Centre d'Études des religions du livre.

Pagel, Walter. 1958. *Paracelsus: An Introduction to Philosophical Medicine in the Era of the Renaissance*. New York: Karger.

———. 1961. Prime Matter of Paracelsus. *Ambix* 9:117–35.

———. 1982. *Joan Baptista Van Helmont: Reformer of Science and Medicine*. Cambridge: Cambridge University Press.

Paracelsus, Theophrastus. 1590. Philosophia ad Atheniensis. Pages 1–47 in *Der Bücher und Schriften*. Edited by Johannes Huser. Vol. 8. Basel: Huser.

———. 1603. *Operum medico-chimicorum sive Paradoxorum*. Frankfurt: Collegio Musarum Palthenianarum.

———. 1658. Philosophia ad Atheniensis. Pages 239–52 in *Opera omnia medico-chemico-chirurgica*. Vol. 2. Geneva: Ioan Antonii & Samuelis de Tournes.

———. 1660. *Paracelsus: His Archidoxis Comprised in Ten Books*. London: J.H.

———. 1894. Philosophy Addressed to the Athenians. Pages 249–82 in *The Hermetic and Alchemical Writings of Paracelsus*. Vol. 2. Edited and translated by Edward Arthur Waite. London: Elliott.

———. 1931. *Sämtliche Werke*. Vol. 13. Edited by Karl Sudhoff. Munchen: Oldenburg.

———. 2007. Opus Paramirum. In *Essential Theoretical Writings*. Edited and translated by Andrew Weeks. Leiden: Brill.

Plato. 2003. *Timaeus*. Translated by Benjamin Jowett. Mineola, N.Y.: Dover.

Ruland, Martin. 1612. *Lexicon Alchemiae*. Frankfurt: Andrea.

———. 1964. *A Lexicon of Alchemy*. Translated by Edward Arthur Waite. 2nd ed. London: Kessinger.

Sherwood Taylor, Frank. 1953. The Idea of the Quintessence. Pages 247–65 in *Science, Medicine and History: Essays in Honour of Charles Singer*. Vol. 1. Oxford: Oxford University Press.

Stonehouse, Ned B. 1957. *Paul before the Areopagus and Other New Testament Studies*. Grand Rapids: Tyndale.

Vaughan, Thomas. 1651. *Lumen de lumine*. London: Blunden.

Walton, Michael T. 1998. Genesis and Chemistry in the Sixteenth Century. Pages 1–14 in *Reading the Book of Nature: The Other Side of the Scientific Revolution Image*. Edited by Allen G. Debus and Michael T. Walton. Kirksville: Truman State University Press.

———. 2011. *Genesis and the Chemical Philosophy: True Christian Science in the Sixteenth and Seventeenth Centuries*. New York: AMS.

Webster, Charles. 1980. *From Paracelsus to Newton: Magic and the Making of Modern Science*. Cambridge: Cambridge University Press.

Part 3
From Modern to Post-Postmodern (Re)Visions

Beyond Postmodernism? Esoteric Interpretations of Gen 1–3 by E. Swedenborg, R. Steiner, and S. D. Fohr

Susanne Scholz

During the rise, heyday, and demise of the modern worldview, three esoteric interpretations of Gen 1–3 appeared. They were published in the eighteenth century C.E., the turn from the nineteenth to the twentieth century C.E., and toward the end of the twentieth century C.E. by Emanuel Swedenborg, Rudolph Steiner, and Samuel D. Fohr. In contrast to academic biblical studies ruled by an empiricist-scientific epistemology, these three readers rely on very different methodologies and assumptions than those advanced in biblical studies insofar as they interpreted Gen 1–3 with an esoteric hermeneutics. Consequently, their biblical exegetical works have been left unexamined although Swedenborg and Steiner influenced significantly religious and cultural life and thought.

This essay remedies this situation, at least on a rudimentary level, but it also wants to do more. It suggests that the three commentaries have the potential to contribute to a renewed cultural and religious understanding of the Bible in our post-postmodern age. As is well-known, the modern worldview was challenged in the second half of the twentieth century. Epistemologically and intellectually, we moved into the postmodern age. Some thinkers even propose that we have moved beyond postmodernity. For instance, Nicolas Bourriaud (2009), Alan Kirby (2009), and Raoul Eshelman (2000/2001) argue eloquently that we live in a post-postmodern era, a "new dark age of dogma" (Toth and Brooks 2007, 10), in which fundamentalisms of all kinds, including religious fundamentalism, and corporate globalization run rampant. In their views, postsecularity defines our politically conservative age. Sometimes also classified as "altermodernity" (Bourriaud 2009, 19), our age also contests the once taken-for-granted principles of modern exegesis, even though some Bible readers repeatedly affirm these principles, which merely gives witness to their demise. In the post-postmodern era, the question therefore becomes how to read the Bible when the historical-critical establishment of dates, settings, and authorial meanings remains disputed and contested and when privatized, personalized, and sentimentalized (PPS) biblical interpretations are theopolitical endorsements of the status quo. The following analysis suggests that the Genesis commentaries of Swedenborg, Steiner, and Fohr may help us in answering this question. After all, their spiritual-religious observations, insights, and comments may have something to offer to people living under the conditions of post-postmodernity.

A word of disclosure: I discovered the three commentaries when I felt dissatisfied with the dominant historical-literalist paradigm in biblical studies. In my view, the post-postmodern era represents an opportune moment to investigate "modern" esoteric readings of the Bible, because they have stood so far outside the hermeneutical mainstream. Could it be that they provide tools for resistant Bible readings against the trends of corporate conformity and neocolonialism so prevalent in today's global economic infrastructures? Or do they merely provide spiritualized escape mechanisms for the discontented elite? The following analysis is a test case. In a close reading, I explore the selected esoteric works to evaluate whether Swedenborg, Steiner, and Fohr offer more than just vague possibilities for a post-postmodern biblical hermeneutics of resistance to the current political, economic, and socioreligious status quo.

From the Body-Oriented to the Spiritual and Heavenly Persons: Emanuel Swedenborg's Esoteric Reading of Gen 2–3

Emanuel Swedenborg (1688–1772) was a Swedish scientist, philosopher, Christian theologian, and mystic whose visions for religious reform of Christianity led to the founding of the Swedenborg Church. He influenced countless people in the West, among them Helen Keller and Carl G. Jung. Swedenborg published many works on religious-spiritual topics after he experienced a spiritual awakening at the age of fifty-six in 1744. Among his writings is an eight volume commentary on the Bible that includes hundreds of pages on the first chapters of the book of Genesis entitled *Arcana Cœlestia* ("Secrets of Heaven"). He published the commentary anonymously between 1749 and 1756, but his work received little attention then and is still ignored in today's world of biblical scholarship (Stengel

2008; Körbel 2001, 154–55). Academic studies on Swedenborg's lengthy and detailed discussions of Gen 2–3 do not exist (but see Edmiston 1923).

Certainly, one reason for this utter lack of engagement must be sought in Swedenborg's complete immersion in what he calls "the inner meaning of Scripture." He sees it constituted on three levels of meaning. A first level of meaning presents "the *internal historical sense*, which focuses on the history of the 'churches,' or what we might refer to as the dominant religious cultures in Western history." A second level is "the *spiritual sense*, which deals with the human process of preparation for heaven known as 'rebirth.'" A third level uncovers "the *heavenly sense*, which concerns the divine process of transformation, elsewhere translated as 'glorification,' that is, the process whereby God became a human being and a human being became God" (Woofenden and Rose 2008, 25; also see Dole 1997; Cooper 1994). In contrast to exegetical conventions, as developed since Baruch Spinoza's *Tractatus Theologico-Politicus* (1670), Swedenborg rejects the literal-historical meaning of the Bible, because, in his view, it misses the deeper symbolic meaning hidden away in the texts (e.g., *Secrets of Heaven* §§277, 293, 294; see also Scherer 2005; Benz 1975).[1] His dismissive stance toward the literal-historical approach has been unpopular ever since the modern worldview came to dominate the epistemological and methodological understanding of the world and literal-historical approaches became the norm. Swedenborg's esoteric hermeneutics breaks with this newly emerging norm, and, as a consequence, his work has been sidelined.

Swedenborg understands the daring proposition he makes and pays a heavy price for it. For instance, some of his contemporaries went so far to diagnose him as mad or epileptic (Donat 2007). Yet undeterred, he emphasizes that "without this interior life, the Word in its letter is dead" (*Secrets of Heaven* §3) and "the Word's literal meaning alone, when it monopolizes our thinking, can never provide a view of the inner contents" (§4). To him, literalist interpretations miss the point, and only symbolic readings excavate the "secrets of heaven" that have "to do with the Lord, his heaven, the church, faith, and all the tenets of faith" (§1). In his view, spiritual understanding is the exclusive goal of biblical exegesis.

---

1. Swedenborg uses paragraphs to number his explanations. They will be referenced in the following analysis with § followed by the paragraph number, as provided by Swedenborg. All translations follow that of Lisa Hyatt Cooper in Swedenborg 2008.

Swedenborg further holds that he knows the inner scriptural meaning, because God "in his divine mercy" revealed it to him "over the past several years of interaction with spirits and angels" (§67). At the very outset of his Genesis interpretation, Swedenborg states: "Except at a very few points, those inner depths never show on the surface" (§1). It is up to interpreters to identify the inner depths of God's word by separating the "outer" from the "inner," because, as Swedenborg believes, "the inward being is what lives and allows the outward being to live," and so "in the same way, the letter of the Word by itself is a body without a soul" (§3).

The articulation of the Bible's inner meaning is, however, not as simple as it sounds, because, as Swedenborg explains, direct contact with the heavens is necessary. Since he experienced this contact, he uses it to establish biblical meanings and to assert his authority. He writes:

> I realize many will claim that no one can talk to spirits and angels as long as bodily life continues, or that I am hallucinating, or that I have circulated such stories in order to play on people's credulity, and so on. But none of this worries me; I have seen, I have heard, I have felt. (§68)

His approach relies on personal contact with the heavens through the physical senses, as in "I have seen, I have heard, I have felt." Hence, he claims that he has the authority to present the Bible's inner meaning, refuting the standards of modern-scientific methodology that require evidence, facts, and the study of nature. Swedenborg encourages people to understand, as he did, by letting go of "body-driven concerns" and by becoming free to encounter "spirits" and "life together with them" (§69). After all, to Swedenborg, people are one with spirits and angels, and he regards humans as spirits "clothed in flesh" (§69). He was in touch with them and thus he acknowledges that none of his ideas originated from him but came "with utmost clarity … from outside, and sometimes I have seen where it came from and how it entered" (§150). To establish the Bible's inner meaning, Bible readers are advised to distinguish scientific-exoteric principles of knowing from those of spiritual-religious truth, because, as Swedenborg states repeatedly, science itself does not teach anything about the spirit world and God (Hanegraaff 2008, 74).

Swedenborg's actual commentary on Gen 1–3 extends from paragraph 67 to paragraph 319, covering over 250 paragraphs that fill more than ninety pages. Discussions on Gen 2–3 are gathered in two chapters of a similar basic organization. In the case of Gen 2, Swedenborg begins with a general explanation on his esoteric hermeneutics (*Secrets of Heaven* §§67–72). He subdivides the commentary on Gen 2 into two sections. The first section covers Gen 2:1–17. It begins with a translation, continues with a summary in Swedenborg's words (§§73–80), and presents his interpretation of the text's inner meaning (§§81–130). The second section covers Gen 2:18–25. Again, he translates the biblical text, summarizes the verses (§§131–136), and offers their inner meaning (§§137–167). A section on "Our Resurrection from Death and Entry into Eternal Life" (§§168–181) concludes the commentary on Gen 2.

Swedenborg's interpretation on Gen 3 follows a similar structure (§§182–319). It offers general comments on "Our Entry, Once Received, into Eternal Life (Continued)" (§§182–189). Subdivided into three parts, the commentary begins with Gen 3:1–13, a translation, a summary, and explanations on the inner meaning of these verses. The same procedure is applied to Gen 3:14–19 and Gen 3:20–24. The chapter concludes with a reflection on "Our Entry into Eternal Life (Continued)" in which Swedenborg reflects on the notion of eternal life. The following analysis highlights two major concepts prevalent in Swedenborg's exegesis on Gen 2–3. They relate to his ideas on the esoteric-historical developments of humanity and his views on gender in relation to the inner self.

The Inner and the Outer Self in the Esoteric History of Humanity

Swedenborg does not view the Genesis stories as depictions of the exoteric development of life on planet earth. Rather humanity's religious-spiritual development or inner history emerges in four stages. It begins with what he calls the "earliest church," followed by the "ancient church," the "Jewish church," and the "Christian church." Importantly, Swedenborg uses the term *church* not as a reference to the Christian institution but as a term for "the human community sharing particular religious viewpoints" (Woofenden and Rose 2008, 48).

Each church is characterized by certain spiritual manifestations, depending on the timeframe in which each church emerges. Swedenborg distinguishes between the antediluvian (preflood) or postdiluvian (postflood) "spiritual" times, and he outlines four stages that are based on very different "historical" timeframes than customary in the empiricist-scientific paradigm. He explains that the events depicted in Genesis refer "to the earliest church on earth, to the spiritual developments that surrounded its fall, and to its replacement by what is here referred to as the 'ancient church'" (Woofenden and Rose 2008, 48). More specifically, Gen 2–3:19 describes those "who lived like animals and finally became spiritual people" (*Secrets of Heaven* §286). Their growth made humans into "heavenly people" who then formed the "earliest church," namely, those generations of people living prior to the flood, as reported in Gen 6 (§286). Said differently, Swedenborg does not view Gen 1–3 as a historical-literal depiction of the earth's creation but as an allusion to humanity's collective inner development. With Gen 3:20, people developed from the prefallen to the fallen state, which lasted until the flood, as described from Gen 3:20–6:6. The flood story signifies closure to humanity's early development (§286), and afterwards the second phase of humanity's development begins.

According to Swedenborg, the main difference between the first and second phases of humanity's inner development consists of "the difference between having perception and having conscience" (§597). Swedenborg explains:

> The states of these two churches were entirely different. That of the earliest church was to receive a perception of good, and so of truth, from the Lord. In the ancient church—'Noah'—the state changed to one of conscience concerning goodness and truth.... The earliest church was heavenly, but the ancient church was spiritual. (§597)

To Swedenborg, then, the Genesis narratives feature different eras in humanity's spiritual-historical development in which the collective awareness becomes increasingly worse. The earliest phase is "heavenly" (§§281, 287–88), because at this point people have "direct revelation through personal contact with spirits and angels and also through visions and dreams sent by the Lord" (§597). Swedenborg finds this earliest stage represented by the first woman, Eve, the mother of all and loved by God "above all others" (§290), as well as by the first seven generations during the earliest stage described in Gen 1:1–3:24 (§§281–82).

Swedenborg asserts that at this stage of humanity's spiritual-religious development people easily knew right from wrong, because their perception was direct, clear, and guided by the general principle based on what he calls "eternal truths." These truths include "the idea that the Lord governs the universe, that he is the source of all goodness and truth and of all life, that our selfhood is pure evil and of itself is dead, and other ideas like these" (§597). During this era, so Swedenborg asserts, love defined faith

(§597; see also §§202 and 398), a situation that he believes changes in the spiritual-religious development of humanity, as articulated in the ensuing Bible stories (§598). In the earliest era people communicated "in ideas or mental expression" and "breathed internally" like "angels" and "any external breathing was silent" (§607). This condition enabled humans to know intuitively and immediately right from wrong, Swedenborg explains.

Yet this ability changed over time. When humans moved to the next spiritual-religious stage, as depicted in the stories of Noah and the flood, it decreased. At this point the ancient church people's internal breathing started to disappear, and they began talking to each other, because "with external breathing came verbal speech—the speech of articulated sounds" (§398). The different form of breathing made it impossible for humans to understand by way of the inner self, as the earliest people had done. Now they relied on their "outer self" (§608), and it was then that doctrines were grasped through the physical senses, shaped into concrete images in the memory, and then reshaped into ideas (§608). Thinking moved from the outside toward the inside in contrast to the earlier stage when people understood intuitively and did not need to rely on the outside. At the same time, love ceased to be the most important principle, and the intellect began to dominate. Thus, to Swedenborg, the entire "psyche" of the ancient church is different from the previous level. He elaborates on this change: "The inner pathways were now blocked off, preventing any contact with heaven except that which lay hidden to consciousness. No channel of instruction lay open but the external one through the senses, as just noted" (§609). Swedenborg describes a process of declining spiritual-religious sensitivity among humans. It is an inner psycho-spiritual-religious drama expressed in the biblical tales. This process moves from an inner perception of the heavenly realm to outer levels of consciousness, eventually leading to the complete dismissal of inner meaning and understanding. Thus, to Swedenborg, only the complete withdrawal from the attachment to outer body-driven concerns enables people to regain access to the heavenly worlds.

Woman and Man as Will and Intellect of the Inner Self

Another notion stands out in Swedenborg's interpretation of Gen 1–3. It has to do with the symbolic meaning of woman and man in the story. To Swedenborg, Gen 3:6 demonstrates that "the fourth generation of the earliest church ... allowed themselves to be seduced by self-love." By "self-love" Swedenborg means that people at this spiritual-religious stage only believed when "they saw it confirmed by evidence from the senses and the facts" (§208). Genesis 3 illustrates this stage in the three considerations that the woman makes about the tree. She ponders that it is good for eating, appealing to the eyes, and desirable for giving insight, all references to "sensual pleasure" and "the properties of our selfhood (or the woman)." To Swedenborg, the female character personifies this unfortunate quality in humanity whereas the eating man "symbolizes the rational mind's consent" (§207). In other words, the woman stands for selfhood which, according to Swedenborg, has negative ramifications for the spiritual-religious development of humanity. He describes this drama in the following way:

> Human selfhood is everything evil and false that wells up out of self-love and materialism. It is the tendency not to believe in the Lord or his Word but in ourselves and to think that what we do not grasp on a sensory or factual basis is nothing. The results of these tendencies is nothing but evil and falsity, which cause us to see everything backward—evil things as good, good things as evil, false things as true, and true things as false. That which exists we consider to be nothing, while that which is nothing we consider to be everything. We call hatred love, darkness light, death life, and the other way around. The Word calls people who succumb to this way of thinking lame and blind. This, then, is human selfhood, which in itself is hellish and damnable. (§210)

Swedenborg's characterization of selfhood, as symbolized in the character of woman in Gen 3:6, is harsh and negative. His focus is on the inner meaning of woman as selfhood, as a reference to "nothing but evil and falsity." Swedenborg explains that his understanding of the symbolic meaning comes from his contact with "spirits" (§215). The spirits are certain that their beliefs are true, because they do not doubt themselves. They resemble people on earth doing the same (§215). As such they are self-centered, permeated by "undiluted falsity" and "an abyss of darkness" (§215). Swedenborg declares the first woman in Genesis resembles them, and so he views her as a symbol for evil, a heavily androcentric characterization for sure.

Yet his main interest in the symbolism of woman and man relates to a larger point. It has to do with a symbolic view on gender, as he states in his discussion on Gen 1:27, "The earliest people ... called the intellect in the spiritual being *male* and the will there *female*" (§54). He defines man as intellect and woman as will, and both intellect and will are part of the human mind. They are "two basic faculties" (§35) linked in the ongoing internal spiritual-religious drama of human development. He writes: "The will holds love or goodness, the intellect holds faith or truth. From love (goodness) the people of that time perceived what belonged to faith (to truth), so that their minds were unified" (§310). In this system of thought, the male is identified with the intellect which consists of faith or truth whereas the female is identified with the will, consisting of love or goodness. Both function in harmony. Hence, Swedenborg states that "the will regulates the intellect, the two together make one mind and as a result one life; under those circumstances, what we will and do is also what we think and intend" (§35). Both love and faith, symbolized in the biblical tale as woman and man, are indispensable and related intimately to each other. The will (woman) needs to regulate the intellect (man), because "[w]hen the intellect is at odds with the will ... our single mind is torn in two" (§35) This inner conflict makes one of them rise up to heaven and the other lean toward hell.

Since, according to Swedenborg, the will (woman) drives everything, he sees us rush into hell "heart and soul if the Lord did not take pity on us" (§35). The woman is the negative foil to man even when she or the will (love) are characterized as the regulating force of the intellect (faith, man). Such an interpretation of woman and man as will and intellect is at once surprisingly egalitarian, but it is also conventionally androcentric, because the will (woman) moves toward hell. As a side note, the interpretation also advances the heterosexist assumption of female and male as exclusively related to each other.

Swedenborg would claim that these issues are germane to the biblical story in which female and male appear as the paradigm of human relationship. He bemoans the lack of balance between will and intellect among people living after the flood, as well as among "those who live in modern times" (§310). In his interpretation, the female quality of love, the will to do good, is absent today. We are dominated by the intellect, which he identifies with man in the Genesis story. As Swedenborg writes:

> [People after the flood] have no love and therefore no will to do good. Faith is still possible, though; in other words, they are able to comprehend truth. Faith or an understanding of truth can lead them to a kind of charity, although they arrive at it by another way. Their way lies through conscience, which is instilled in them by the Lord and is formed out of a knowledge of truth and of the good that results from it. (§310)

In other words, Swedenborg's genderized view of will (love, woman) and intellect (faith, man) permeates humanity's inner development. The woman, in particular, symbolizes the church that Swedenborg finds corrupted by self-dependence (§262; see also §§155, 156), but he also criticizes man's sole reliance on "rational capacity" (§261). Although Swedenborg does not state it explicitly, his interpretation offers a sharp critique of a male-dominated or intellect-driven culture and society. He regrets that the balance between female and male is corrupted, a situation that the biblical narrative symbolizes with the eating of the fruit.

Yet then again, Swedenborg also struggles with his egalitarian conceptualization of female and male. He reminds his readers that an explicit hierarchy ought to exist in heterosexual marriage, and so he states: "A wife should be under the influence of her husband's good sense." Swedenborg's negative assessment of woman provides the reason for this androcentric prescription, and he goes even further when he proclaims that a wife "acts on desire, which is self-centered, and not so much from reason as a man does" (§266). In other words, when push comes to shove, Swedenborg does not escape privileging maleness and reason. He finds men superior to women, attributing androcentric privilege to married men in "real" life. Although he insists on the symbolic and not the historical-literal meaning of the Bible, in the end his sexist assumptions (as well as his racist and anti-Jewish views) prevail (Woofenden and Rose 2008, 51–56).

Still, Swedenborg emphasizes repeatedly that his interpretation refers to humanity in general. For instance, he states that the eating of the fruit is the moment when "our selfhood" is no longer filled with "innocence, peace, and goodness" and abandons its "heavenly, angelic identity received from the Lord" (*Secrets of Heaven* §252). He declares that the eating of the fruit turns humanity's love into "self-love," which led us away from God and heaven toward "sensory evidence and secular knowledge" (§205). Swedenborg laments this spiritual-religious decline:

> Telling more about the inner meaning of these things, however, would be difficult, as people today know nothing about them. They have no concept, for instance, of a faith based on love, of wisdom, or of the intelligence that comes from these. Shallow people know hardly anything but secular facts, which they call understanding and wisdom, and also faith. They do not even know what love is, and many are unacquainted with the will and intellect and the fact these two combine to form the mind. (§111)

In short, to Swedenborg, the early Genesis narratives depict the earliest stages of humanity's spiritual-religious development, moving from an inner grasp of God and faith in love to an externalization of knowledge due to a focus on "ourselves," "our self-absorption," and the "material world" (§152). Thus the biblical texts depict humanity as striving for "autonomy" (§131), being dissatisfied with God's authority, and seeking autonomy in the world (§138). They portray symbolically how humans move from being heavenly to spiritual people (§81), from people who perceive truth and goodness from love (§81), to people who understand only with the intellect (§61). Since the fall, humans seek religious knowledge and acknowledge truth and goodness only from a stance of faith, not from a stance of love (§81). They apply "secular knowledge when investigating religious mysteries" (§127). Yet to Swedenborg, the religious-spiritual path cannot be found in nature, and the Genesis stories detail the proper approach when they are read with a hermeneutics grounded in direct contact with the divine realm.

The True Version of Evolution: Rudolf Steiner's Esoteric Reading of Gen 1–2

Rudolf Steiner (1861–1925) was an Austrian philosopher, social thinker, architect, and esotericist who founded a new spiritual movement called Anthroposophy and initiated developments in education (Waldorf schools), medicine, agriculture, and art (eurythmy) (McDermott 1992). Like Swedenborg, he was a prolific writer and lecturer, and his publications have been translated into many languages. In a series of lectures delivered in August of 1910,[2] Steiner elaborates on the seven-day creation account in an esoteric way. In his view, "we would be quite mistaken to take the words of the first sections of Genesis as referring to things or events which can be seen with the physical eye" (Steiner 2002, 2–3). Like Swedenborg, Steiner asserts that Genesis does not describe events of the external world but refers to internal-historical developments that become obvious when the text is read with "the spiritual scientific method" (2002, 3). Only then, so Steiner asserts, will readers "acquire a living picture of what lived in the ancient Hebrew sages when they let those most powerful

---

2. These lectures were published together in 2002 in *Genesis: Secrets of Creation*. References from these lectures will be taken from this published collection.

words work on them which, as words, do at least still exist in the world" (2002, 4). So while the biblical tale does not depict historical events in the world, it offers clues for "understand[ing] the spiritual origin of our physical world" (2002, 172). Steiner explains key Hebrew phrases and concepts, as they appear in Gen 1–2. Again, like Swedenborg, he interprets the biblical creation stories as one narrative. He rejects explicitly the idea of "modern biblical criticism" that the account of Gen 1:1–2:4a is different from the story in Gen 2:4b–3:24 (2002, 127).

Steiner invites his readers to meditate on the very first term (*bereshit*), to visualize it, and to imagine the sounds it produces. He states:

> *Bet*, the first letter, called up the weaving together of the substance of the outer shell, *resh*, the second accompanying sound, called up the countenances of the spiritual beings who did the weaving within the shell, and *shin*, the third sound, called up the prickly force that was working its way out to manifestation. (2002, 7)

This meditative, visualizing, and imaginary technique aims to identify the eternal principle behind the term. Steiner wants to get a sense of "the spirit of this language which combined with a creativity of soul of which the people of today, with their abstract languages, can have no idea" (2002, 8). In other words, Steiner's hermeneutics looks for the original meaning of the Bible's first words as intended by the spiritually attuned scribes. To Steiner, the ancient scribes saw the world as "a sphere in which fiery, gaseous and watery elements weave," as they listened to the sounds of the words in Genesis. They remembered that

> within this active weaving, elemental sphere there is a group of spiritual beings who are engaged in thinking creatively, and the goal of their creative thinking is to direct the whole force of the joint activity towards the image of man [*sic*]. The first fruit of their thinking is the conception of something manifesting itself outwardly and of something else inwardly active (2002, 12–13).

Accordingly, the sounds of Hebrew words matter greatly in Steiner's effort to recapture the spiritual meaning of the biblical text.

To Steiner, then, the biblical accounts do not refer to literal-historical events; they need to be understood symbolically. He believes that "the content of these mental images is not the point; the point is that the soul devotes all its energies to having nothing in its consciousness other than the mental images in question" (1997, 290). The goal of the sounds is "to tear the soul away from sensory perception" (1997, 295). We ought to read the text to forget our physicality and to make mental images explicit as they emerge from the texts. In this way, the texts teach about "our own origin" (2002, 13), which is spiritual and not physical. Steiner states: "It's not important *what* is imagined, but only that the process of visualizing the image frees the soul from dependence on anything physical" (2002, 13). The technique is available to anybody "choosing to apply the gifts of unbiased reasoning and a healthy sense of truth" (2002, 422). The goal is to develop interiority, and Steiner's description of human history explains why this is more necessary today than ever before.

A Preparatory Stage of Human Existence: A Male-Female Human Being, Undifferentiated, and Etheric

Steiner's interpretation of the creation stories makes another unique point. It characterizes humanity's creation in Gen 1–2 as an "extremely complicated process" (2002, 143). This process did not take place on what we call earth but in "higher, spiritual realms." Steiner describes a cosmic process that took place to form the earth, eventually leading to the planet as we know it today. His explanations are based on the central esoteric principle from the spiritual as moving down to the physical realm. He sees this principle in action during the cosmic dynamics of earth's development, and he explains this process: "This is how the Earth developed from a spiritual cosmic being into a physical plant: Everything materially connected to it condensed out of what was formerly spiritually connected to it" (1997, 120). Similar to other esoteric thinkers, including Swedenborg, Steiner's hermeneutics assumes that the spiritual level comes down to the material level. The material emanates from the spiritual realm (1997, 120). This idea is based on a strong hierarchy that also applies to humanity's evolution. Accordingly, humanity emanated from the spiritual to the physical level, a development that, according to Steiner, was linked to the cosmic movements of sun, moon, and earth. The sun and the moon had to separate from the earth, which made the forces on earth less spiritually and less materially intense. The separation created some balance between the spiritual forces of the sun and the "coarse" forces of the moon (2002, 123–25). Only after the withdrawal of the sun and the moon did it become possible for humans to live on earth (2002, 125). Steiner states:

> Whereas the forces would have been, so to say, too spiritual if the earth had remained united with the sun, they would have had to become too coarse had it remained united with the moon. Thereupon the moon also withdrew, and the earth remained behind in a state of balance brought about because sun beings and moon beings both influenced it from outside. The earth prepared itself in this way to be able to be the bearer of human existence. (2002, 125; see also 131–32)

Steiner develops specific terminology to describe the various eons in which these processes took place. The separation of the sun, moon, and earth occurred during the so-called Lemurian and Atlantean ages, and it was then that the earth began to cool down. Steiner also explains that at that time the earth's atmosphere was saturated with a watery substance resembling a mixture of water and fog, perhaps as described in Gen 1:2: "The earth was a formless void and darkness covered the face of the deep, while a wind from God swept over the face of the waters" (NRSV). Steiner contrasts this early developmental stage of the earth to today's conditions when he writes:

> The difference that exists today between whether it is rainy or whether the atmosphere is clear of rain did not exist in those ancient times. Everything was shrouded in watery fog, laden with all sorts of fumes and smoke and other substances which had not at that time assumed solid form. Much of what is solid today still streamed through the atmosphere in the form of steam. And everything was pervaded by these masses of watery fog until far into Atlantean times. (2002, 127; see also 128)

Clearly, his explanations go far beyond the literal biblical account when he contends that the withdrawal of the sun and the moon, as well as the watery atmosphere enabled "what had previously existed in a much more spiritual condition … to take on physical form'" (2002, 127). He sees this process described during the "third day" of Gen 1:9. In other words, Steiner's interpretation links biblical details with ideas taken from other sources that remain unspecified.

This hermeneutical liberty makes it possible for him to state that most souls/spirits had left earth when the sun and the moon withdrew from the earth, thriving "on the planets surrounding the earth," namely Mars, Jupiter, and Saturn, and further developing there (2002, 131). He explains that some of "the strongest, toughest human soul/spirits" remained on earth, and they were the first ones "coming into being of the etheric and physical bodies we now live in during the day" (2002, 131). Steiner surmises that with the help of the "elohim forces" (2002, 134) these early human beings resisted "mummification" or "hardening" after the sun and the moon had withdrawn from union with the earth. The withdrawal made another "cosmic advancement" possible. Based on the linguistic plurality of the noun *elohim*, Steiner theorizes that the elohim advanced to "Jehovah-Elohim" which enabled human beings to progress as well (2002, 134). With a reference to Gen 2:7, Steiner declares that it was the advanced version of elohim called Jehovah-Elohim who created "man" from the dust of the earth (2002, 136).

To Steiner, the biblical description of humanity's "essential nature" is "a model of accurate and appropriate wording" (2002, 139). Humanity's descent into physical, solid matter did not happen together with the other "living creatures" (2002, 139) but required a separate step. It is outlined in Gen 1 where animals, living on earth prior to human life, descended first. After some time, so argued Steiner, "did the conditions gradually arise favorable to the formation of the prototype of humankind" (2002, 140). It was then, in a separate step, that humans appeared.

Steiner's reading makes much of the mention of elohim in Gen 1, whom he characterizes as "the great directing forces" in the process of populating earth (2002, 134). He refrains from translating the masculine plural of the Hebrew elohim into a singular noun in English. Instead, he insists on this noun's plural meaning, because, in his view, it refers to the creative forces during the early evolutionary developments on earth. The elohim created physical humanity although the first human "was of course not yet like he is today" (2002, 134), as the elohim built humans "before earthly dust had been imprinted into the human body" (2002, 140) and before gender differentiation was created. Steiner also notes that "the physical body which man [*sic*] inhabits today only arose later when Jehovah-Elohim breathed into man the living breath" (2002, 140). Still the elohim created the "essential nature" of humans as found in humans today. Steiner elaborates:

> At that time human beings still had the same kind of body. We can describe it best, as far as we can imagine it at all, by saying that the physical body was more etheric still, whereas the etheric body was somewhat denser than today. In other words, what is our dense physical body today was not as dense at the time it was formed by the elohim, and the etheric body was denser than today. A densification towards becoming more physical only occurred later under the influence of Jehovah-Elohim. (2002, 141)

The first step produces humans closer to the heavenly realm, an idea also found in Swedenborg's interpretation. Humanity descends into the human physical form as part of a process of decline from the spiritual, etheric body into the material body, as we know it today.

Interestingly, Steiner stresses that the mere spiritual-etheric human being, created by the elohim, was not yet gender differentiated (2002, 141). Again this idea resembles Swedenborg's insistence on the androgynous nature of the initial human being, but Steiner argues this point differently than Swedenborg. Steiner maintains that the biblical account of Gen 1:26, "Let us make humankind" (NRSV), remembers the early androgynous stage of humanity. The story indicates that once each human was an "undifferentiated human being, the male-female human being … created in the image of the elohim" (2002, 141). Hence, in Steiner's interpretation, too, gender differentiation belongs to a later developmental phase.

The idea of different steps being part of the creation process comes through in yet another consideration in Steiner's reading, which relates to the terminology of *nefesh* and *neshimah*. Steiner attributes the different terms to the text's recognition that humanity developed in an evolutionary process on its own. He observes that the first term, *nefesh*, appears in Gen 1:21, 24, where it refers to both animals and humans. In Steiner's view, the term presents "a premature act of creation" (2002, 142) with human beings "at the peak of animal creation" (2002, 142–43). Only after the appearance of the second term, *neshimah* in Gen 2:7, does the term refer to "a higher member" of the soul/spiritual realm imprinted on humanity. Steiner asserts:

> With this imprinting of *neshama* it now became possible to give a man [*sic*] the potential to become an ego. For these old Hebrew expressions *nefesh*, *ruach*, *neshama*, are none other than what we have described as corresponding to our spiritual scientific terms of sentient soul, intellectual soul and consciousness soul. (2002, 143)

He observes that the terminology hints at yet another important evolutionary aspect of human beings. Steiner highlights them in his reading of Gen 2:4a ("These are the generations of the heavens and the earth when they were created," NRSV). He explains that the term for "descendants" and "generations" is the same in Hebrew (*toledot*). Thus, in his opinion, Gen 2:4a should be understood in line with Gen 10:1, which "speaks of the descendants of Noah" (2002, 147). When terminological consistency is kept in the translation, it becomes clear that the biblical text recognizes the ongoing emergence of different groups of "humans" from the spiritual realm to earth. Accordingly, Steiner translates Gen 2:4a as: "These are the *descendants* of the heavens and the earth."

Steiner maintains that the biblical account knows of a threefold creation process during which several versions of human beings appeared. In a first step, which occurs on the sixth day in the biblical account, the elohim create the "more etheric, more delicate human being" (2002, 146), whom Steiner calls the "elohim human beings." In a second step, Jehovah-Elohim forms them into the "Jehovah human beings" (2002, 146), and they are imprinted with the dust of the earth. In a third and final evolutionary step, "the descendants of those beings of heaven and earth who were created by the elohim and whose development was continued by Jehovah-Elohim" (2002, 146) came into existence. The identification of this threefold process in Genesis is important, because, in Steiner's view, it agrees with "what we can establish through spiritual or esoteric science" (2002, 147). In other words, Steiner posits that "clairvoyant experience" (2002, 147) verifies the biblical account, as he acknowledges in this statement: "It was by clairvoyant experience that the facts originally given to us were acquired" (2002, 146). Like Swedenborg, therefore, Steiner develops his interpretation with an esoteric hermeneutic that combines a symbolic-inner methodology with "experience." While he calls it "clairvoyant," Swedenborg describes it as direct contact with the heavens.

Central to Steiner's clairvoyant stance is the notion that "physical existence emerges like a crystallization" (2002, 148). He applies this idea to the entire evolutionary process of the cosmos, life on planet earth, the emergence of humans, and also to his reading of Gen 1–2. Accordingly, spirit crystalizes or descends into matter, in sharp opposition to the modern scientific theory of evolution that Steiner rejects, because it contradicts the fundamental esoteric principle that higher beings do not develop from evolutionary lower beings. Steiner is not shy to confront the scientific community about this difference, and so he contends:

> Man [*sic*] did not arise through lower creatures progressing to acquire human form. It is incredible that people can think that an animal form turned into the higher form of a human being. Whilst these animal forms were arising, forming their physical bodies below, man had already existed for a long time, but it was only later that he descended and took his place beside the animals. Anyone who cannot look upon evolution in

> this way is beyond help; he is hypnotized, as it were, by modern concepts, not by scientific facts but by contemporary opinion. (2002, 149)

In his view, then, the modern position has it all wrong. Steiner even declares that those who subscribe to evolution are "beyond help" and "hypnotized," strong words indeed. Yet read within his system of thought, his critique of the scientific idea of evolution is congruent. His interpretation of Gen 1–2 reinforces it.

Symbolic Meaning as Support for Spiritual Growth: Samuel D. Fohr's Esoteric Reading of Gen 2–3

A third esoteric interpretation of the biblical creation account comes from Samuel D. Fohr (born 1943), professor emeritus of philosophy at the University of Pittsburgh in Bradford, Pennsylvania. He received his doctorate in philosophy from the University of Michigan and taught courses on Eastern and Western philosophy. He edited more than a dozen books on René Guénon, a French author, intellectual, and metaphysician (1886–1951), who published extensively on esoteric spirituality. Fohr also published books on the symbolic meaning of the Grimm's fairytales (Fohr 2004) and the spiritual symbolism of Genesis and Exodus (Fohr 1986). His work on the esoteric meaning of Gen 2–3 is included here not to suggest that it is on par with Swedenborg or Steiner. Rather, it stands in the same hermeneutical tradition and offers a fascinating example of the esoteric reading tradition on Genesis at the end of the twentieth century.

In his book, *Adam and Eve* (Fohr 1986), Fohr offers a symbolic or inner reading of the two first biblical books, Genesis and Exodus, in which he integrates insights from Jewish and Christian interpreters since 200 B.C.E. His interpretation also makes extensive comparisons to the Sufi, Buddhist, Hindu, and Tao traditions. In fact, Fohr acknowledges the Vivekananda-Vedantu Society of Chicago, particularly Swami Bhashyananda, for teaching him about the Hindu tradition (Fohr 1986, v). In addition, Fohr's work on René Guénon provides ample background information on the symbolic hermeneutic Fohr advances in *Adam and Eve*. In the study on the Grimm's tales, Fohr acknowledges his dependence on Guénon, which also applies to *Adam and Eve*:

> I will be using a conceptual schema based on the writings of René Guénon, the outstanding interpreter of the traditional worldview in the

> twentieth century. Guénon himself commented on the significance of folktales, most notably in his article "Tradition and the Unconscious," found in the collection *Symbols of Sacred Science*. (2004, 2)

Fohr expounds on this "traditional" worldview steeped in "the symbolic dimension," because he wants to make esoteric meaning "accessible and rewarding to the specialist and layman alike" (1986, xiii). He explains that this approach helps in gaining "knowledge of one's innermost being, for God is understood as the center point or heart of the believer" (1986, 2). It assumes that God is neither "other" nor "totally external," a key notion of the exoteric view of religion. Rather, an esoteric interpretation provides information and insight into "really knowing ourselves" as "tantamount to knowing God" (1986, 1). He further states that in an esoteric interpretation, "liberation or deliverance involves penultimately a residing in consciousness at the still center point of one's being (the point of the 'actionless activity' of God), and ultimately an awareness of one's essential identity with God" (1986, 2). To Fohr, then, an esoteric hermeneutics needs to facilitate the deepening of an individual's inner quest for God.

Similar to other venerated texts, the narratives of Genesis and Exodus support such a psycho-religious deepening if they are read as reminders of metaphysical or "primordial truths" (1986, 15). The truths become clear when an individual makes progress on the spiritual journey, which Fohr finds best described by Friedrich von Hügel in 1923. Fohr writes:

> Adapting Friedrich von Hügel's masterful analysis we may say that all people first become acquainted with religion through their exoteric dimension. It cannot be otherwise since, as we have already said, religion is basically exoteric in character. A majority of people never go beyond this first stage, which we will call the childish stage of belief. It is childish because we are urged to accept what we are told without question, even if what we are expected to believe is highly implausible, e.g., the historical truth of all the stories in the Bible. A significant minority questions the historical truth of these stories as well as the dogmas of their religion. Some of these people, feeling that religion is a tissue of lies, never go beyond this stage and become atheists, or at best agnostics. Or perhaps they do not have quite so strong a reaction and grudgingly accept Bible stories as fictional tales whose purpose is to teach certain lessons. People in the latter group live out their lives in a state of lukewarm faith bordering on atheism. But some realize that there is another dimension to religion and go beyond this second stage. They discover the esoteric

> writings of those connected with initiatic groups and learn of the inner life and the inner meaning of Bible stories. These people take up the life of the spirit as best they can, and we may call this third stage the mature practice of religion. (1986, 5–6)

These different yet related dimensions of religious deepening constitute the hermeneutical basis for Fohr. The esoteric approach constitutes the final stage, as it is a spiritually mature reading of the Bible. Leaving behind the literalism or historical meaning, it advances a symbolic, esoteric, or inner biblical meaning. Fohr observes that Bible readers of earlier centuries, such as Origen and Maimonides, read biblical texts accordingly (1986, 7). He recognizes that a literal meaning is not valueless, as "laws and morals drawn from the many stories are beneficial externally for societies and individuals alike" (1986, 7). A literal meaning may also serve as a preparatory stage for learning to appreciate the symbolic meaning, because, as Fohr explains, "there are always two stages in spiritual growth, one preparatory and the other active" (1986, 7). He knows that the symbolic approach requires understanding, because "there are no symbols without intellects to comprehend them as such" (1986, 8). Fohr also acknowledges that he brings information to the text and reads Genesis and Exodus "with a background understanding of basic metaphysical truths" (1986, 15). He elaborates on these truths in twelve chapters that discuss the stories of Cain and Abel, Noah and Babel, Abraham and Isaac, Esau and Jacob, Jacob and Joseph, Moses and Aaron, Moses and Pharoah, and at the end of the volume also Gen 1 and Gen 2–3. His discussion on Gen 2–3 is the focus of the following analysis (1986, 119–29).

From "Edenic Man" to Male and Female: Gender Duality as a Symbol for the Loss of the Golden Age

Like other esoteric readers, Fohr assumes a literary coherence of Gen 1 and Gen 2–3. He posits that Gen 1:27, presenting "Edenic Man" as female and male, is central for understanding "the nature of Edenic Man" (1986, 115). This "Edenic Man" is androgynous, "balancing in himself the masculine and feminine aspects of Existence and integrating in himself all of the elements of our particular state of existence" (1986, 115). Similar to Swedenborg and Steiner, Fohr thus emphasizes that the first "Adam" is "the androgyne Adam-Eve" (1986, 116), "the prototype of man, rather than a human being" (1986, 117), and this human "prototype is split into two parts, female and male, in Genesis 2" (1986, 117). Yet also here Fohr emphasizes in accordance with his psycho-spiritual hermeneutics that the text does not report an historical event. Rather, the depiction is true for all times and persons, and "it is in this respect that we all suffer the effects of 'original sin'" (1986, 121). Like Swedenborg and Steiner, Fohr reads the biblical tale as memory of a golden age from which humans fell away, and due to humanity's central position in the cosmos, the human fall resulted in the fall of the whole of creation.

Thus, Fohr's interpretation focuses on the fall, which is symbolically expressed in the act of creating gender duality, "in the splitting of the androgynous Adam into Adam and Eve" (1986, 121). Interestingly, Fohr's notion of the fall differs significantly from the traditional Christian reading that locates the moment of the human fall in the couple's eating of the fruit. Fohr finds the idea that the fall begins at the moment of the emergence of gender duality also articulated in the Hindu tradition:

> And just as the splitting of Adam necessarily results in the imperfection of Adam and Eve which leads to their fall, the splitting of the Unity of Existence into the duality of Purusha and Prakriti (Heaven and Earth, the wind and the waters) necessarily results in the imperfection of the cosmos which leads to its fall. (1986, 121)

Fohr's interpretation stresses that the splitting into duality is necessary for the cosmos to exist, which the Genesis account articulates symbolically in the duality of male and female and the Hindu tradition in the duality of Purusha and Prakriti. Hence, in the biblical account the human prototype is split "in two incomplete halves," which describes the psycho-spiritual "loss of completeness" in the individual, a "loss of balance between the active and passive poles of creation as objectified in us" (1986, 122).

According to this reading, humans try to remedy the disconnection with God on the physical, emotional, or mental levels, but, as the story teaches, only the spiritual level brings a lasting sense of union with the divine. Thus only when "the masculine and feminine poles of creation" reunify within a person, when the androgynous state is spiritually experienced, spiritual regeneration becomes attainable, and "paradise" or "the fruits of the Tree of Life" are experienced on earth (1986, 123). He recognizes that this "Terrestrial Paradise has been called by many names: the Garden of Eden, the Land of Hyperboreans, the Isle of the Blessed, and Ultima Thule" (1986, 123). These symbolic expressions refer to "the center of Divine Influence on earth, and their indestructibility despite all the cataclysms and the degeneration of the world symbolizes the persistence of this influence" (1986, 124). Yet Fohr also observes, similar to other esoteric thinkers, that people of our era do not understand these expressions, because this era is permeated by a worldwide spiritual ignorance (1986, 124). Fohr's reading is thus pessimistic about today's spiritual condition, a situation that he finds already articulated in the biblical account. In this sense, then, Fohr's interpretation resembles classic Christian readings that negatively assess the nature of humanity and the world. It is also similar to Steiner's interpretation that outlines an esoteric process of continuous decline in humanity's development.

Fohr's approach is also similar to the classic Christian reading in yet another aspect. To Fohr, sexuality is a symbolic expression of humanity's fallen state. Therefore, in his view, religious texts and writers have intentionally linked sexual awareness with the fall, as "humans lose the last vestige of the primordial world-view" during puberty (1986, 125). He writes:

> Before it they had been complete (not needing a sexual partner) and balanced (containing male and female aspects in nearly equal amounts). Intellectually they were neuter and externally they treated others in this way. But with the dawning of sexual awareness they begin to see people first and foremost as males and females who are to be treated differently and viewed as objects for the fulfillment of their desires. To sum up, puberty and the coming of sexual awareness is an example on a certain level of the division of androgynous man. (1986, 125)

Fohr's interpretation points out that the Genesis account remembers the connection between human sexuality and the human feelings of separation from the world. Fallenness brings awareness to the human dualistic existence in the world. It is an inherent part of the created order, implying the existence of what is "other-than-the-self" (1986, 121). This "other-than-the-self" is often called evil, because, so Fohr argues, it represents our dislikes, a dynamic represented in the character of the serpent, which symbolizes the pull of the world "away from the center of our being" (1986, 126). Fohr explains:

> Just as a snake entraps a victim by coiling around it, the world can be said to entrap us by envelopment. In leading us away from our center it causes us to feel incomplete and thus puts desire in the place of peace. Actually, desire is but one side of a coin whose other side is aversion, and

> together they lead us to divide the world into what is good and what is evil. The cherubim which God sets to guard the entrance of the Garden of Eden after He has exiled Adam and Eve can be seen as symbolizing this judgmental view of the world. (1986, 126)

In the story the serpent entices the human couple to move away from divine union and to disrupt the state of consciousness of the complete person. In Fohr's psycho-spiritual hermeneutics, this drama plays out in each person as everybody faces this condition, challenged to overcome one's alienation. Genesis 2–3 describes this "development of the psycho-physical individuality" (1986, 126), and, accordingly, it depicts the sense of separateness from the rest of creation, leading people to evaluate what is good and what is evil. This dilemma occurs in all of us, Fohr stresses. Consequently, we experience "a loss of joy or bliss and the beginning of suffering due to either not getting (or losing) what we desire or getting what we have an aversion to" (1986, 126). In a nutshell, we are indeed cast out of paradise, as depicted in Gen 3 (1986, 126).

Fohr's interpretation does not only work with classic Christian theology but also integrates the Buddhist notion of the wheel of existence. Fohr makes this connection explicit when he writes:

> The Buddhist wheel of existence is comparable as a symbol to a section or cut of the tree surrounded by the snake. In the wheel we observe a place of central repose or peace surrounded by the moving spokes and rim. Typically we find ourselves on the rim of that wheel as it spins around. Our proper goal is to slide down one of the spokes toward the center and thus reach a point where we have stopped spinning—the Terrestrial Paradise.... This journey is an inner one, taking place in the consciousness of the human being. (1986, 127)

Relying on multireligious images and ideas, Fohr presents a psycho-spiritual interpretation of Gen 2–3 that highlights an inner process, transforming the consciousness of the individual. Fohr draws on Sufism, Hinduism, Buddhism, and classic Christian concepts while stressing human suffering as the basic human condition from which we need to liberate ourselves to experience union with God and "our already existing identity with God" (1986, 127). The ultimate purpose of Gen 2–3, then, is a deepening psycho-spiritual understanding of the human purpose and directing our attention toward the divine-spiritual realm, away from the world.

Toward a Future for Esoteric Readings of the Bible: Concluding Comments

We engaged in this investigation on the three esoteric readings of Gen 1–3 to explore the hermeneutical possibilities for an ongoing "meaningful" reception of the Bible at the beginning of the post-postmodern era. Do the three approaches provide tools for resistant Bible readings, or do they merely provide spiritualized escape mechanisms for the discontented elite?

Predictably, a simple yes-or-no answer does not offer an intellectually or hermeneutically satisfying response to the epistemological challenges we are facing in the post-postmodern era. Clearly, Swedenborg, Steiner, and Fohr forcefully remind us that the literal-historical study of the Bible misses the point, because it turns the reading of the Bible into an antiquarian project. Faiths have been lost and careers been changed because of this view of the Bible. Foremost among such people is Julius Wellhausen, who journeyed from the theology department at the University of Greifswald to the philology department at the University of Halle in 1882, and after him many Bible readers have wrestled with this hermeneutical challenge. Only few asserted what Swedenborg, Steiner, and Fohr proclaim without hesitation, namely, that interpreters ought to concern themselves with the inner, spiritual-religious meaning of the Bible.

The three esoteric thinkers do not agree in every aspect on the nature or extent of what constitutes the inner meaning of the Bible. Swedenborg grounds himself in visionary insights and experiences, which nurture his conviction that only the inner biblical meaning communicates the truth about "the Heavens." Genesis 2–3 demonstrates to him that humanity has moved away from God, and this development needs to be reversed. Steiner puts his reading of Gen 1–2 into a cosmic-historical framework. He proclaims that humanity's evolution occurred from the above to the below in opposition to the modern-scientific theory of evolution. Fohr stresses the psycho-spiritual processes that have to take place in each person. He sees them broadly depicted in the biblical creation account, as well as in other religious traditions. His comparative religious framework suggests that these processes are true for all humans anywhere and at any time. In short, the interpretations of Swedenborg, Steiner, and Fohr offer different interpretative emphases, but they agree on the obsoleteness of literal-historical approaches. Their readings emphasize uniformly that the Bible provides access to religious mystery, and it is the task of interpreters to uncover at least some of it.

Such a hermeneutic is, of course, a dangerous proposition even in a post-postmodern age when the irrationality of all kinds of fundamentalisms battles against the presumed rationality of the secular-modernist stance. Luckily, in the realm of biblical studies this tension does not lead to loss of human life or the violation of the "Convention against Torture and Other Cruel, Inhuman or Degrading Treatment of Punishment." Yet the field's struggles with the issue of academic credibility make many exegetes suspicious of intellectual methodological modifications toward a spiritual meaning of the Bible. Hence, the interpretations of Swedenborg and Steiner have not received much hearing in biblical studies despite these thinkers' intellectual and religious standing in Western culture.

So back to the question what these interpretations may offer to the study of the Bible in the post-postmodern age. In my view, they provide a way out of a rigidly literalist worldview, whether it is religiously or secularly defined. This, after all, is the problem of our post-9/11 age, as postmodern scholars observe: "Religious, economic, political and nationalist fundamentalisms have rapidly expanded their 'empires' and prosecuted their grand narratives of global history" (Toth and Brooks 2007, 10). In contrast, the esoteric interpretations of Swedenborg, Steiner, and Fohr advance innerly defined and hence more tentatively articulated biblical interpretations. Moreover, Fohr's comparative religions approach stresses union among the religions rather than division or exclusivity. Inner unity of all religions appears in yet another aspect in the selected esoteric interpretations. They regard all humans as confronted with the same spiritual-religious challenges. To them, there is neither West nor East, neither North nor South but the same spiritual-religious challenges for all humans. In a time of political, economic, social, and religious division and strife, such a unifying vision has many benefits. In Steiner's view, it may provide a chance to move humankind beyond a mummified, dense, and coarse state and encourage spiritual-religious maturity, depth, and sophistication.

In short, the interpretations remind us that there is a better reason than war, hatred, and fear for human life on planet earth. They teach that we need to move beyond a dualistically perceived world and open our sensors toward ultimate reality. They advise against separating what we love from how we live, because this split creates alienation, despair, and oppression in the world (Sölle and Cloyes 1984). Only a mind split off from itself, the world, and the divine manages to fly into buildings, to invade non-attacking countries, and to pollute the oceans disregarding whales, fish, birds, and all the other creatures, big and small. Swedenborg, Steiner, and

Fohr hold up an understanding of the self in the inner and outer world that might help shed light on such splitting tendencies wherever and whenever they appear. In this sense, then, these esoteric interpreters give biblical literature an important role to play in our post-postmodern world. They propose reading the Bible as sacred literature that teaches about the inner path toward individual and collective wholeness and living more justly and peacefully not only in the inner but also in the outer world.

Works Cited

Benz, Ernst. 1975. Die Signatur der Dinge: Aussen und Innen in der mystischen Kosmologie, in Schriftauslegung und Physiognomik. Pages 517–80 *in Correspondences in Man and World: Lectures Given at the Eranos Conference in Ascona (1973)*. Edited by Adolf Portmann and Rudolf Ritsema. Leiden: Brill.

Bourriaud, Nicolas. 2009. *The Radicant*. New York: Lukas & Sternberg.

Cooper, Lisa Hyatt. 1994. Problems of Scriptural Translation in Swedenborg's Writings. *Studia Swedenborgiana* 9. Online: http://www.shs.psr.edu/studia/index.asp?article_id=27.

Dole, Andrew. 1997. Re-evaluating Allegorical Interpretation in Swedenborg. *Studia Swedenborgiana* 10:41–75.

Donat, James G. 2007. Wesley, Swedenborg, and the Accusation of Madness. *Wesleyan Theological Journal* 42:83–97.

Edmiston, Llyod H. 1923. Creation of Man: A Divinely Ordered Evolutionary Process. *The New Church Review* 30:38–53.

Eshelman, Raoul. 2000/2001. Performatism, or the End of Postmodernism. *Anthropoetics* 6. Online: www.anthropoetics.ucla.edu/ap0602/perform.htm.

Fohr, S. D. 1986. *Adam and Eve: Spiritual Symbolism of Genesis and Exodus*. Lanham, Md.: University Press of America.

———. 2004. *Cinderella's Gold Slipper: Spiritual Symbolism in the Grimm's Tales*. 3rd rev. ed. Hilldale, N.Y.: Sophia Perennis.

Hanegraaff, Wouter J. 2008. Swedenborg's Magnum Opus. Pages 63–129 in *Secrets of Heaven*, by Emanuel Swedenborg. Vol. 1. New Century Edition of the Words of Emanuel Swedenborg. West Chester, Pa.: Swedenborg.

Kirby, Alan. 2009. *Digimodernism: How New Technologies Dismantle the Postmodern and Reconfigure Our Culture*. New York: Continuum.

Körbel, Thomas. 2001. *Hermeneutik der Esoterik: Eine Phänomenologie des Kartenspiels Tarot als Beitrag zum Verständnis von Parareligiösität.* Münster: LIT.

McDermott, Robert A. 1992. Rudolf Steiner and Anthroposophy. Pages 288–310 in *Modern Esoteric Spirituality*. Edited by Antoine Faivre and Jacob Needleman. New York: Crossroad.

Scherer, Stephen P. 2005. A Comparison of Swedenborg and Skovoroda's Biblical Thought. *Logos* 46:45–71.

Sölle, Dorothee, and Shirley A. Cloyes. 1984. *To Work and to Love: A Theology of Creation*. Philadelphia: Fortress.

Steiner, Rudolf. 1997. *An Outline of Esoteric Science*. Translated by Catharine E. Creeger. Great Barrington, Maine: Anthroposophic.

———. 2002. *Genesis: Secrets of Creation: The First Book of Moses: Eleven Lectures Given in Munich, 16–26 August 1910*. Forest Row, East Sussex: Steiner.

Stengel, Friedemann, ed. 2008. *Kant und Swedenborg. Zugänge zu einem umstrittenen Verhältnis*. Tübingen: Niemeyer.

Swedenborg, Emanuel. 2008. *Secrets of Heaven: Genesis 1–8*. Translated by Lisa Hyatt Cooper. West Chester, Pa.: Swedenborg Foundation.

Toth, Josh, and Neil Brooks. 2007. Introduction: A Wake and Renewed? Pages 1–14 in *The Mourning After: Attending the Wake of Postmodernism*. Edited by Neil Brooks and Josh Toth. Amsterdam: Rodopi.

Woofenden, William Ross, and Jonathan S. Rose. 2008. A Reader's Guide to *Secrets of Heaven*. Pages 17–61 in *Secrets of Heaven*, by Emanuel Swedenborg. Vol. 1. New Century Edition of the Words of Emanuel Swedenborg. West Chester, Pa.: Swedenborg Foundation.

Restoring a Broken Creation during Times of Apocalypse: An Essay on the Analogical Symbolism of Fall and Integrity in the Metaphysics of Béla Hamvas (1897–1968)

László-Attila Hubbes

> In 1955 in Hungary there lived only one single person who could have not only conversed but actually exchanged views with Heraclitus, Buddha, Lao Tzu, and Shakespeare, and that in each one's mother tongue. If these four prophets of the human spirit had gotten off the plane in Tiszapalkonya and if they had addressed the first laborer they came across and if this had happened to be Béla Hamvas himself, after talking for three nights straight—during the day Hamvas had to carry mortar, but perhaps his guests would have given him a hand—well then, what might they have thought: if in this country the unskilled laborers are like this man, what then might the scholars be like? But had they looked around the country, they would have understood everything. (Szőcs 1987–1989, 852)[1]

Introducing the Thinker

Béla Hamvas was author of dozens of volumes, but most of his writings had never been published during his lifetime. One of his volumes—actually printed in his life—bears the title *The Invisible History* ([1943] 1988),[2] which,

1. The motto of this essay is taken from a footnote to the poem "... és akiket nem" ["... and whom not"] added by Géza Szőcs himself. This anonymous translation is quoted from a website dedicated to the work of Béla Hamvas, online: http://www.hamvasbela.org/2012/07/szocs-geza-es-akiket-nem-ajanlom.html.

2. Unless stated otherwise, all titles and quotations translated from primary and secondary sources are mine. See the list of Works Cited at the end of this essay.

though not self-referencing, is adequately describing his life and activity. He studied philosophy, cultural history, cultural anthropology, music, arts and literature, and ancient and oriental languages on a lifelong quest to find and realize the lost normality of the human soul. In this essay I invoke him briefly through a narrow, though central issue of his opus: the nature of human integrity—an authentic Christian anthropology organically embedded into the universal metaphysical tradition. I wish to bring Hamvas into the spotlight of international attention, paying homage to a grand spirit forgotten, misunderstood, or never even known in his own nation. Since he is relatively unknown, some basic biographical data are given first.

Son of a Lutheran pastor, Hamvas was born in 1897 in Eperjes (today Prešov, Slovak Republic), grew up and finished school in Pozsony (today Bratislava, Slovak Republic), to where his family later moved. Following the example of his fellow classmates, he volunteered for army service in the First World War and between 1915 and 1917 was wounded twice on the Austro-Hungarian-Russian front. In 1919, after his father refused to take the oath for Czechoslovakian citizenship, his family was expelled from Slovakia and moved to Budapest. Here, he studied German and Hungarian Philology at the Pázmány Péter University of Budapest between 1919 and 1923. After finishing university he worked several years (from 1923 to 1926) as a journalist for the Hungarian newspapers *Budapesti Hírlap* and *Szózat* with a high sensitivity for the illnesses of society, but he quickly got disappointed by this vocation. It was a real self-fulfillment when he got in 1927 the job of librarian at the Metropolitan Library of Budapest, where he worked until 1948. Together with mythologist Károly Kerényi, in 1935 he founded *Sziget*, a spiritual workshop and publication that ran for two years. In 1937 he married the writer Katalin Kemény, a genuine spiritual match. During the Second World War, between 1940 and 1944, he was drafted three times into military service; once in 1942 he was posted to the Russian front, from where he managed to escape. Near the end of the war, in 1945 his house was hit by a bomb; his library and manuscripts were entirely destroyed. In the short postwar regeneration period of 1945–1948, he was the editor of the *Leaflets of the University Press*. In 1948 he was placed on the B-list.[3] Forced to quit his job, he retreated to work as farmer

3. The B-list was compiled by the new Communist Hungarian authorities in the 1940s and 1950s to cleanse the public institutions of undesirable, politically unreliable personae non gratae. Around 100,000 civil servants and public personalities were made redundant during this procedure only between 1946 and 1948 ([sulinet], n.d.).

in Szentendre in his brother-in-law's garden. In 1951 he registered as a simple worker to avoid harassment from authorities; he was interned as an unskilled laborer then as a storeman on labor camp-like building sites and factories at Bokod, Inota, and Tiszapalkonya. Finally in 1964 he retired from work at the age of sixty-seven and, four years later in 1968, died in Szentendre, where he rests.[4]

He first faced human insanity in the trenches of the First World War, then among the turmoil of a disintegrating homeland[5] and European civilization; he found an unsettling consolation in the embarrassing moral inquiries of Nietzsche and Kierkegaard. These philosophical works, together with his worldly and inner experiences, made him sensible to all the crises of his contemporary world. While he compiled a bibliography on the international crisis literature of the thirties ([1937a] 1983), he discovered striking similarities with ancient laments over the depreciation of the world. In fact, as Katalin Kemény noted (1987), he turned to the study of crisis inspired by his deep concern for the lost human existential integrity: "The main sense of his Opus lies not in revealing this or that segment of the crisis, but in the empathy and transilluminating of the existential corruption, of the separation of life from existence" (164). Thus, in parallel with analyzing the contemporary social and material crisis, Hamvas set out for a spiritual archaeology and tried to reach the origins of humanity's turbulent decay, which he named *apocalypse*. In this quest his first station was the classical Hellenic culture. Very much like Nietzsche in his *Geburt der Tragödie* (1872, 1884), he originally approached the archaic Greeks from an existential perspective, viewing their culture in a tragic, pessimistic light as the archetype of heroic existence ([1937b] 1993). At the same time he also got closer to the poetic approach of Hölderlin, Rilke, and the *George Kreis*.[6] There he found a special affinity with Orphic poetry, which

4. Biographical data compiled from Dúl 1987; Kemény 1990; Darabos and Szathmári 1999; Darabos 2002; Miklóssy 2002; Szakolczai 2005.

5. In 1919–1920, as a consequence of the First World War, the Treaty of Trianon lead to the dismemberment of Old or Greater Hungary and the loss of approximately two-thirds of its territory and population in favor of the surrounding nation states (Austria, Czechoslovakia, Romania, and Serbia). This was followed by the instauration of Red (Communist) and White (Nationalist) terror regimes (see Szász 2001–2002).

6. The mystical and aristocratic spirituality of the *George Kreis* formed around the German poet Stefan George at the end of the nineteenth century and its vision of the archaic Greek culture was a direct inspiration for Hamvas (see [1937b] 1993) to establish together, with mythologist Károly Kerényi, the *Sziget kör* ["Island" literary

he thought to be an authentic expression of the original human integrity. He saw a major breach in ancient Greek thought, a corruption of the ideal archaic existence, a departure from the authentic golden age when men and women still walked with the gods from the myths. The original integrity transparent from the mythic and mystic language of Orphic poetry and Pythagoreism suffers a rupture, and this crisis is what Hamvas hears from the warnings of Heraclitus and Pythagoras (1936a, see also *Scientia Sacra* [1943–1944] 1995). For him this turn observed in ancient Greek history signaled a spiritual fall. He tried at the same time to historically situate the Greek crisis into a larger picture of what might have happened in the world's spirituality after he recognized similar phenomena in the contemporary ancient cultures of Egypt, the Near East, Persia, China, and India.[7] He found spiritual kins for Heraclitus in the "furious sages" of the Orient: Zarathustra, Buddha, Lao-Tzu, K'ung Fu-Tzu (Confucius), Isaiah, and Jeremiah, all of them contemporaries. Something went wrong, something was lost, something changed.[8] Thus, he searched for the critical origins and dug ever deeper and wider in the history of culture only

---

group], a spiritual workshop and journal centered on the study of archaic and classic Greek culture and mythology.

7. "Around six hundred B.C. there lived Lao-Tzu in China, Buddha in India, Zarathustra in Iran. Humanity entered a new eon: placing itself in a new world situation. These representatives of human spirituality all point to this great fact. What is the essence of this new universal situation?… Not the one (personality) did emerge, but the multitude sank. And from that time the strive of the one will be directed to revert humanity onto its way. This new situation emerged at about six hundred B.C. uniformly all around the world, and independently of each other in China, India, Iran and Greece" (1936a; see [1940–1964b] 2005, 325–26). This idea—which later became one of his central concepts—appeared already in his 1936 study concerning the new Hungarian translations of the 137 fragments of Heraclitus (1936a). The principle of a worldwide spiritual change is almost identical with the idea of *Achsenzeit* (Axial Age) developed later by Karl Jaspers (1949). It is worth noting that Hamvas was among the first to introduce Jaspers's existential philosophy to the Hungarian public (1941b).

8. For a better understanding, it must be said that although Hamvas never used the term "Axial Age"—as Szakolczai explains (2005)—he saw the laments, warnings, and teachings of these great ancient spirits as the expression of a great worldwide crisis of the seventh century B.C.E. reaching from China to the Mediterranean. But, unlike in Jaspers vision, "for Hamvas, the Axial Age was not a sovereign, autonomous development, but a symptom: a product of unprecedented confusion, chaos and decline" (Szakolczai 2005, 110).

to discover that the roots of foul are omnipresent from the earliest to the farthest civilizations of the world.

Unitary Spiritual Tradition

Learner of many ancient languages,[9] Hamvas not only studied but also translated and interpreted, to name only some of the more representative texts or traditions in no specific order, kabbalah, Tao Te Ching, Zohar, Lun Yu, Mysterium Magnum, Bardo Thodol, Pert em Heru, 1 Enoch, Empedocles, pre-Columbian traditions, the Avesta, Pythagoras, the Vedas, the Samkhyakarika, the Sefer Yetzirah, Zen, the Katha Upanishad, the Corpus Hermeticum, and Buddha's Diamond Sutra. In all these texts or legacies, he came to presume a unitary spiritual tradition. He discovered that the recognition of evil but also the cures for our crisis are to be found everywhere in the great sacral books of humanity.[10] In the many myths, oral traditions, scriptures, and mysticisms, he recognized one single universal metaphysical tradition of humanity. These teachings are unitary not in the sense that all of them somehow originated from one source or came down one from another, but rather by the fact that each of them knows of the perfection of origins. In various ways they reflect the original human *status absolutus*.

In this respect Hamvas is close to other European contemporary traditionalists (see Szőnyi 1996, 2011), such as René Guénon, Giulio Evola, or Leopold Ziegler, whom he often cited, commented, and criticized,[11] but without adopting their or their followers' ultraconservative political ideology. He rather based himself on the great European mystics such as Jacob Böhme, Franz Xaver von Baader, and Louis Claude de Saint-Martin.[12]

---

9. Some authors mention seventeen languages, including Latin, Greek, Hebrew, Sanskrit, Persian, and Chinese (Szakolczai 2005, 107).

10. Hamvas uses de term "sacral" to denote the universal knowledge of humanity's divine nature and origin.

11. Hamvas referred to them, consented, or argued with their ideas throughout his entire lifework too often to list here the references, but still there are some essays worth mentioning in this respect on Evola ([1935] 1983) and Guénon ([1942] 1987), in which he discusses these traditionalist authors in more detail.

12. Again, the ideas of these mystic authors are so much woven into Hamvas's work that it is nearly impossible to give a representative list of references. The most important writings in which they are discussed are the *Scientia Sacra*, the *Magia Sutra*, or the *Tabula Smaragdina*.

His main preoccupation was to understand and actualize the message of Eden, the *status absolutus* of Adam Kadmon, also known as the *état primordial, Urstand,* originary state, the unspoiled human of the original creation observed in all narratives of origin. To this issue he dedicated major treatises like the *Scientia Sacra* ([1943–1944] 1995),[13] *Tabula Smaragdina: Magia Sutra* ([1947–1950] 1994), and his commentaries on 1 Enoch ([1945] 1989), the Pert em Heru ([1948] 2005), Milarepa ([1943] 1988), the Bardo Thodol, Lun Yu, or Lao Tzu ([1940–1964a] 2003), the Sefer Yetzirah ([1940–1964b] 2005), or the Sufi mystics ([1940–1964b] 2005).

The farther Hamvas reached into ancient and distant lores of the Orient, the more he realized that the crisis and its resolution are also very close at hand, within our reach in our own legacy, in the message of the Gospels. Beginning with the study of Alexandrine gnostics through interpreting medieval and later mystics like Meister Eckhart, Angelus Silesius, Saint John of the Cross, Franz von Baader, or Louis Claude de Saint-Martin to the great Russian philosophers of religion Nikolai Berdyaev, Vladimir Solovyev, Lev Shestov, Dmitry Merezhkovsky, and Sergei Bulgakov, he sought for the essence of Christianity. Mostly, he relied on Jakob Böhme, some of whose works he translated,[14] interpreted, and integrated into his own opus. He always worked to (re)integrate the Judeo-Christian wisdom about the primordial perfection of creation into the consciousness of modern humanity.

Analogies

There is still another important aspect of his thinking that must be mentioned for a better understanding of his concept concerning the unitary spiritual tradition of the ancients. Many would question the validity of

13. The *Scientia Sacra* was meant to be a single complex work. It consists of six books on the spiritual tradition of archaic humanity. This is the *Scientia Sacra* proper, which was published in two volumes ([1943–1944] 1995). There was also a vast project in twelve prospected books interpreting Christianity: the *Scientia Aeterna*, which—although Hamvas continued to work on it until his death—remained unfinished. The first four complete books and a fragmentary fifth of this work were published as a third volume of the *Scientia Sacra* series ([1960–1964] 1996). For this reason it is often referred to misleadingly as *Scientia Sacra II*. For clarity I use in what follows the abbreviation *SS* for the *Scientia Sacra* properly speaking and *SA* for the *Scientia Aeterna*.

14. *Aurora oder Die Morgenröte im Aufgang; Psychologia vera* (*Vierzig Fragen von der Seele*) ([1946–1947] 2013).

such a concept, bringing as argument the great diversity of the various cultural traditions and the ideas, principles, and myths contradictory to other traditions contained in each. But Hamvas is not an adept of any of the cultural diffusionist theories, which claim that all civilizations developed from only one or a small number of early cultures,[15] nor does he propose the sameness of all archaic cultures. He simply states that there are common universal characters in all ancient spiritual legacies known to us. Besides the shared knowledge of the perfection of origins, the corruption of ages, and the moral *status absolutus* of the human, he emphasizes that all this wisdom is based on a different kind of thinking, which he most often names analogical logic. This archaic, mythical, mystical thinking—so alien to us today—is expressed in a highly visual language of analogies. Hamvas developed his concept of analogy in most detail in his commentary on the *Tabula Smaragdina* ([1947–1950] 1994), dedicated to the hermetic language of arithmology and alchemy, where he distinguished three patterns of thinking: the logic of analogy, the logic of identity (opposition), and the logic of unity. The following quote explains a contrast between the first two:

> The logic of analogy is the logic of seeing. The logic of identity is the logic of deciding. The former is epic (lyric), the latter is dramatic. Tradition teaches that every analogy highlights and proves one essential and basic correspondence. This single correspondence is the analogy between the empirical (visible) and beyond-empirical (invisible) worlds. That, which is above corresponds to that, which is below. The sphere between the visible and the invisible spheres, which turns the visible into invisible and the invisible into visible, this turning point is the number. (4.26)

A useful summary of his analogy thesis comes from the *Scientia Sacra*, where, on explaining the archetypes, he states:

> The vision and thinking of historical man relies on logical oppositions; the vision and thinking of archaic man relies on analogy. The main principle of analogy is what the *Tabula Smaragdina* expresses this way: 'That, which is below corresponds with that which is above, and that which is above corresponds to that which is below.'... There is analogy between

15. This idea was widespread in the nineteenth century and the first half of the twentieth, especially among German and British archaeologists and cultural historians, with exponents like Leo Frobenius (1897–1898) and Grafton Elliot Smith (1929).

> the way of the stars and human fate; there is analogy between the life of humankind and the life of a single individual; there is analogy between colors and sounds, numbers and bodies. Each is different, still yet each is the same. This always new and never repeating singularity, which still is always the same and unchangeably one, they called analogy. And the archaic man saw the world through the differences and also through the similarities beyond this diversity." (*SS* 1.2.3.2)

This is the language of mythologies and the language of revelation; this is why Hamvas spoke of the unity of all traditions. Hermetic and occult as it seems to us, this is the language in which art and poetry find expression, and Hamvas himself wrote in this language. All the central notions and keywords of his opus are such analogical symbols, and so they are the guiding terms in this analysis to elaborate on his interpretation of Genesis.

From Creation to Restoration

The Hamvasian interpretation of the Genesis story of Eden and the fall should be understood within the framework of the metaphysical traditions. The following presentation does not perform a makeshift analysis but allows Hamvas to speak through quotations[16] taken from his major relevant works and arranged according to key terms. They are chosen in such a way that his ideas unfold in a narrative process. Thus, the following key notions in his opus organize our discussion as follows: creation, golden age, apocalypse, the fall, the feminine principle, love: revelation and cultivation, love: restoration (*inqualieren*), and salvation.

One thing should be clear from the start: Hamvas never wrote a direct exegesis on Gen 1–3. Rather, he was concerned in his work with this founding myth of our world: our creation, our fall, and consecutively, our restoration. In fact, he translated for modern Western readers the message, the legacy, and the interpretations of the biblical revelation on the human condition in the created world, based on the best available explanations. He stated:

> The Mishna writes: "the whole story of creation must be told to only two people from a generation; while the Merkabah to only a single one,

16. Since few of his works are translated into English, I rely on my own translations. However, when a translation is available, I use it with a reference to the source.

> but one with a mind bright enough to be able to guess all by oneself from hints and allusions." About this hidden sense were written as commentaries the Zohar from ancient history, the book of Maimonides from later times, then Jakob Böhme's *Mysterium Magnum*. From these works one can understand—even if not so easily—the mystery of revelation. (*SS* 1.2.2.1)

Creation

Hamvas, drawing from many archaic traditions, relied steadily on ancient gnosis.[17] Thus, his cosmological visions are emphatically gnostic. Concerning Genesis, he made a distinction between the spiritual and material creation and considered the former the original creation and the latter a secondary emanation. He turns to the Zohar for his argument:

> Wondering upon the mystery of creation—the Zohar writes—I was walking on the seashore, when Elijah appeared and asked me: "Do you know the meaning of the words MI BARA ELLEH?"[18] I answered: "These words mean: 'These are the arrays of Heaven all God's creation.'" Elijah spoke: "When the Concealed One verged on being revealed, at first a Something, a Single Point was produced that had no expansion, but was the beginning of the world's expanse. This Point was the idea by which the Creator formed what he intended to form. And from this idea the great universe emerged, called MI, the unnamable Being, who created the world. Seeking to be revealed in full splendor and uttered by full name, the Creator garbed itself in a splendid radiant mantle and from the rays created ELLEH, which means: 'These, all the things of the world.' Now MI and ELLEH have joined, as sounds join in a word, and the Unnamable descended into Nature." (*SS* 1.2.1.2)

17. Hamvas himself cannot be considered a genuine gnostic. Still, his work contains strong gnostic elements, mainly regarding the duality of spirit and matter, and in *Scientia Aeterna* he blamed Christianity for expelling Gnosticism, thus cutting away the possibility of transcendental cognition (see *SA* 3.76–80).

18. MI BARA ELLEH ("Who created these?" capitals original). Hamvas often uses the original untranslated words and expressions for greater accuracy in essential points, while he usually quotes, or rather paraphrases, narrative texts more freely and with superficial reference. For such inaccuracies he is frequently blamed by philologists and other scholars. This text is from the Zohar 1:2a.

In Hamvasian terms, nature or this material world does not correspond to creation—and in this respect Hamvas contradicts ancient gnostics. The material world is only a place where the primordial spirits have sunk: "Matter is not creation. The material world has never been created by anyone or anything. This is the closed space, to where the Powers expelled from the ancient and primordial spiritual creation have fallen. It came into being, when a part of the world has separated from the great creation" (*SS* 1.2.2.4).[19]

As concerns the place of humanity within this creation and among the spirits, Hamvas is clearly in accordance with the Genesis story: the human being was created as the last creation of Genesis.

> Man is the last opus of creation. Last and comprising creature, the lord of nature, supernatural being, an image of the creator Spirit, ruling over all creatures, and the only one who is in direct connection with the Creator.... The archaic man is the divine spirit, lord of the open, free bright spiritual universe: Adam Kadmon, the primordial man, the first man, the One, the highest ability of the immortal soul, reason. (*SS* 1.2.2.3)

Based on Baader,[20] Hamvas sees the first human as the realization of creation and as being above the cosmos: all creation fits into human existence, the visible cosmos, and the supersensory soul and spirit alike. This is why humans have ethics and metaphysics and religion. And this is why the human is not a minor universe (microcosmos), but a minor God (microtheos) (*Mágia Szútra* 6).

For this reason the human is the central issue in the Hamvasian cosmogony and eschatology: humanity is the youngest and smallest part of creation but also its essence and responsible for the whole creation. As *imago Dei* and *imago mundi*, humanity is part, holder, and maintainer of the perfection of creation, the so-called golden age or Eden. Yet humanity is also part and originator of creation's corruption, just as humans are the vehicle of its restoration. The circle is closed.

---

19. It must be mentioned here that Hamvas raises a paradox: in his opinion contrary to previous or other religions forming the unitary tradition, "Christianity hasn't got a doctrine on genesis" (*SA* 1.45). To be accurate, the quoted statement continues: "nor has it got any doctrines of cosmology, anthropology, psychology, or sociology."

20. Given his essayistic genre, Hamvas rarely gave exact or accurate references. In the quoted statement he refers to Baader, most probably to one of his works on Böhme ([1852] 1963; 1855).

Golden Age

Turning now to the perfection of origins, Hamvas uses a whole range of synonymous analogical symbols with wide connotations in meaning: golden age and paradise and Eden and Satya Yuga, to name only some. All these terms denote some kind of perfection, integrity, wholeness, beatitude, and communion that are not even necessarily related to the temporal aspect, to the beginnings. When Hamvas refers to this state as a *golden age*, he brings quotations into his discourse that situate the golden age at the dawn of time, close to the moment of creation, even if it spanned aeons. It means bliss and wholeness, both from an individual perspective and from the point of view of the human community—whether it occurred at the beginning or at the end. He writes: "The collective beatitude is what the Iranian 'asha' means, which is called gold in alchemy, which is named by various myths as Satya Yuga, or paradise, or the garden of Eden, or Elysion. This collective beatitude is what humanity must achieve" (*SS* 1.3.4.6).

Usually, the term *golden age* simply means existence, unbroken intact being.

> The golden age is the time of peace, beauty and bounty, the actual reality coming true on earth. While the spiritual and divine powers freely and richly flew into nature and matter, the process enlightened, sanctified, and integrated all that lived on earth. The visible world was naturally completed by the invisible. This made life integral: it made it whole, total, and unitary. This is the nature of the golden age: being. (*SS* 1.1.1.4)

This existential aspect prevails over the temporal, and Hamvas emphasizes it by contrasting the golden age with the apocalypse not as the beginning and the end of times, but rather as two states. One state signifies integrity and the other corruption. He elaborates:

> The golden age is no less than existence. This whole totality, the visible and the invisible together. Earth and Heavens, God and Man. This is the Great Community. They are together because they belong to one another and one without the other is only half, only fragment. The apocalypse is this fragment. The fragmentary existence, which is only material, only earthly, only: life. The fragmentary existence, the closed existence. (*SS* 1.1.1.5)

Apocalypse

The title of this essay refers to this apocalypse as the revealed state of crisis. Hamvas set out on his spiritual quest to search for its roots. He wanted to unveil the present imperfect condition, as he states: "Apocalypse means literally: *revelatio*, manifestation, judiciary revealing. Golden age means: blissful gladness. The two expressions are the two ultimate states of existence" (*SS* 1.1.1.6 and passim). Already in his *Világválság* (The World Crisis; [1937a] 1983) Hamvas states:

> The assertion that crisis is nothing else than the manifestation of the eternal human eschaton (apocalypse, revelation, Enthüllung, Offenbarung), naturally alludes to the concept that this recognition of the eternal state today, when the recognizance has happened, must have been conjured up by some circumstances. And what is that what evoked it? The radical crisis of the universal status of humanity. (1.2)

In other words, Hamvas does not consider apocalypse to be a catastrophe that ends the world as we know it but a revelation showing us the world as we have not known it. It is the manifestation of the corrupt existence of humanity turned away from the original state, having fallen out of the golden age (see *SA* 1.119). He explains elsewhere: "The apocalyptic character of post-golden age mankind is that it is under judgment" (*SS* 1.1.1.6).

The Fall

If the golden age evoked such a polysemantic cloud of words, the same applies to the idea of a fall. To Hamvas, it denotes the concept of corruption with its many relations, including the original sin known from Gen 3. The gnostic approach that blames the confusion of the creator spirit for the fault in perfection is a basic idea in the *Scientia Sacra*:

> Creation was the moment when the soul identified itself with the world. The spirit remembered this moment and confused itself with the evil. In this moment the force of the Powers has boiled up and they have sprung onto the impersonal powers. Who were these Powers? Their Greek names are Phthora, Thanatos, Eris, Penia, Hybris, Hamartia—Corruption, Death, Strife, Penury, Pride, Rebellion. The transfer has undone the equilibrium of the world. Part of creation was torn apart, separated and closed into itself. Unity disappeared. The world has broken into two. This

> was the universal catastrophe, which the archaic traditions call the rebellion of the spirits. (*SS* 1.2.2.3)

Hamvas also states elsewhere: "The place where the fallen spirits have sunk: the matter. The divine reason remained in the spiritual world, but could not resist the lure of the fallen Powers and it also fell into the material world. This is the catastrophe, what the archaic traditions name Fall [into sin]" (*SS* 1.2.2.4). A similar but not gnostic view is expressed in Hamvas's commentary on the 1 Enoch apocalypse. There Hamvas explains why the seven rebel stars (angels) or Watchers have corrupted innocent humankind. It was the turn away from the measure and the turn toward the illegitimate use of knowledge combined with seduction and violence ([1945] 1989, also [1940–1964b] 2005, 84–92). Whether he refers to power spirits or angelic Watchers, all of these external agents refer to humanity's spirituality and moral stance in Hamvas's analogical language. Since, as shown above, humanity is of central importance in the Hamvasian cosmology, the origin of corruption is human fault. He states:

> The primordial vision and sight of the human soul was naturally oriented "inside" and was indeed "insight." The outward turn coincides with the "fall," the immersion into matter, the fallout from the spiritual world. Man started to see outward very late, and this vision "came to life as a consequence of the catastrophic inhibition" and intervened in internal sight. When the human soul began to see outward, it in fact looked in the direction opposite to spirit: towards material nature, towards the heavy and brute world—towards darkness. (*SS* 1.2.4.5)

Turning and seeing outward, humanity fell. Divine spirit was lost, and human spirit has totally sunk into matter. And since humanity, lord of nature, forgot the word of rule, it drew down with itself nature as well. As a consequence, with its own wrench and fall humanity corrupted the whole creation (*SS* 1.2.2.4).

Humanity's immersion into the material nature and nature's consecutive fall has caused a general disorientation of the whole creation, which Böhme calls *turba*. This perturbation is known to all traditions. It means the obscuring of reason for Hindus, sin for the Hebrews, or disease for the Greeks (*SA* 1.36). A consequence of this fall and disorientation, of losing the primordial state, is a degraded existence that results in a sense of heavy emptiness twinned by an unscrupulous desire for life. "The uninhibited thirst for life is not the original human attitude, but it appeared because man has lost something more important than life" (*SA* 1.4; see also 5). Still, as Hamvas explains referring to Baader, we today cannot understand anymore the sin committed by ancient humans, because we cannot commit it anymore (*SS* 1.2.4.2).

The Feminine Principle

Hamvas and much of the tradition, especially the oriental, the gnostic, and the hermetic systems link the matter into which the primordial soul has fallen and for which it bears an insatiable hunger to the feminine principle. The feminine, in its many hypostases, plays a crucial role in the Hamvasian opus. In his first interpretation in the *Scientia Sacra*, the feminine is matter and mother of all nature due to her origin, her creation. Hamvas relies on Böhme when he states that the Creator did not create Eve by halving Adam, but rather from the essence of Adam. The Creator sublimated the quintessence of Adam's being and created Eve from this condensed existence. In other words, "Eve came into existence as the essence of man and being. As *matrix mundi*, as Böhme puts it: the matrix, the archetype, the Ur-form: mother of the world" (*SS* 1.2.5.1).

The second aspect of the feminine according to Hamvas is a direct consequence of her material nature. Matter—just as the world itself—in the Hindu tradition is closely linked to Maya, the delusion or mirage, again a feminine concept. Based on various traditions of the East, Hamvas relates the carnal, seductive Eve to this magical, charming material nature:

> Eve is the being who entirely identifies herself with the body, and the independence of the soul never even emerges or even looms in her mind. The more she confuses herself with her bodily being, the more insatiable, the more voracious, the more ravening she is. (*SS* 1.2.5.5)

While Eve is presented as the *incarnation* of the feminine principle, there is also Sophia, the chaste spiritual woman of the hermetic tradition. Sophia is the ideal, the ancient Virgin Mother of the cosmos, the Matrix, the Wisdom, in whom love recognizes itself; she is the Shining Maiden, the Celestial Woman. Thus, Sophia the virgin stayed with God, and Adam fallen into the material world received the "woman," the carnal Eve instead of her (*SS* 1.2.5.2).

At the same time, Hamvas argues that salvation for women does not come by returning to the spirit. He exemplifies with another analogical image that the feminine holds the key to realizing the restoration of the broken creation: "The symbol of salvation: Isis with little Horus in her arms, Magna Mater, holding in her arms the child, which is humanity. The celestial affection awaken in the womanly soul. Because: love is the highest degree of wakefulness" (*SS* 1.2.6).

Love: Revelation and Cultivation

Thus we have arrived at another central term of Hamvas: love. He considers the first word to be a manifestation of love, writing: "The mystery of creation is that the Creator, in the mysterium of love, has transformed into the essence of the World. This mystery is purported by the word. The divine Ur-word reveals itself for man only and exclusively in revelation" (*SS* 1.2.3.6). He continues that the restoration is also a deed of love and depends on a person's openness to divine revelation. "When man becomes sensible to the word of revelation, he is not in an extraordinary state, he is not exalted, but on the contrary, he then reaches his normal and legitimate primordial *status absolutus*: he returns to his place, beside the Creator" (*SS* 1.2.3.6).

There is another perspective on love in Hamvasian interpretation: while creation is the revelation of divine love, a more human aspect of love that is beyond understanding this revelation is the realization of creative love through cultivation. If humanity is of divine origin, as all traditions state and if the human is not only lord but also corrupter of creation and bears responsibility for it, humanity must partake in the act of restoration.

Before returning his attention to Christianity, Hamvas points to this concept already in the *Scientia Sacra*, bringing an argument from the ancient Iranian tradition: "Man, says Zarathustra, is either father of nature or its robber. Man either realizes the spirit of love and then is father of nature, or he does not realize it, and then he is robber of nature" (*SS* 1.5.2). Hamvas explains further that the realization of this spirit of love (derived from the concept of *asha)* is cultivation to realize the paternal spirit in everything that pertains to the material and natural world, be it land, or neighbor, or community (*SS* 1.5.5).

But as he later elaborates in the *Scientia Aeterna*, love is more than cultivation: love is a power, it is the ultimate mean of salvation, of restoration. Hamvas describes this act of restoration as follows:

> Jesus has revealed the roots of the central corruption beneath the fall as it has been taught by many traditions. The symptoms of corruption are

> degraded reason, immoral deeds, and insanity, but in the core of it all is the overflow of corruption, the power of existence-perversion. The power brought by Jesus is not opposed to the existence-corruption; it is a greater power. It is even purer than the ultimate purity of the original being. Curiously, it is not an incredible and triumphant power, but a poignantly gentle and powerless overpower that renounces to all power. It is weaker, softer, fonder, and more tender than all powers. The Gospel calls it love. Love is the power that restrains and corrects the corruption of existence so that it creates an even higher level of being than the original. (*SA* 2.38)

Restoration and Salvation

The power of love taught by Jesus makes the difference for Hamvas between tradition and Christianity. He saw tradition as the revelation of the original perfection and also as revelation of the crisis: the loss of this primordial golden age and the fall under judgment, which is the apocalypse. And he sought in all ancient tradition the revelation of the means of restoration, which he found in the realization of the state of normality by wakefulness, return to measure, balance, and order (*SS* 1.3.4.6; also see Szakolczai 2005, 117–18); and finally, he saw in Christianity the realization of tradition: by bringing in the ultimate power through which all the means of restoration are achievable: love. To understand Hamvas's vision of restoration, we must refer to his understanding of salvation. He states that each sacral tradition has a concept of salvation, which depends on its interpretation of the nature of initial corruption. Since in India it is viewed as mental error, salvation comes from the restoration of the original reason; since in Hellenic tradition ethical and aesthetic decay is strongly interconnected, salvation results from the joint reparation of the primordial soundness of existential beauty and moral integrity; respectively, in Hebrew tradition corruption is moral evil, and consequently redemption is gained by good deeds (*SA* 3.37). In all cases, the central problem is that of existential corruption. Regardless of the specific interpretations, in all traditions restoration is achieved by a return to the primordial state, to the golden age of creation. In this return to the primordial state, Hamvas elaborates that humanity has an active role to play: "The duty of man is not to wait and contemplate, but to act, to be an active participant in the redemption of the world" (*SS* 1.3.4.4). In the interpretation of Hamvas, Jesus was the first to dare to accomplish this task of salvation by acting with the utmost power: love, and from this love, offering the supreme sacrifice (*SA* 2 passim, especially 19, 71, 79). Jesus also has shown the way and nature of this task to all humans: not back to Eden, but forward. As Hamvas explains elsewhere: “If we know that salvation is a deeper opus than creation, then we must germinate the beginning of salvation from even deeper; we must recognize: a redeemed man does not turn back to Adam but goes forward to Christ” (*Mágia Szútra* 49).

Hamvas interprets Christianity through this optic of salvation. Therefore, he separates Christianity from tradition, arguing that it offers the step forward towards reintegration. Christianity teaches the restoration of normality through the sacrifice of love, first and irrevocably made by Jesus. Hamvas insists that Christianity is not meant to be a religion, and it differs from other sacral traditions, because it has no teaching concerning creation; it has neither cosmology, nor anthropology, psychology, or sociology. This is the fact that has confused even the greatest thinkers. They believed that Christianity, since it is not a so-called complete tradition or a total archaic unit, is only a fragment. It only touches at corruption at its deepest point and reveals the *status absolutus* (*SA* 1.45).

We conclude our exploration of the Hamvasian interpretation of creation and anthropogony with a contrasting reflection on the words from the opposite end of Genesis: apocalypse and eschatology. The solution offered by Jesus through his sacrifice is to end the apocalypse and bring forward the world to its ultimate state, the eschaton. Hamvas writes:

> Apocalypse is to get saturated with intellectual obscurity, sin, and sickness in the continuous flow of corruption (world history) and finally to arrive at the catastrophe in which the world dissolves. In apocalyptic the earth stays earth; the world stays world; man remains man. The apocalypse is situated in time. Eschaton means the final situation. The first and the last. Alpha and omega. It is situated outside of time. The *status absolutus* is eschaton. The kingdom of God is such an ultimate state outside of time and above it. In eschatology earth, world, man, nature, being, God is all one. Christianity is integrally eschatology. (*SA* 2.83)

Conclusion

Hamvas, by his personality and also due to his existential circumstances, was highly sensible to the crisis of modernity. From his early career, he refused both the materialistic scientifism[21] and the conservative national

21. Hamvas's term *scientifism* bears a pejorative connotation, meaning a rigid positivistic scientific rationalism.

Christian discourses of his times and did not accept the superficial and symptomatic solutions offered by these paradigms. Following the footsteps of the rebellious Nietzsche in search for the roots of desolation, he first inquired the Greeks. He understood that the crisis was neither modern, nor European, not even ancient Hellenic. He recognized a liminal time in the years around 600 B.C.E., when great spirits and prophets all around the world, in China, India, Persia, the Middle East, and Greece spoke about the fall and tried to warn, to wake up their contemporaries to return to normality. Hamvas realized that the roots of the crisis are universal, and all the great sacral scriptures and oral wisdoms speak of it univocally from Far East Asia to Hellas, and from Egypt to pre-Columbian America. He found paradigmatic the biblical story of creation and fall told in Gen 1–3; it was repeated everywhere, preserving a universal knowledge of the golden age and human failure, but also of the promise and the means of final restoration. This universal knowledge of humanity's divine nature and origin he named sacral tradition in accordance with his western counterparts Guénon and Evola. But unlike these contemporary traditionalist philosophers,[22] he believed that Jesus brought the resolution to the fall described in Genesis by the power and sacrifice of love and that genuine Christianity may realize the restoration of the world.

Hamvas never wrote a detailed analysis of Gen 1–3,[23] but he did have an esoteric reading of it, as he strived in all of his writings to interpret the major questions regarding creation, humanity's place in it, and the reasons for the fall, all for the sake of finding the way, understanding the way of restoration, and realizing this goal in his writings and his life. Hamvas saw the answers in the sacral tradition and found the way of realization in the Christian hermetic legacy. As we could see in this brief review of the essential Hamvasian works, creation was one of the central issues that preoccupied him throughout his life. Everything he wrote revolved around the basic questions raised and elaborated in the first book of the

22. Guénon converted to Islam, while Evola praised Paganism (see Szakolczai 2005).

23. Still, it is worth mentioning that in one place in the *Scientia Aeterna* he refers in this context specifically to the story in Gen 4. There he interprets Cain's murder and Seth's birth in the light of kabbalah, showing that Seth, the first genuine human was the one, who preserved and handed down till Noah the book of Adam: the ancient knowledge of the original perfection of creation, thus he was the first bearer of the sacral tradition (*SA* 1.74–75).

Holy Scripture: how was the world and humanity created? What is the human role within creation? But the answer he gave was no theology, nor was it science or philosophy. It was, what he suggested describing the nature of the Sefer Yetzirah, the *poetics of creation* ([1940–1964b] 2005, 202–3) meaning by that the original sense of *poiesis*—the art and craft of creation. It is in this light that we should understand Hamvas's writings as well in the noblest sense of poetry, as a poetics of creation, about creation. Read in this poetic register, the book of creation unfolds its hidden, esoteric meanings—enriching our understanding of the biblical tradition with new insights.

This essay offered only a brief glimpse of Hamvas's vast opus of esoteric philosophy. His academic reception at home started laboriously in recent years, and his international presentation has scarcely begun[24]—partly because of his long-time inaccessibility but also partly because of his esoteric spirituality and apocalyptic tone. Hamvas is part of the group of modern European traditionalists. Comparative readings with contemporary philosophical and theological works would certainly show the manifold influences he integrated in his work. It also ensures that his work will influence future thinkers sensitive to esoteric hermeneutics.

Works Cited

Baader, Franz von. (1852) 1963. Vorlesungen über J. Boehme's Theologumena und Philosopheme. Pages 357–436 in *Sämtliche Werke*. Vol. 3. Edited by Franz Hoffmann. Aelen: Scientia.

———. 1855. Vorlesungen und Erlaeuterungen zu J. Boehme's Lehre. Pages 57–392 in *Sämtliche Werke*. Vol. 3. Edited by Julius Hamberger. Leipzig: Bethmann.

Böhme, Jacob. (1612) 1977. *Aurora oder Die Morgenröte im Aufgang*. Freiburg: Aurum. Online: http://www.zeno.org/nid/20009159436.

———. (1620) 1960. *Psychologia vera, oder Viertzig Fragen von der Seelen*. Vol. 3 of *Jakob Böhme: Sämtliche Schriften*. Facsimile reprint of the edition of 1730. Edited by Will-Erich Peuckert. Stuttgart: Frommann-Holzboog.

Darabos, Pál. 2002. *Hamvas Béla: Egy életmű fiziognómiája*. 3 vols. Budapest: Hamvas Intézet.

24. See here Szakolczai 2005; Szőnyi 1996; 2014.

Darabos, Pál, and Szathmári Botond, eds. 1999. *A nevezetes névtelen: 30 éve hunyt el Hamvas Béla*. Budapest: Osiris.

Dúl, Antal. 1987. *Bevezető* [*Preface*] to *Hamvas Béla 33 esszéje*, 5–9. Budapest: Tartóshullám.

Frobenius, Leo. 1897–1898. Der westafrikanische Kulturkreis. *Petermanns Mitteilungen* 43:225–236, 262–67; 44:193–204, 265–71.

Hamvas, Béla. (1935) 1983. Modern apokalipszis [Modern Apocalypse]. *Társadalomtudomány* 2–3:113–27. Repr. pages 9–33 in *A világválság*. Gondolkodó Magyarok. Budapest: Magvető.

———. 1936a. Hérakleitos helye az európai szellemiségben [The Place of Heraclitus in European Spirituality]. Pages 58–81 in *Hérakleitos múzsái vagy a természetről*. Edited by Kerényi Károly and Kövendi Dénes. Budapest: Stemma.

———. (1936b) 1983. Krízis és katarzis [Crisis and Catharsis]. *Társadalomtudomány* 1–3:1–20. Repr. in pages 34–62 in *A világválság*. Gondolkodó Magyarok. Budapest: Magvető.

———. (1937a) 1983. A világválság [The World Crisis]. *Fővárosi Könyvtár Évkönyve* 7:39–48. Repr. pages 63–80 in *A világválság*. Gondolkodó Magyarok. Budapest: Magvető.

———. (1937b) 1993. Hexakümion [Hexakymion] in *A babérligetkönyv* (1932–1945): *Hexakümion* (1937). Szombathely: Életünk.

———. (1940–1964a) 2003. *India, Kína, Tibet, Japán* [India, China, Tibet, Japan]. Vol. 1 of *Az ősök nagy csarnoka* [*The Great Hall of the Ancients*]. Budapest: Medio Kiadó.

———. (1940–1964b) 2005. *Egyiptom, Héber hagyomány, Iszlám, Görög hagyomány* [*Egypt, Hebrew Tradition, Islam, Hellenic Tradition*]. Vol. 3 of *Az ősök nagy csarnoka* [*The Great Hall of the Ancients*]. Budapest: Medio Kiadó.

———. (1941a) 1998. Scientia Sacra: Írás és hagyomány [Scientia Sacra: Scripture and Tradition]. *Athenæum* 4:376–77. Repr. page 20 in *Tradíció évkönyv*.

———. 1941b. *Szellem és exisztencia: Karl Jaspers filozófiája* [*Spirit and Existence: Karl Jaspers's Philosophy*]. Szeged: Dunántúl Pécsi Egyetem.

———. (1942) 1987. René Guénon és a társadalom metafizikája [René Guénon and the Metaphysics of Society]. *Társadalomtudomány* 1:76–85. Repr. in *Hamvas Béla 33 esszéje*. Edited by Dúl Antal. Budapest: Tartóshullám.

———. (1943) 1988. *A láthatatlan történet* [*The Invisible History*]. Budapest: Egyetemi Nyomda. 2nd ed. Budapest: Akadémia Kiadó.

———. (1943–1944). 1995. *Scientia Sacra*. 2 vols. Repr. *Az őskori emberiség szellemi hagyománya* [*Spiritual Tradition of the Ancients*]. Vol. 1 of *Scientia Sacra*. 2nd ed. Budapest: Medio Kiadó.

———, trans. (1945) 1989. *Henoch Apokalypsise* [*The Apocalypse of Henoch*]. Budapest: Bibliotheca. Repr.: Budapest: Holnap Kiadó.

———, trans. (1946–1947) 2013. Jakob Böhme: Psychologia vera, A lélekről szóló negyven kérdés (Vierzig Fragen von der Seele), in *Mexikó, Santa soledad, Alkímia, Jakob Böhme, Csuang-ce, Eksztázis*. [Mexico, Santa Soledad, Alchemy, Jakob Boehme, Zhuangzi, Ecstasy], vol. 4 of *Az ősök nagy csarnoka* [The Great Hall of the Ancients]. Szentendre—Budapest: Medio Kiadó.

———, trans. 1947. *Hérakleitos 131 fennmaradt mondata* [131 Preserved Sentences of Heraclitus]. A dialektika klasszikusai. Budapest: Röpirat és Vitairat Könyvtár.

———. (1947–1950) 1994. *Tabula smaragdina: Mágia szútra*. Szombathely: Életünk Könyvek. Online (in English translation with unknown translator and parameters): http://www.hamvas.comlu.com/hamvastabulasmaragdina.htm.

———, trans. (1948) 2005. *Pert em Heru: az egyiptomi halottaskönyv* [*Pert em Heru: The Egyptian Book of the Dead*]. Pages 9–74 in *Egyiptom, Héber hagyomány, Iszlám, Görög hagyomány* [*Egypt, Hebrew Tradition, Islam, Hellenic Tradition*]. Vol. 3 of *Az ősök nagy csarnoka* [*The Great Hall of the Ancients*]. Szentendre: Medio Kiadó.

———. (1960–1964) 1996. *A kereszténység* [Christianity]. Vol. 3 of *Scientia Sacra*. Budapest: Medio Kiadó.

———. 1983. *A világválság* [The World Crisis]. Gondolkodó Magyarok. Budapest: Magvető.

Jaspers, Karl. 1949. *Vom Ursprung und Ziel der Geschichte*. Zürich: Artemis.

Kemény, Katalin. 1987. *Élet* és *életmű*. Pages 139–44 in *Szellem* és *egzisztencia*. By Hamvas Béla. Pécs: Baranya Megyei Könyvtár.

———. 1990. *Az ember, aki ismerte saját neveit: Széljegyzetek Hamvas Béla Karneváljához*. Budapest: Akadémiai Kiadó.

Miklóssy, Endre. 2002. *Hamvas Béla*. Magyar Pantheon 15. Budapest: Új Mandátum.

Nietzsche, Friedrich. 1872. *Die Geburt der Tragödie aus dem Geiste der Musik*. Online: http://www.gutenberg2000.de/nietzsche/tragoedi/tragoedi.htm.

———. 1884. *Die Geburt der Tragödie oder Griechentum und Pessimis mus*. Online: http://www.gutenberg2000.de/nietzsche/tragoedi/tragoedi.htm.

Smith, Grafton Elliot. 1929. *The Migrations of Early Culture*. Manchester: Manchester University Press.

(sulinet). n.d. Magyarország *1944–1953*. The Institute for the History of the 1956 Hungarian Revolution. Online: http://www.rev.hu/sulinet45/index.htm.

Szakolczai, Árpád. 2005. Between Tradition and Christianity: The Axial Age in The Perspective of Béla Hamvas. N.p. in *Axial Civilizations and World History*. Edited by Johann P. Arnason, S.N. Eisenstadt, and Björn Wittrock. Jerusalem Studies in Religion and Culture. Leiden: Brill. Online: http://www.scribd.com/doc/79954614/Axial-Civilizations.

Szász, Zoltán. 2001–2002. Revolutions and National Movements after the Collapse of the Monarchy (1918–1919). N.p. in *From 1830 to 1919*. Vol. 3 of *History of Transylvania*. Edited by Köpeczi Béla and Szász Zoltán. Hungarian Academy of Sciences: Atlantic Research and Publications. Social Science Monographs. Online: http://mek.oszk.hu/03400/03407/html/.

Szőcs, Géza. 1987–1988. "… és akiket nem" ["… and whom not"]. Online: http://www.hamvasbela.org/2012/07/szocs-geza-es-akiket-nem-ajanlom.html.

———. 2007. "… és akiket nem" ["… and whom not"]. *Életünk: Irodalmi, művészeti és kritikai folyóirat: Hamvas Béla* 45: 852.

Szőnyi, György. 1996. Occult Ascension in Troubled Times: The Ideals of Mankind in Rudolf Steiner and Béla Hamvas. Pages 29–43 in *Ideals of Mankind*. Edited by M. Kronegger and Anna-Teresa Tymieniecka. Analecta Husserliana 49. Dordrecht: Kluwer Academic.

———. 2014. "His Dark Materials": The Early Apocalypticism of Enoch Recycled in Modern and Postmodern Times. N.p. in *The Apocalyptic Complex: Origins, Histories, Permanence. Proceedings of the International Conference "The Apocalyptic Complex."* Edited by Nadia Al-Bagdadi, Matthias Riedl, and David Marno. Budapest: Central European University Press.

The Zohar. 2004. Translation and Commentary by Daniel Chanan Matt. Pritzker Edition. Stanford: Stanford University Press.

The Bible and Africana Esotericism: Toward an Architectonic for Interdisciplinary Study

Hugh R. Page Jr.

> Oh, won't you tell me, what can the whole world be hiding?
> I want to know.
> "The World's a Masquerade," Earth, Wind, and Fire (1973)

The spectrum of themes, pivotal figures, and primary sources animating the study of the Western esoteric tradition, particularly those branches found in Europe and North America, has received considerable scholarly attention in recent years (e.g., Hanegraaff et al. 2005; Hanegraaff and Kripal 2008; Kripal 2010; Stuckrad 2005; Faivre and Rhone 2010; and Goodrick-Clarke 2008). Unfortunately, some of the distinct tributaries feeding this larger intellectual and religious stream, such as those originating in Africana (i.e., African and African Diaspora) milieus or typically navigated by peoples of African descent, have not been sufficiently studied. Moreover, the utilization of the Bible as a foundational resource, occasional point of reference, or primary interlocutor in the construction of Africana esoteric cosmologies and epistemologies—in both historical and contemporary perspective—presents opportunities for interdisciplinary research that have yet to be fully exploited.

The current study proceeds in several steps. First, it proposes both a tentative definition of Africana esotericism and basic protocols for the study of the phenomenon. Second, it offers guidelines for identifying "core texts"[1] (such as primary literary, artistic, and other sources)

1. My perspective on the concept of "core text" is informed by the broad and inclusive understanding animating the Association for Core Texts and Courses (ACTC), whose mission is to "advance and strengthen the integrated and common study of world classics and texts of major cultural significance" (Association for Core

through which manifestations of Africana esotericism may be accessed, and it also provides a very selective preliminary listing of such texts. Third, it considers the role that Africana esotericism has played, and continues to play, in the quest for human rights in the Americas. Fourth, it will touch upon the impact of unknown authorship, pseudonymous attribution, intertextual discourse (e.g., with the Christian Bible), and commodification on the ways that these sources have been interpreted within Black communities. Fifth, it concludes with a set of questions and issues that might serve as a *heuristic architectonic* for future research. The study has two aims: it wants to stimulate greater interest in Africana esotericism and the hermeneutical strategies employed in the reading and appropriation of authoritative texts, such as the Bible, by African and Black Diaspora esoteric thinkers. It also wants to help in the creation of a subfield within Western esoteric studies devoted to the examination of the aforementioned and related phenomena.

Definition, Protocols for Investigation, and Methodology

In the volume, *Modern Esoteric Spirituality* (Faivre and Needleman, 1992), Antoine Faivre notes the implicit difficulty in defining *esotericism*. He and his editorial colleagues eschew use of the term in favor of the more inclusive designation *esoteric spirituality* as a way of denoting "a range of spiritual forms" (Faivre 1992, xi).[2] He identifies four "intrinsic" and two "relative" characteristics of Western esoteric spirituality. The former consist of a concern with correspondences, nature (as alive), imaginative and mediatorial capacities, and transmutation. The latter are comprised of an emphasis on concordance and transmission of traditions (xv–xx).

I define Africana esotericism as a diverse, dynamic, and constantly evolving corpus of ideas and practices hailing from Africa and the African Diaspora that calls attention to "secrecy" and "concealment" as elements fundamental to both the cosmic landscape and the human experience

Texts and Courses and ACTC Liberal Arts Institute at St. Mary's College of California 2011). Core esoteric texts in the Africana tradition would be those identified as vital for the construction or decoding of the hidden topography of the cosmos within a given African or African Diaspora *Sitz im Leben*.

2. He also notes, quite rightly, that the noun *esotericism* could well be used in the plural so as better to indicate the multiplicity of extant esoteric systems (Faivre 1992, xi–xii).

overall. Whether one has in mind veiled languages used to disguise meaning in some African and African American settings (Richards 1992, 42), the "unseen" verities affirmed by the so-called "Black Sacred Worldview" (Floyd-Thomas et al. 2007, 80), the protocols for the "hush arbors" (Holmes 2004, 83) that served as sanctuaries for enslaved Africans in the American South, the encoded messages of African American quilts (Page and Bailey 2010, n.p., gallery fig. 25), the double meanings encountered in spirituals (Raboteau 2001, 48), Africana initiatory rituals and healing practices in the Caribbean and the Americas (see Johnson 2007, 71; Harding 2000; Murphy 1993, 2; Dow 1997, 2–3; Hurston [1935] 1990: 183–285; and Mitchem 2007), or—in the words of Jon Michael Spencer—"the synchronous duplicity of the blues" (Spencer 1994, xxvi), the epistemological importance of those things that are hidden, at times in plain sight, is clear. In certain Africana contexts, this body of lore is in conversation with, at times partially derived from, or in the process of deconstructing Jewish, Christian, Islamic, Western esoteric, and other traditions in the creation of ways of life that foster wholeness, construct identity, and promote liberation. Certain aspects of Africana esotericism can be said to flow out of, or perhaps into, one or more of Faivre's "rivers" and "streams" of Western esotericism, such as alchemy, astrology, magic, kabbalah (Christian), Hermeticism (neo-Alexandrian), Paracelsian nature philosophy, theosophical thought, and Rosicrucian ideas (Faivre 1992, xiv), while at the same time being nurtured by the "headwaters" of Africana traditions hailing from Africa, Europe, the Caribbean, and elsewhere in the New World.

The study of a phenomenon of this kind is tremendously difficult. The reasons for this are varied and complex, not the least of which are the fact that a field dedicated specifically to the critical examination of Africana esotericism, as defined above, has yet fully to emerge[3] and that esotericism—as manifest specifically in Africa and the African Diaspora—does not appear to be one of the primary foci of the newly emerging discipline of Western esoteric studies. A few examples of entries included, or lacking in, the *Dictionary of Gnosis and Western Esotericism* (Hanegraaff et al. 2005) are illustrative of this fact. The *Dictionary* contains a sizeable article on the relatively well-known figure Paschal Beverley Randolph (Deveney 2005) but only brief references to Pamela Colman Smith (Laurant 2005,

---

3. The forthcoming volume co-edited by Stephen C. Finley, Margarita S. Guillory, and I, entitled *Esotericism in African American Religious Experience: "There Is a Mystery"*... (Leiden: Brill), promises to pave the way for the establishment of such a field.

1112; Gilbert 2005), the artist responsible for illustrating the widely used *Rider-Waite Tarot Deck* (Waite and Smith 1971).[4] An entry on the topic of secrecy in the modern world does not address the implications of this trope in Africana cultures (Faivre 2005). The entry on "Unidentified Flying Object" (UFO) lore (Mayer 2005) is silent on the tradition of the "Mother Plane" central to the Nation of Islam (see Muhammad 2004), an image that has found its way into African American popular culture.[5] Furthermore, no specific topical entries are found on African, African American, or African Diaspora esoterica per se. Thus, the role of the esoteric in the lives of peoples of African descent, the impact of such persons in shaping esoteric thought and practice in Europe and the Americas, and the sources to be culled in the study of the aforementioned topics are left largely untouched.

In spite of this absence, prior research in this field has, in fact, been undertaken. One can point to work on individual figures such as Randolph (Deveney 1996) and Pamela Colman Smith (Kaplan 1990, 1–45; 2009). There are also studies too numerous to mention—critical and popular—devoted to groups such as the Nation of Islam (Lincoln 1994), the Moorish Science Temple of America (Moore 2005), the Five Percent Nation of Gods and Earths (Allah 2007), the Spiritual Baptists (Duncan 2008), and a host of others, which are exemplars of Africana esotericism. Insofar as scholars have noted that African-American *conjure* is a site where one can see both an emphasis on secrecy as well as the confluence of indigenous African, European, Christian, and Jewish kabbalistic ideas, it too can legitimately be classified as an Africana esoteric construct.[6] To date, these appear not to have been studied primarily as examples of a larger universe of Africana esoteric discourse. The time has come for these and other representative sources to be gathered and assessed within such a paradigm.

What steps might be taken to begin such a process? First, one must retrace the historical evolution of Africana religious thought on the Afri-

4. On the possibility of Smith's Jamaican ancestry, see Kaplan 2009 (5).

5. For an example of how this image has been adapted for the branding and marketing of Nike products, see the "Funk Ship" advertisement produced by the Hughes Brothers, online at http://www.youtube.com/watch?v=j3WE0fM70X4.

6. *Conjure* is that creolized amalgam of protective and healing lore originating in the southern United States and sometimes designated *hoodoo* or *rootwork*. On the various elements constituting *conjure*, see for example Long 2001 (3–16, 122), Chireau 2003 (55–56), and Anderson 2008 (32, 45).

can continent, in Europe, in the Atlantic World, and elsewhere with an eye toward the place that esoteric phenomena, whether African, European, or Native American, have occupied in it. In so doing, one must look not only at the development of Christianity, but also at the role of indigenous African survivals, new religious amalgams developed in the Black Diaspora, as well as the development of novel approaches to religious belief and practice that fall outside of the Judeo-Christian mainstream. An illustrative case in point within the Americas is African American *conjure* mentioned above. Another consists of influential figures such as Sojourner Truth, Benjamin Banneker, George Washington Carver, and Howard Thurman, whose worldviews have esoteric facets. Yet another case consists in the early development of distinctively Africana forms of spiritualism. The development of the Black Hawk cult by Mother Leaf Anderson is a particularly interesting example of this phenomenon (see Berry and Byrd 1995). Within the Africana Diaspora in Europe, the art and writings of Pamela Colman Smith, particularly the tarot symbolism growing out of her collaboration with Arthur Edward Waite, but also possibly informed by her research on and retelling of Jamaican folktales, is a classic case in point.[7] Another, representing a creative blending of tarot symbolism and Candomblé,[8] is found in the *Tarot of the Orishas* (Zolorak and Dürkön 1995).

Second, one should reexamine resistance movements and institutional structures allied with, ancillary to, or growing out of the Black church. Here, one thinks immediately of the Black Masonic lodge system in the eighteenth century and of figures such as Prince Hall, Absalom Jones, and Richard Allen.[9] In the early twentieth century, one can point as well to the African Orthodox Church, an outgrowth of Black dissent within The Episcopal Church (TEC), and the Universal Negro Improvement Association. The enigmatic George G. M. James appears to have had some affiliation with both institutions. His *Stolen Legacy* (1954) alludes to the existence of

7. Concerning Smith's ongoing interest in such lore and those who expressed an interest in it, such as William Butler Yeats, through whom her introduction to the Order of the Golden Dawn came, see Kaplan 2009 (32–38).

8. Candomblé is an African Diaspora religion originating in Brazil. It represents a blending of Nigerian Yoruba and Roman Catholic traditions. Beliefs focus on the existence of a central administrative deity (*Olorun* / *Olodumaré*), spiritual intermediaries (*orixás*), and the cultivation of power (*axé*) via ritual, initiation, and possession (Myers 2005, 730).

9. On Hall's biblical hermeneutic, see Page 2003.

a body of Africana esoteric lore.[10] Consideration should also be given to the Qu'ran created by Noble Drew Ali for the Moorish Science Temple of America ([1927] 2008). One thinks, as well, of the religion of Rastafari in Jamaica and elsewhere as a manifestation of Africana esotericism.

Third, one needs to look closely at the lives and extant works of Africana artists, musicians, and literary figures for evidence of conscious engagement or embrace of one or more of the major tributaries of the Western esoteric tradition (e.g., alchemical, astrological, or magical thought). Among those who could be placed on such a list are Reginald Arthur, Zora Neale Hurston, Jean Toomer, and even the musical artist Prince.[11] Allan Rohan Crite's collection of brush drawings (1947) inspired by the Anglican mass might also be included insofar as they express his vision of a celestial realm whose *dramatis personae* are reflective of the Africana ethos on earth.

Fourth, one must reconsider the impact of Western esoteric spiritualities and the institutions that served as their primary stewards on the Africana religious imagination from the late eighteenth century to the present. A particularly interesting case in point, African American Freemasonry, has already been mentioned. The early Mormon movement of Joseph Smith is another. Quinn (1998) and Forsberg (2004) have argued convincingly that Smith's intellectual and spiritual formation were heavily influenced by esoteric ideas. If this is the case, the embrace of Smith's movement by African Americans, such as Elijah Abel, one of his earliest followers, needs to be examined.[12]

In sum, what is needed is a gathering and classification of Africana esoteric texts that allows Africana esotericism to be set alongside other exemplars of Western esoteric thought and praxis.[13] The collection of such primary data needs likely to involve several activities. The first is archival work. The second is the conduct of personal interviews and the compila-

---

10. On James and *Stolen Legacy*, see Page 1998.

11. On the visionary experiences of Arthur, Hurston, and Toomer, see Noll's interesting collection of vignettes (1991, 18–19, 44–45, 74–76). An early exploration of some of the theological themes expressed in the lyrics of Prince is an unpublished paper delivered by Page for the African American Biblical Hermeneutics Section of the Society of Biblical Literature (2000).

12. See the Eunice Kinney Letter (1891) for an account of his ministry from an eyewitness observer.

13. Here, I use the term *text* broadly so as to include literature, music, art, and other physical assemblages of cultural artifacts.

tion of oral histories. The third, for those who see information gathered on an "insider" basis as beneficial, would be participant observation within groups in which Africana esoteric spiritualities of one form or another are nurtured. Given that these traditions are nonstatic and constantly evolving, the aspiring researcher must keep a watchful eye for the appearance of new expressions of Africana esoteric genius as well.

Africana Esotericism: A *Very* Preliminary Listing of Core Texts

While the presentation of a truly comprehensive list of Africana esoteric sources is beyond the scope of this study, the following tentative list is *suggestive* of some of the more important texts and other artifacts that might be considered central to what I would term the *Africana Esoteric Tradition* (AET). Informing my partial selection has been the question: "What corpus of texts best reflects major past and present trajectories in Africana esotericism?"

The Bible (King James Version) must head the list of Africana esoteric texts. Given its impact—both positive and negative—on Africana life, it cannot be ignored. In particular, enigmatic biblical figures such as Enoch (Gen 5:21–24), Hiram (1 Kgs 7:13–14), and Moses have fired the imaginations of certain Black writers, such as Zora Neale Hurston ([1935] 1991), and given rise to popular esoteric lore. That it has been used as a text of power by African Americans has been duly noted (Smith 1994). The Psalms in particular have been prominent. This is true of *conjure* practitioners since the early twentieth century (see Anderson 2008, 48). David Adamo has called attention to the prophylactic use of Psalms prevalent within African indigenous churches as well (2004). Thus, interpretive works borrowing heavily from kabbalistic sources and adopted by Africana readers such as Godfrey Selig's *Secrets of the Psalms* ([1958] 1982), along with those produced by and for Africana readers such as J. O. Ogunfuye's *The Secrets of the Uses of Psalms* (1980; see also Adamo 2004) must also be included.

Early on in the North American Diaspora, the Masonic metanarrative appears to have exercised considerable sway among influential free Blacks in Massachusetts and Pennsylvania. The Masonic charges of Prince Hall, founder of Freemasonry among African Americans, encapsulate that story, one that includes the full sweep of biblical and Africana history as understood by the author (1792, 1797). The ubiquitous writings of Randolph offer a glimpse into a different esoteric *Weltanschau-*

ung, that of Randolph's construction of Rosicrucianism.[14] In addition, the life stories of early Black members of the Latter Day Saints movement such as Elijah Abel (1810–1882), Walker Lewis (1798–1856), and William McCary illustrate the interplay of Masonic thought, Mormon theology, religious entrepreneurism, westward expansion in North America, and the movement for the abolition of slavery (see Bringhurst and Smith 2004; Evenson 2012).

The *Rider-Waite Tarot Deck*, brainchild of Pamela Colman Smith and Arthur Edward Waite, brings together the symbolism of the Order of the Golden Dawn and Smith's unique vision. When considered, or read "through," her experience as a child of Caribbean (possible Jamaican mother) descent living in the United Kingdom and her other artistic and literary endeavors (e.g., as *griot*), one wonders whether the symbolism of her versions of the Major and Minor Arcana encode her life experiences as a woman of color living in Diaspora.

For example, the attention of even the most casual observer of the deck might well be drawn toward several biblical images and allusions in the Major Arcana. The "High Priestess" of card 2 sits between the pillars of Solomon's temple (Jachin and Boaz in 1 Kgs 7:21) and holds upon her lap a book labeled "Torah." The "Lovers" of card 6 clearly reflect the primordial man and woman in the Genesis creation story (Gen 2:4–3:24). The "Wheel of Fortune" (card 10) contains the Tetragrammaton and iconographic depictions of the four canonical gospel writers.[15] The "Hanged Man" (card 12) has obvious undertones of the crucifixion of Jesus, as well as the mythology of Odin. The cards representing "Temperance" (card 14), "The Devil" (card 15), the "Tower" (card 16), "Judgment" (card 20), and the "World" (card 21) all contain images alluding to biblical themes. These include angelic figures, scenes reminiscent of pristine nature, the serpentine encounter in the biblical garden of Eden (Gen 3:1–3), symbolic depictions of the canonical gospels, and the resurrection (Matt 24:31; 1 Cor 15:52; 1 Thess 4:16).

However, one might look at the representations of the feminine in these cards and ask whether they also recount the story of Smith's own initiatory journey (her personal *siglum* "PCS" appears in, or near,

14. For a treatment of these, see Deveney 1996.

15. Scholars have noted the connection between the imagery in Rev 4:6–9, that of Ezek 1:5–10, and iconographic depictions of the four canonical gospels.

the lower right corner of each card)[16] and the difficulties that she and other women of African descent encounter in the processes of identity construction, self-actualization, and the navigation of social and class boundaries while living in Diaspora. As a pivotal esoteric artifact, possibly produced by an Africana artist, it merits inclusion as a key resource.

A text that can possibly be utilized in a similar manner for an American context is the Qu'ran of the Moorish Science Temple (Ali [1927] 2008). Added to this should be the "Supreme Mathematics" and "Supreme Alphabet" of the Five Percent Nation—examples of modern Africana esoteric ciphers (see Black Apologetics Ministry 2001–2003), as well as *The Problem Book* attributed to the mysterious W. D. Fard (n.d.) and the various writings of the late Elijah Muhammad such as his *The Mother Plane* (2004).

To round out this preliminary list, one could think of the pseudonymous works attributed to Henri Gamache, in particular his *Master Book of Candle Burning* ([1942b] 1998), *Mystery of the Long Lost 8th, 9th, and 10th Books of Moses* (1993), and *The Master Key to Occult Secrets* ([1942a] 1983). These are miscellanies of astrological, biblical, medieval Jewish, and Africana lore. They have circulated among practitioners of African American *conjure* since the 1940s (Long 2001, 125). Other items could, and should, be put on this list, such as the music of African American musical groups and artists (e.g., Earth, Wind, and Fire; Stevie Wonder; Parliament/Funkadelic; and Prince).

All of the aforementioned represent *touchstones* within Africana esotericism—the talismanic use of sacred texts; identification of biblical characters and images as mediators of secret gnosis; the utilization and selective adaptation of Masonic lore and symbols; creative enculturation of Africana imagery—subtly and overtly—through Tarot; the creation of new secret literatures through sampling, anthologizing, and "framing"; and the conscious resignification of letters and numbers according to Africana esoteric precepts.

A Proposed Architectonic

The development of an architectonic for subsequent engagement of these texts is a necessary next step in the critical analysis of these artifacts and other Africana esoteric lore. Such an interpretive design should be sen-

16. The only one on which it does not seem to appear is card 0, the "Fool."

sitive to cultural domains, themes, and methodologies found in a broad spectrum of Africana life settings. The methods and animating questions for research on the AET must take into account the stigma—in some settings quite pronounced—of religious and ritual practices considered nonnormative in the Black community. Information gathering may well need to be through informal conversation, environmental scans of neighborhoods for practitioners, memoir, autobiographical ethnography, ethnographic poetry, and lived experience.

Once gathered, larger concerns will center on how the sources should be classified by genre and interpreted, as well as the means to be employed in charting their reception history among African and Black Diaspora readers. Some effort should be made to distinguish between works generated by Africana authors; those appropriated—unaltered—by Africana audiences; those originating elsewhere that have been adapted by Africana users; and interpretations that have been generated to "hedge" or "frame" esoteric traditions originating outside of Africana matrices.

The sources should then be queried in a manner that seeks to explore their place within Africana life. A basic set of issues and questions might include:

(1) To what extent do these sources contribute to the formation of Africana identity, lived, imagined, or ritually enacted?
(2) How do they reflect struggles endemic to the experience of dispersion, forced or voluntary?
(3) Are recurring Africana tropes such as concealment, freedom, resistance to hegemony, *et cetera* prevalent in these texts?
(4) In what ways do these sources construe Africana community?
(5) Given that some of the texts in question bear pseudonymous attributions, it is important to ask what bearing the pseudonymous nature has had on their distribution as commodities within Africana communities.
(6) Finally, one must consider the engagement of Africana esoteric texts by peoples of African descent that consider themselves to be part of the Jewish, Christian, and Muslim mainstream.[17]

---

17. Here I have in mind the secret engagement of underground texts in so-called nonesoteric settings.

Conclusion

This preliminary foray into relatively new territory has not been exhaustive. Instead, its aim has been to start a scholarly conversation. Further work to excavate and recover the AET will face inevitable limitations and implicit difficulties, not the least of which are navigating terrain where dialogue partners are not yet in abundance and the primary sources are difficult to pin down. Nonetheless, the potential yield, in terms of our ability more clearly to understand how African, European, and other esoteric traditions were inherited, generated, borrowed, preserved, adapted, and passed on by peoples of African descent is enormous. In the end, such research will no doubt shed much needed light on how this lore was used to construct spiritualities of resistance. It may also help us better to understand the ways in which Africana esoteric cosmologies and texts have been deployed in democratizing access to those tools—numinous and pragmatic—essential to self-empowerment and liberation.

Implications for the Study of Gen 1–3

The extent to which such Africana maps of the mundane and arcane worlds are dependent upon biblical antecedents like those found in Gen 1–3 must certainly receive greater attention. Some branches of the AET appear to embrace, in a literal or symbolic sense, the cosmogonic and anthropological notions woven into the creation stories found in these chapters. Others either bring the aforementioned traditions into conversation with an alternative body of lore whose epistemological and soteriological foundations are decidedly African or African-Diasporan in origin, or reject the Bible's cosmology outright. This strategy applies to other parts of the Old and New Testaments as well.

Basic assertions in Genesis about the providential hand setting the generative process in motion (1:3); the social roles of women and men (1:27–28; 2:23–25; 3:15–16); the essential goodness of the world (1:31); and the power of the created order to sustain humanity implicitly (1:29) and through sustained effort (3:17–19) are invariably called into question by the continuing exploitation of Black bodies, racism, colonialism, and the historic destabilization of Black communities by poverty, political disenfranchisement, and ecological abandonment. In the face of such realities, reactions to these biblical notions have varied—and continue to vary—among peoples of African descent. One might go so far as to suggest that esoteric engagements of

Gen 1–3 and other sections of the book within the AET represent a particular species of the well-known hermeneutic of suspicion characteristically employed by no small number of Africana readers in Africa and elsewhere.

That the Bible, and in particular the primordial lore found in the initial chapters of Genesis, is a major source feeding the larger stream of Western esotericism is without question. The issue as to whether the same may realistically be said of the AET remains to be seen. On the one hand, certain of the phenomena presented above suggest that it can. On the other hand, there are many rivulets that have historically fed, and continue to nurture, the AET whose sources can be traced elsewhere. Establishing the relative import of these sources, and their relationship to Gen 1–3, will certainly be a major item on the agenda of those continuing to define and add to the growing body of research on Africana esotericisms.

Works Cited

Adamo, David T. 2004. Psalms. Pages 151–62 in *Global Bible Commentary*. Edited by Daniel Patte. Nashville: Abingdon.

Ali, Drew. (1927) 2008. *The Holy Koran of the Moorish Science Temple of America*. Online: http://www.hermetic.com/bey/7koran.html.

Allah, Wakeel. 2007. *In the Name of Allah: A History of Clarence 13X and the Five Percenters*. 2nd ed. Atlanta: A-Team.

Anderson, Jeffrey E. 2008. *Hoodoo, Voodoo, and Conjure: A Handbook*. Greenwood Folklore Handbooks. Westport, Conn.: Greenwood.

Association for Core Texts and Courses and ACTC Liberal Arts Institute at St. Mary's College of California. 2011. Online: http://www.coretexts.org/.

Berry, Jason, and Sydney Byrd. 1995. *The Spirit of Black Hawk: A Mystery of Africans and Indians*. Jackson, Miss.: University of Mississippi Press.

Black Apologetics Ministry. 2001–2003. Supreme Mathematics. Online: http://www.blackapologetics.com/mathdetail.html.

Bringhurst, Newell G., and Darron T. Smith, eds. 2004. *Black and Mormon*. Urbana, Ill.: University of Illinois Press.

Chireau, Yvonne P. 2003. *Black Magic: Religion and the African American Conjuring Tradition*. Berkeley: University of California Press.

Crite, Allan Rohan. 1947. *All Glory: Brush Drawing Meditations on the Prayer of Consecration*. Cambridge: Society of St. John the Evangelist.

Deveney, John Patrick. 1996. *Paschal Beverly Randolph: A Nineteenth-Century Black American Spiritualist, Rosicrucian, and Sex Magician*. Albany, N.Y.: State University of New York Press.

———. 2005. Randolph, Paschal Beverly. Pages 976–79 in vol. 2 of *Dictionary of Gnosis and Western Esotericism*. Edited by Wouter J. Hanegraaff et al. Leiden: Brill.

Dow, Carolyn L. 1997. *Saravá!: Afro-Brazilian Magic*. St. Paul, Minn.: Llewellyn.

Duncan, Carol B. 2008. *This Spot of Ground: Spiritual Baptists in Toronto*. Waterloo, Ont., Canada: Wilfrid Laurier University Press.

Eunice Kinney Letter. 1891. Online: http://www.blacklds.org/kinney.

Evenson, Darrick. 2012. Black Mormons and the Curse of Cain Legacy. Online: http://www.angelfire.com/mo2/blackmormon/homepage.html.

Faivre, Antoine. 1992. Introduction. Pages xi–xxii in *Modern Esoteric Spirituality*. Edited by Antoine Faivre and Jacob Needleman. New York: Crossroad.

———. 2005. Secrecy III: Modernity. Pages 1056–61 in vol. 2 of *Dictionary of Gnosis and Western Esotericism*. Edited by Wouter J. Hanegraaff et al. Leiden: Brill.

Faivre, Antoine, and Jacob Needleman, eds. 1992. *Modern Esoteric Spirituality*. World Spirituality 21. New York: Crossroad.

Faivre, Antoine, and Christine Rhone. 2010. *Western Esotericism: A Concise History*. SUNY Series in Western Esoteric Traditions. Albany, N.Y.: State University of New York Press.

Fard, W. D. n.d. *The Problem Book*. Online: www.supremewisdom.webs.com/theproblembook.htm.

Floyd-Thomas, Stacey, Juan Floyd-Thomas, Carol B. Duncan, Stephen G. Gray Jr., and Nancy Lynne Westfield, eds. 2007. *Black Church Studies: An Introduction*. Nashville: Abingdon.

Forsberg, Clyde R., Jr. 2004. *Equal Rites: The Book of Mormon, Masonry, Gender, and American Culture*. New York: Columbia University Press.

Gamache, Henri. (1942a) 1983. *The Master Key to Occult Secrets*. Repr. Bronx, N.Y.: Original Publications.

———. (1942b) 1998. *The Master Book of Candle Burning*. Repr. Plainview, N.Y.: Original Publications.

———. 1993. *Mystery of the Long Lost 8th, 9th, and 10th Books of Moses*. Plainview, N.Y.: Original Publications.

Gilbert, Roberta A. 2005. Waite, Arthur Edward. Pages 1164–65 in vol. 2 of *Dictionary of Gnosis and Western Esotericism*. Edited by Wouter J. Hanegraaff et al. Leiden: Brill.

Goodrick-Clarke, Nicholas. 2008. *The Western Esoteric Traditions: A Historical Introduction*. Oxford: Oxford University Press.

Hall, Prince. 1792. *A Charge Delivered to the Brethren of the African Lodge on the 25th of June 1792 at the Hall of Brother William Smith in Charlestown*. Edited by C. K. Shipton. Readex Microprint ed. Early American Imprints. Worcester, Mass.: American Antiquarian Society.

———. 1797. *A Charge Delivered to the African Lodge, June 14, 1797, at Menotomy*. Edited by C. K. Shipton. Readex Microprint ed. Early American Imprints. Worcester, Mass.: American Antiquarian Society.

Hanegraaff, Wouter J., Antoine Faivre, R. van den Broek, and Jean-Pierre Brach, eds. 2005. *Dictionary of Gnosis and Western Esotericism*. 2 vols. Leiden: Brill.

Hanegraaff, Wouter J., and Jeffrey J. Kripal. 2008. *Hidden Intercourse: Eros and Sexuality in the History of Western Esotericism*. Aries Book Series. Leiden: Brill.

Harding, Rachel E. 2000. *A Refuge in Thunder: Candomblé and Alternative Spaces of Blackness*. Bloomington: Indiana University Press.

Holmes, Barbara A. 2004. *Joy Unspeakable: Contemplative Practices of the Black Church*. Minneapolis: Fortress.

Hurston, Zora Neale. (1935) 1990. *Mules and Men*. Repr. New York: HarperPerennial.

———. (1939) 1991. *Moses: Man of the Mountain*. Repr. New York: HarperPerennial.

James, George G. M. 1954. *Stolen Legacy*. New York: Philosophical Library.

Johnson, Paul Christopher. 2007. *Diaspora Conversions: Black Carib Religion and the Recovery of Africa*. Berkeley: University of California Press.

Kaplan, Stuart R. 1990. *The Encyclopedia of Tarot*. Vol. 3. Stamford, Conn.: U.S. Games Systems.

———. 2009. *The Artwork and Times of Pamela Colman Smith: Artist of the Rider-Waite Tarot Deck*. Stamford, Conn.: U.S. Games Systems.

Kripal, Jeffrey J. 2010. *Authors of the Impossible: The Paranormal and the Sacred*. Chicago: University of Chicago Press.

Laurant, Jean-Pierre. 2005. Tarot. Pages 1110–12 in vol. 2 of *Dictionary of Gnosis and Western Esotericism*. Edited by Wouter J. Hanegraaff et al. Leiden: Brill.

Lincoln, C. Eric. 1994. The Black Muslims in America. 3rd ed. Grand Rapids: Eerdmans.

Long, Carolyn Morrow. 2001. *Spiritual Merchants: Religion, Magic, and Commerce*. Knoxville: University of Tennessee Press.

Mayer, Jean-François. 2005. UFO Traditions. Pages 1139–44 in vol. 2 of *Dictionary of Gnosis and Western Esotericism*. Edited by Wouter J. Hanegraaff et al. Leiden: Brill.

Mitchem, Stephanie. 2007. *African American Folk Healing*. New York: New York University Press.

Moore, Keith. 2005. *Moorish Circle 7: The Rise of the Islamic Faith Among Blacks in America and its Masonic Origins*. Bloomington: AuthorHouse.

Muhammad, Elijah. 2004. *The Mother Plane*. Repr. Maryland Heights, Mo.: Secretarius Memps.

Murphy, Joseph M. 1993. *Santería: African Spirits in America*. Repr. Boston: Beacon.

Myers, Asron. 2005. Candomblé. Pages 730–31 in vol. 1 of *Africana: The Encyclopedia of the African and African American Experience*. Edited by J. Kwame Anthony Appiah and Henry Louis Gates. Oxford: Oxford University Press.

Noll, Joyce Elaine. 1991. *Company of Prophets: African American Psychics, Healers and Visionaries*. St. Paul, Minn.: Llewellyn.

Ogunfuye, J. O. 1980. *The Secrets of the Uses of Psalms*. 3rd ed. Ibadan: Opcol Occult and Spiritual Centres.

Page, Hugh R., Jr. 1998. Some Reflections on G. G. M. James' Stolen Legacy and its Place in the Black Athena Debate. Pages 10–14 in *Anduraru: The Bulletin of the Institute for Ancient Near Eastern and Afroasiatic Cultural Research*. Edited by J. Hugh R. Page. Wilmington, Del.: Institute for Ancient Near Eastern and Afroasiatic Cultural Research.

———. 2000. 'I Was Dreaming When I Wrote This': Biblical Appropriation and Interpretation in the Music of Prince. Paper presented at the annual meeting of the Society of Biblical Literature. Nashville, Tenn. November 21.

———. 2003. A Case Study in Eighteenth-Century Afrodiasporan Biblical Hermeneutics and Historiography: The Masonic Charges of Prince Hall. Pages 103–22 in *Yet With A Steady Beat: Contemporary U.S. Afrocentric Biblical Interpretation*. Edited by R. C. Bailey. Atlanta: Society of Biblical Literature.

Page, Hugh R., Jr, and Randall C. Bailey, eds. 2010. *The Africana Bible: Reading Israel's Scriptures from Africa and the African Diaspora*. Minneapolis: Fortress.

Quinn, Michael D. 1998. *Early Mormonism and the Magic Worldview*. Rev. ed. Salt Lake City, Utah: Signature Books.

Raboteau, Albert J. 2001. *Canaan Land: A Religious History of African Americans*. Oxford: Oxford University Press.

Richards, Dona Marimba. 1992. *Let the Circle Be Unbroken: The Implications of African Spirituality in the Diaspora*. Repr. Lawrenceville, N.J.: Red Sea Press.

Selig, Godfrey A. [1958] 1982. *Secrets of the Psalms: A Fragment of the Practical Kabala, with Extracts from other Kabalistic Writings, as Translated by the Author*. Repr. 8th printing. Fort Worth, Tex.: Dorene.

Smith, Theophus. 1994. *Conjuring Culture: Biblical Formations of Black America*. Oxford: Oxford University Press.

Spencer, Jon Michael. 1994. *Blues and Evil*. Knoxville: University of Tennessee Press.

Stuckrad, Kocku von. 2005. *Western Esoterisicm: A Brief History of Secret Knowledge*. London: Equinox.

Waite, Arthur Edward, and Pamela Colman Smith. 1971. Rider-Waite Tarot Deck. Stamford, Conn.: U.S. Games Systems.

Zolorak, and Dürkön. 1995. *The Tarot of the Orishas*. 2nd ed. St. Paul, Minn.: Llewellyn.

Responses

Strategies of Esoteric Exegesis

Elaine Pagels

> … both read the Bible day and night;
> but you read black where I read white.
> (William Blake, "The Everlasting Gospel")

Where did we come from? Who are we? How are we to live? The creation stories of Gen 1–3 show how some people have been asking—and seeking to answer—such questions for thousands of years, most likely for millennia. Yet the two stories most familiar to those influenced by Jewish and Christian tradition are themselves paradoxical. In the first place, gaps and unexplained leaps in both stories leave huge spaces in which the imagination may roam; thus each may open up for the hearer more questions than it claims to answer. Furthermore, since each of these stories is over three or four thousand years old in written form and likely told for countless years before that, each derives from an ancient cultural setting virtually unimaginable to the great majority of readers, so that they often become a kind of cultural Rorschach test.

Hidden Truths from Eden, edited by Caroline Vander Stichele and Susanne Scholz, offers a wide range of contributions from scholars from diverse fields, each one—and the entire collection—demonstrating just how far such interpretations may range—and how practical their consequences can be.

In the opening essay, for example, Anna Rebecca Solevåg challenges conventional Christian interpretations of the Adam and Eve story, noting that countless Christians have taken their cues from church fathers like Tertullian, who interprets this story as showing that the woman, naturally weak and gullible, "shed Adam's blood" by seducing the man into sin (*Cult. fem.* 1.1.1–2). Yet those whom Tertullian denounced as heretics read Eve as the revealer of a higher spiritual truth who defied the tyrannical Lord of the world. Here, however, Solevåg explores an avenue of interpretation different from either of these; a kind of interpretation articulated by groups of early Christian advocates of asceticism—in this case, the anonymous author of the Acts of Andrew.

Members of such circles, as Solevåg shows, tended to encourage believers to take from the story a salutary warning, as well as moral encouragement to "each person" to "correct his or her own fall" (Acts Andr. 37). Here the purported author, Andrew, addresses a woman convert, exhorting her to "undo the sin of Adam and Eve" by rejecting illicit carnal intercourse; thus the celibate woman may become "a new Eve" (Solevåg, 16). Solevåg rejects the view that this author advocates repudiating marital sexual union altogether (as Pagels 1989 and Klauck 2008 previously have interpreted the text), she notes that the text characterizes the woman's husband as the devil, the serpent incarnate, which suggests the only pure option open to her is a chaste and spiritual union with Christ (13).

Solevåg adds to previous discussions significant insight in applying to this text what some scholars call an "intersectional perspective" (12). In this case, she notes how the author contrasts the upper-class heroine, Maximilla, with her slave woman, Euclia. While the former demonstrates a superior, masculine capacity for self-control, her slave is depicted as lustful, deceptive, a braggart, and a thief, whom her master justly kills for betraying family secrets. Thus the account contrasts such an evil slave with "faithful slaves" who remain obedient to their masters, thus reinforcing ancient ideologies of slavery (15–16).

Next, Tuomas Rasimus raises a provocative question: "Imperial Propaganda in Paradise?" Rasimus notes a puzzling detail found in the Apocryphon of John—that the author of this ancient and widely read text pictures Christ appearing to Adam and Eve in the form of an eagle that perches on the tree of knowledge and attempts to persuade them to eat of its fruit. Having previously argued that what scholars call "Sethian" mythology consists of three distinct clusters of mythological ideas (Rasimus 2009), Rasimus here reviews a remarkable range of readings of the Adam and Eve story and then discusses the use of this image among extant manuscripts, as well as the ways that various scholars have proposed to interpret it. Finally, after reviewing eagle symbolism in ancient imperial and religious sources, Rasimus persuasively concludes that the implied context in this text is baptismal and that "the image of the eagle was borrowed from imperial propaganda" (49) to place Christ in counterpoint to the Roman emperor and to depict the former as true victor and ruler.

In the following essay, Peter W. Martens takes up another provocative detail: what does Gen 3:21 mean by saying that "the Lord God made garments of skins for the man and his wife, and clothed them" (NRSV)? When Origen responded to the second century philosopher Celsus's ridicule of this story—and to the intense arguments it elicited among Christian readers—he insisted that the story must have "a certain secret and mystical meaning" (*Cels.* 4.40). Deciphering what meaning he found there, however, is no easy task—not only because Origen's opponents destroyed much of what he wrote on Genesis, but also, Martens shows, because Origen himself apparently offered different—and conflicting—interpretations. Twice, in extant passages, he suggests that the "garments" figuratively refer to the bodies God bestowed on previously incorporeal souls (*Comm. Gen.* 125.20–23; *Cels.* 4.40; see Martens, 58–70). Later, however, in his *Homilies on Leviticus,* he suggests a more literal interpretation—that God actually *did* provide clothing for them that was made from the skin of dead animals—clothing that symbolized the deadly consequences of human sin (*Hom. Lev.* 6.2.7; see Martens, 73). In this finely researched study, Martens points out, too, that Origen, like such exegetes as Philo, sometimes juxtaposed Gen 1:26–27 with Gen 2:7 as referring to two sequential stages in human creation. Yet he could also read other passages—Gen 2:7 and 3:21, for example—as if they refer to the *same* event. Martens notes that although such an exegetical choice may look like a minor point, it illustrates what became a central question of interpretation: whether—or when—to take different passages to refer to the same event—or to two distinct events.

Elliot R. Wolfson's contribution then takes us into fascinating territory, exploring medieval Jewish sources of kabbalistic exegesis that explicate various perceptions of body, gender, and sexuality. Wolfson first shows that "the typical approach to anthropomorphism"—that is, seeing it as an accommodation to the limitations of human perception—fails to understand the approaches taken by kabbalists, who instead see anthropomorphism informing us about its divine source—that is, seeing in the human body clues to the divine mystery (88). Readers will immediately note analogies between what is found in these medieval texts and the discussion of what Origen had written nearly a millennium earlier—visions of Adam as divine *anthropos,* whose luminous and androgynous body was replaced with "garment of skins," interpreted as the mortal and gendered flesh that took its place after sin.

Wolfson here takes up a theme that recently has engaged considerable controversy among scholars of kabbalah: how kabbalists read the implications of the two creation accounts in terms of gender and sexuality. Some, notably including Moshe Idel (2005a, 2005b), professor of Jewish Mysticism at the Hebrew University of Jerusalem, interpret kabbalistic statements that the divine image (Gen 1:26–27) includes both masculine and feminine elements as theological affirmations of equality between the sexes. From such interpretations some scholars go on to draw a positive contrast between medieval kabbalists and exegetes with encratic tendencies, especially Christians, claiming that kabbalistic teachings "celebrated heterosexuality as the means to bring about the rectification of the schism within the divine" (96–97).

Wolfson argues instead that a closer and more accurate reading of the texts reveals that "the deep structure undergirding the kabbalistic construction of gender … is that of a masculine androgyny" (103). Challenging views that he derides as "romantic" (inferring, as I read him, that his opponent's views conveniently reflect values too contemporaneous and politically correct; see Wolfson [102]), Wolfson reads these texts as consistently androcentric. So, he argues, kabbalistic interpreters read the creation accounts of Gen 1 and Gen 2 together as part of a unified Scripture, thus seeing woman's emergence from Adam as an aspect of the male androgyne's original endowment. From this he concludes that kabbalistic readers, like the Gen 2 account itself, appropriate both the power to give birth and nourishment to the male, denying them to the female (105–6). Analogous with this, he suggests, are kabbalistic associations of the feminine with the evil impulse and with the moon, and thus only with reflected light, while associating the masculine element with the good impulse, as well as with the sun, as primary source of light (105).

What I find striking about this scholarly debate is that it resonates so closely with recent controversies about Christian exegesis of Genesis in the earliest centuries of the Common Era. For when I first read such so-called gnostic sources as the Apocryphon of John, the Gospel of the Egyptians, or Trimorphic Protennoia, I was struck by the way such texts describe divine emanation in feminine as well as masculine imagery. On closer investigation, however, I came to see that with few exceptions, such texts most often maintain, to one degree or another, the androcentric perspectives reflected in the biblical sources they interpret. Certain other scholars, however, excoriated such "historical" readings, insisting instead that these ancient texts supported contemporary feminist convictions about gender equality—in terms both human and divine. What is at stake here, of course, is the central historiographical question of how we relate contemporary concerns to our understanding of sources, especially ancient or medieval ones. Consequently, having read this essay along with Wolfson's major study, *Language, Eros, Being: Kabbalistic Hermeneutics and Poetic Imagination* (2005), as well as such books of his critics as Moshe Idel's *Kabbalah and Eros* (2005b), I find Wolfson's analysis more persuasive.

Peter J. Forshaw's article, "The Genesis of Christian Kabbalah," follows Wolfson's contribution, showing how some Christians sought to appropriate kabbalistic speculation. Foreshaw relates how Pico della Mirandola astounded Christians in fifteenth century Europe by disclosing that "the Jews possessed a secret, mystical interpretation of Scripture" (127)—or, rather, whole ranges of such interpretations. After first investigating these as well as he could, Pico had some translated for him into Latin and then sought to apply them to the Genesis account, notably in his "Kabbalistic Conclusions according to My Own Opinion." Convinced that applying kabbalistic strategies of exegesis could support Christian views of Christ and the Trinity, Pico ignited the enthusiasm of others who sought to practice both speculative kabbalistic exegesis and practical kabbalah, the latter involving amulets believed to be invested with powers of exorcism, healing, and acts of power. What Pico could hardly have known is that the kind of exegetical strategies he found in such texts had been engaged by some Christians over a millennium earlier—anonymous authors of some of the Nag Hammadi texts—before their efforts were rejected as heretical and censored by certain bishops.

Georgiana Hedesan's "The Mystery of *Mysterium Magnum*" adds another dimension to this remarkable collection with a discussion of the treatise *Philosophia ad Atheniensis* (ca. 1600), which sets forth an influential alchemical interpretation of Gen 1 attributed to Paracelsus. This treatise suggests that the work of creation proceeded by a process of catalyzing separations in the *mysterium magnum*—mysterious indeed, since interpreters intensely debated whether this "mother of all the elements" was actually a form of matter or some kind of "formless potentiality" (Hedesan, 148–49)—above all, whether speaking of such a primal substance—substantial or not!—would contradict the doctrine of *creatio ex nihilo*. In her conclusion, Hedesan briefly sketches later interpretations of these speculations, most powerfully in the last treatise written by Jacob Böhme. Characterizing the *mysterium magnum* as a "spiritual essence," Böhme then alludes to a primordial creation that precedes cosmology, which he then seeks to integrate with the Genesis creation accounts (Hedesan, 161).

The final three papers take up a range of more contemporary interpretations, beginning with Susanne Scholz's intriguing discussion of Emanuel Swedenborg, Rudolph Steiner, and Samuel D. Fohr. Having found the "historical-literalist paradigm in biblical studies" too narrowly focused (170), Scholz finds wider scope for the imagination in the work of interpreters who seek what Swedenborg calls "the inner meaning of Scripture" (171). Setting aside traditional claims of religious authority while exploring the symbolic power of the texts, Swedenborg declares that his interpretations rely instead on what he himself has experienced. Scholz traces Swedenborg's psychospiritual reading of the story of Adam and Eve, acknowledging its idiosyncratic reading of gender, while appreciating his effort to seek "direct contact with the divine realm" (179).

She next considers the work of Rudolph Steiner, who founded the nineteenth-century school that he called the "Anthroposophical Society." Following practices known to esoteric interpreters for millennia, Steiner reads the two Genesis creation accounts as a unified source, suggesting that one must read this through what he called his "spiritual scientific method" (see Scholz, 179). While his own exegesis, largely based on a reading of the Hebrew words and letters, seems grounded in Jewish traditions, he clearly sought to open up what he saw as universal forms of spiritual insight.

Scholz's third example involves Samuel D. Fohr, professor of Philosophy at the University of Pittsburgh, who published books on the spiritual symbolism of Genesis and Exodus. Yet Fohr draws not only upon Jewish and Christian sources, but also on sources from Sufi, Buddhist, Hindu, and Taoist traditions. Hoping to extend his readers' vision beyond simply historical, dogmatic, or moralistic readings of biblical narrative, Fohr offers his own, rather richly complex, reading of those texts.

Having presented three such different readings of Gen 1–3, Scholtz suggests that such examples might offer new hermeneutical possibilities for reading the Bible, suggesting that "such a unifying vision … may … encourage spiritual religions maturity, depth, and sophistication" (193). In her conclusion, she notes acutely how such practices may be particularly apt in the present, especially for those in the twenty-first century who share her concerns with conflict, war, and ecological damage.

Next, László-Attila Hubbes discusses the work of Béla Hamvas (1897–1968), a remarkable Hungarian author and visionary who has remained, until now, largely unknown in the West. After enlisting in the army around the age of seventeen to fight in World War I and having become a writer and publisher concerned with social problems, Hamvas was drafted three times into military service during World War II (Hubbes, 198). Shortly afterwards, forced into unemployment by the Hungarian government because of his outspoken political views, Hamvas worked as a field hand while continuing to read widely and write about what he saw as the spiritual crisis of his time (199). Like Fohr, Hamvas explored a wide range of cultural traditions, from ancient kabbalah to Jacob Böhme's *Mysterium Magnum* and from the Corpus Hermeticum to the Diamond Sutra. After immersing himself in the sacred lore of many cultures, he set out to write his own version of a founding myth: how the world was created, what was its golden age, its crises, the forms of divine revelation, and how humankind could achieve salvation and restoration to moral integrity and spiritual wisdom. Hubbes suggests that what he sought, above all, was to write his sacred science as a kind of "poetics of creation"—one that, Hubbes suggests, may yet inspire generations to come (215).

The collection concludes with what Hugh Page Jr. calls "An Architectonic for Interdisciplinary Study," which opens up an enormous range of potential study of Africana esotericism that not only would embrace indigenous African sources, but also would require investigating how these have developed in the black Diaspora throughout such areas as Europe, America, and the Caribbean. Secondly, Page notes the movements and structures that have emerged from the black church—not only such movements as the African Methodist Episcopal church, but also the black Masonic lodge system, temples of Moorish Science, and the Rastafarian movement in Jamaica. Finally, Page enumerates a third source: the work of artists, musicians, and writers who have developed what he calls Africana traditions.

Page also notes the enormous influence—positive and negative—of the Bible in the creation of what he calls "Africana esoteric texts" (224), which display a profusion of imaginative extension and reinterpretation of biblical sources. Noted, too, is the influence of the Qu'ran for various movements, perhaps especially for the writings of W. D. Fard and Elijah Muhammad.

Hidden Truths from Eden offers, as its editors note, a richly suggestive starting place for further investigations. Here I mention only two directions that such research might take; no doubt other readers will come up with many more. First, and most obvious, we could continue investigating connections and analogies between the many traditions mentioned here. As an example, I mention only the research project that engages me right now: namely, exploring how strategies of esoteric exegesis that developed in certain Jewish circles in antiquity (ca. 100–400 C.E.) were adopted by disciples of the Egyptian Christian teacher Valentinus (ca. 140 C.E.). Yet within a generation such strategies were denounced by Irenaeus, bishop of Lyons, as "evil exegesis," forms of "falsely so-called *gnosis*" (*Haer.* 1, Praefatio), and Valentinus's followers were accused of having invented them from Greek philosophic sources—pointing toward interpretations followed by many historians ever since—perhaps because few Christian scholars are familiar with Jewish esoteric traditions.

Second, further research could serve to integrate our understanding of these various forms of esoteric exegesis with the political, social, and historical circumstances and concerns of each exegete and of the audience each addresses. Such questions may strike some readers at first as too literal, prosaic, or merely "historical." Yet the contributions by Scholz, Hubbes, and Page, for example, show with special clarity how such considerations can add significant perspectives to our understanding of what motivates people to create esoteric interpretations and what such interpretations can offer.

Consider, for example, what Georg Simmel points out in his 1906 article, "The Sociology of Secrecy and of Secret Societies": "Secrecy secures, so to speak, the possibility of a second world alongside of the obvious world, and the latter is most strenuously affected by the former" (462). Taking into account the interpreters' social, political, and historical situation may demonstrate how symbolic and imaginative exegesis has enabled people to deal with—and sometimes resist and transcend—particular social and political constraints. Take, for example, the case of Rudolph Steiner. Was Steiner Jewish as certain elements of his biography indicate? In the material presented here, the question is neither asked nor answered, perhaps because the biographical evidence suggests that he intentionally deflected that question. That would not be surprising, of course, since he lived in an Austria rife with anti-Semitism just at the time when his fellow Austrian, Adolph Hitler, himself partly Jewish, was working to ignite racist hatred. Yet considering such a question could suggest some very practical effects of the spiritual exegesis he sought to pioneer, since, as he envisioned it, such exegesis could open up universal forms of spiritual insight that he believed could bypass, or transcend, classification as either "Jewish" or "Christian."

Hubbes's essay offers a stunning example, having opened his article on Béla Hamvas with a brief but detailed account of the political and social circumstances from which his writing emerged, including the two world wars, repressive governments, and social ostracism that intensely preoccupied this remarkable man. Hubbes clearly indicates that Hamvas wrote his "spiritual scientific method" in response to the horrors he had witnessed and suffered.

Finally, Page mentions in his summary of Africana esotericism a wide range of strategies that such practices could serve: as forms of resistance to oppressive social orders and strategies to ridicule, subvert, or escape them, such as the messages encoded in quilts or in spirituals; further, as Page says, such esotericism could serve to "foster wholeness, construct identity, and promote liberation" (221), as they often have in situations that involve slavery and colonialism.

Hidden Truths from Eden encourages those of us who are scholars and students to look beyond our specialized research and learn from that of colleagues in many fields—a welcome and valuable collection!

Works Cited

Idel, Moshe. 2005a. Androgyny and Equality in the Theosophico-Theurgical Kabbalah. *Diogenes* 52:27–38.

———. 2005b. *Kabbalah and Eros*. New Haven: Yale University Press.

Klauck, Hans-Josef. 2008. *The Apocryphal Acts of the Apostles: An Introduction*. Translated by Brian McNeil. Waco, Tex.: Baylor University Press.

Pagels, Elaine. 1989. *Adam, Eve, and the Serpent*. New York: Vintage.

Rasimus, Tuomas. 2009. *Paradise Reconsidered in Gnostic Mythmaking: Rethinking Sethianism in the Light of the Ophite Evidence*. Nag Hammadi and Manichaean Studies 68. Leiden: Brill.

Simmel, Georg. 1906. The Sociology of Secrecy and of Secret Societies. *American Journal of Sociology* 11:441–98.

Steiner, Rudolf. 2002. *Genesis: Secrets of Creation: The First Book of Moses: Eleven Lectures Given in Munich, 16–26 August 1910*. Forest Row, East Sussex: Steiner.

Wolfson, Elliot R. 2005. *Language, Eros, Being: Kabbalistic Hermeneutics and Poetic Imagination*. New York: Fordham University Press.

Esotericism and Biblical Interpretation

Samuel D. Fohr

Like many words, *esoteric* has attracted a number of meanings over the centuries. And it could be argued that any one person's understanding is just that and not entitled to any special importance. One could compare it to the word *scientism*, which to me means the worship of science and/or technology and viewing the scientist as a kind of priest. But there are at least half a dozen understandings of this word, and I suppose it would be rather childish to insist on my meaning, even if I have good reason to prefer it as the most significant one. Then, too, the meanings of words tend to degenerate over time, just as words themselves degenerate. So it has come about that the word esoteric refers sometimes to the occult, sometimes to the outré, and sometimes just to whatever is considered arcane (another term whose meaning has degenerated) or out of the ordinary ken of most people, like some out of the way facts in a particular discipline.

Moreover, the term *esoteric* is often contrasted with the term *exoteric* and taken to refer to the two sides of a spiritual tradition: the inner secret side and the outer public side. Again, there is nothing objectionable in this, but it is still superficial. What is essential to understand is that these terms point to the two ways of relating to God, the ultimate reality, which are open to humans. The following description of these ways has been greatly influenced by the writings of René Guénon, whom I take to be the most insightful explicator of esotericism in the twentieth century.

In the exoteric approach, God is up in the heavens, while we are down here on earth, and our goal is to be loving servants who will finally meet God in heaven after we die. In the esoteric approach, we are nothing other than God, and the spiritual goal is to become aware of this. Looking at the distinction between the two approaches from another angle, we can say that from the exoteric point of view, God is in the world, in heaven, while from the esoteric point of view the world is in God. There are several well-known statements of the latter view, including Augustine in book 1 of his *Confessions*. Similarly, the ancient Jewish philosopher Philo of Alexandria, in book 1 of his work *On Dreams*, refers to God as a place (*hamakom* in Hebrew), because of God containing things without God being contained in anything. According to the early modern kabbalist Isaac Luria, God created a space (*tsimtsum*) within God in order to provide a place for the world to form. But for the sake of fully understanding the contributions in this volume as well as my response, we need to say more about God's relationship to the world as understood from the esoteric point of view.

We can speak of God unmanifested and God manifested. God unmanifested is the Infinite (*Ein Sof* in Kabbalism), but it has also been called the Ground of Being, the *Ungrund*, and various other names in spiritual traditions all over the world. The first manifestation or appearance of God is Being, which is one. Again, every tradition has different names for God manifested, but they almost all describe it as three in one. Even in the Jewish biblical tradition, God visits Abraham in the guise of three persons (Gen 18).

God as Maker or Creator of the world is but one aspect of God manifested (and not an evil being as the gnostics held). Being polarizes to produce the active and passive poles of universal manifestation. In kabbalistic terms, *Hokhmah*, the second *sefirah* or aspect of *Ein Sof*, projects the third, *Binah*. The passive pole is the substance of the world, and it is originally in a chaotic state. The beginning of Genesis really starts at this point, with the "wind" hovering over the "waters" (1:2). The active pole is Aristotle's Unmoved Mover, and by its influence on the passive pole the latter is formed into a three-fold world. Although they have different names in different spiritual traditions, I have found it helpful to refer to these three worlds as the world spirit, the world soul, and the world body. The world spirit cuts through the middle of the world, functioning as the world axis, and in many traditions it forms the trunk of the world tree. It is also the center point of every human. If the world is the macrocosm, then we who are microcosms are also tripartite, having a spirit (or intellect in the original meaning of the word), soul, and body (*pneuma*, *psyche*, and *soma*). One way of explaining the esoteric spiritual path is to say that we are to reverse in consciousness the manifestation of the world by God, going back to our origin. We are to reach this state through initiation into a genuine esoteric tradition and then through practices, which are usually referred to as various kinds of meditation. Augustine refers to such practices in book 11 of his *Confessions*, where he twice urges his readers to hold their minds still so that they might taste of eternity.

Practitioners of the esoteric approach to God believe that the venerated writings of all spiritual traditions have an outer meaning intended for most people and an inner "hidden" meaning expressed symbolically for those who are more interested in penetrating the mysteries of God. They believe this because they know of spiritual teachers from ancient to modern times who explained the symbolism of their respective sacred texts and of other traditional stories from their cultures. We cannot here go into why such teachers prefer to express esoteric truths symbolically. What we can say is that while there may not a be a universal symbolic language, there are certain natural symbols, like the sun, which are given the same symbolic meaning in almost all spiritual traditions. Furthermore, it turns out that the "hidden truths" contained in the writings of almost all spiritual traditions are very similar. László-Attila Hubbes touches upon the reason for this similarity in the first part of his paper on the metaphysics of Béla Hamvas. According to Hamvas, there is a unitary spiritual tradition in the world. Hamvas did not mean that all spiritual traditions of the world originated from one source, but that "there are common universal characters in all ancient spiritual legacies known to us." In other words, the same ideas show up in different traditions, ideas such as "the perfection of origins, the corruption of ages" and many more (Hubbes, 203). Guénon believed in one earthly primordial tradition from which all the others derive. Although this idea is certainly possible given that humanity originated in one place, I believe Hamvas is probably right. The similarities in the different traditions are most likely due to our common humanity, or to diffusion, or to there being one God inspiring us all, or possibly to all three. Whatever the reasons, the result is that once one understands the basics of spiritual symbolism it is easy to spot and interpret that symbolism in practically every spiritual tradition.

When we consider a second-century C.E. work like the Gospel of Andrew, we have to ask two questions: is it a symbolic esoteric story, and does it understand the story of Adam and Eve in a symbolic esoteric way? After explaining all the ramifications of the story from various points of view, Anna Rebecca Solevåg makes the following comment: "In my view, the use of Gen 3 in the Acts of Andrew is similar to Nag Hammadi uses of Adam and Eve. In both cases, Gen 3 is 'understood as spiritual allegory—not so much *history with a moral* as *myth with a meaning*'" (emphasis original; quoting Elaine Pagels). She continues:

> On the one hand, the story of the fall is interpreted typologically in order to give meaning to events in the present. The fall is not something 'that happened' but a divine reality that corresponds to the challenges at hand. On the other hand, from the gender-analytical perspective the interpretation of Genesis resembles those of other mainstream proto-orthodox Christian interpretations. (Solevåg, 19).

Thus according to her "on the one hand" comment, the Acts of Andrew takes the Adam-Eve story not as history but as true for all time.

As a help in determining whether or not the Acts of Andrew is indeed a spiritual allegory, we need to begin with a little exegesis of the biblical account. The story of the fall is prefigured by the split of the androgynous Adam-Eve mentioned in Gen 1 into the pair of Adam and Eve mentioned in Gen 2. Thus we have a complete being falling into incompleteness, which all humans feel especially after they reach puberty. The fall of Adam and Eve in Gen 3 results in them gaining knowledge of good and evil. This idea signifies going from a unitary consciousness centered in the spirit, which is supraindividual, to a consciousness of myself and others, mine and thine, liking and disliking, grasping and rejecting. It is a development that is true for all humans for all time, since it happens to all of us as we mature. The idea of the esoteric path is to reverse this process through spiritual practices and, as the Gospel of Thomas states, "to make the two one" (logion 22).

The Acts of Andrew is a rather strange document, perhaps because of its mixed heritage. Throughout most of it, Andrew prays to God to save him from death, but in the last episode, he cannot wait to die. In that episode he is trying to convince Maximilla to refrain from sexual relations with her husband Aegeates. Aegeates threatens to have Andrew killed if Maximilla does not submit to him. Andrew is willing to go to his grave to keep Maximilla from sinning again. It appears that according to the Acts of Andrew it is sexual intercourse that is the original sin of humanity. What is not clear is whether it assumes Eve's first intercourse was with Adam or the serpent. In any case, Andrew compares himself to Adam and Maximilla to Eve and asks her not to make the same mistake as Eve. He refuses to act like Adam, even when he is invited into her bedroom.

We could read the Acts of Andrew as an esoteric symbolic story where Maximilla is the soul caught between the pull of the body (Aegeates) and the spirit (Andrew). Or we could say she is caught between her lower tendencies and higher tendencies, or even between the devil and God. But there is a peculiarity in this story which argues against this sort of interpretation. In the end, Maximilla refuses to submit to her husband,

and Aegeates has Andrew crucified. Now if the soul chooses the side of the spirit, then it is odd that the spirit is, as a result, eliminated. Or to put it another way, if the higher tendencies in a person win out over the lower tendencies, why should that spell death for the higher tendencies? It may be that Maximilla's transformation shows that she has overcome "the primordial gender divide" and restored "the androgynous image," as Solevåg puts it (21), and thus has "made the two one" (Gos. Thom. 22). This transformation would certainly be true for anyone who has gone far on the esoteric path. But such a reading is not clearly indicated to either Solevåg or myself. The problem is that the whole account revolves around overcoming one's sexual impulses, and this is not in itself sufficient for attaining the goal of the esoteric spiritual path; it is not even necessary. How the Acts of Andrew views the story of Adam and Eve is also murky. Andrew's linking Maximilla with Eve and himself with Adam could mean that he takes the story of Adam and Eve as one which is true for all people for all time. On the other hand, the author of the Acts of Andrew could view the Adam and Eve story as history with the message that one can reach salvation by not making the same mistake. It is difficult to choose between these interpretations, and certainly there is nothing in the Acts of Andrew about the esoteric meaning of the fall.

In reading Tuomas Rasimus's exhaustive analysis of the second century C.E. Apocryphon of John, which purports to be a secret teaching given by Jesus to the apostle John after the former's ascension, whether one calls it *gnostic*, *Sethian*, or anything else, I cannot help but recall that old philosophical standby, Ockham's Razor: do not multiply entities beyond necessity. Not only is God's creation increased by all sorts of entities not mentioned in the Bible, but the whole story of the fall of Adam and Eve is twisted inside out. Furthermore, Jesus is portrayed as an eagle, something atypical but not unknown, as Rasimus points out. And this is just one version of what has been generally known as the gnostic account of creation.

There is one aspect of the Apocryphon of John which makes sense from the esoteric point of view. "The tree of knowledge is simultaneously the *real* tree of life," as Rasimus puts it (35). The tree of knowledge and the tree of life are really two aspects of the world tree. Its branches are the various planes of existence. Falling into duality (the knowledge of good and evil) is in effect falling away from the center. The snake (or serpent) around the tree is a dual symbol. Its coils are another symbol of the various planes of existence. But at least in the ancient world, it also symbolized immortality and wisdom. As to the first, the Epic of Gilgamesh tells how a snake stole the herb of immortality from Gilgamesh. As to the second we have the instruction of Jesus: "So be wise as serpents and innocent as doves" (Matt 10:16, NRSV). The snake was considered a symbol of immortality, because it shed its skin and thus was seen as being constantly reborn. So it is not surprising that in the garden of Eden it is connected to the world tree. But this is not how the author of the Apocryphon of John sees things. Perhaps his own view of the snake is due to the peculiar milieu of its composition that Rasimus describes, namely, the principate era of the Roman Empire when the eagle was the symbol of Roman military power. There was a well-known story of an eagle killing a serpent, and an emperor's apotheosis was signaled by the release of an eagle from his funerary pyre.

Peter W. Martens's discussion of Origen's interpretation of the garment of skins, which God bestowed on Adam and Eve after their fall, is fair and comprehensive. However, it points to the truth that not any old interpretation will count as allegorical. We can applaud Origen's eschewing a literalistic view of Genesis without accepting all of his particular symbolic interpretations. Again, we can accept his view that, as Martens says, "Moses, like a 'distinguished orator,' composed Genesis in a twofold manner. He paid attention to 'the outward form' of his text, but he also gave 'opportunities for deeper study for the few with more understanding and who are capable of searching out his meaning' (*Cels.* 1.18, Chadwick)" (Martens, 79). The sentiment would be true whatever the authorship of Genesis. And again, we should not "cling to the letter of the Scripture as if it were true, but rather search for the 'hidden treasure' [see Matt 13:44] in the letter" (Origen, *Comm. Gen.* 125.23–29; quoted in Martens, 66). Certainly the opening chapters of Genesis should be interpreted allegorically, but in doing so one has to begin with the plain meaning of the text.

As Origen claims, Adam can refer to all of humanity and not just a person. His complete view is that before the fall Adam and Eve did not have bodies, but after the fall God forced them into bodies, which are the garments of skins mentioned in Genesis. We can see the problems with this interpretation by noting the contortions Origen has to go through to deny the obvious bodily existence of both Adam and Eve in the Genesis account. In effect, Origen wants to take the earth out of the earthly (terrestrial) paradise.

There are individual symbols and allegories (or symbolic stories). In an allegory, one group of events is meant to symbolize another group of events. Thus Adam and Eve's fall can symbolize what happens within the consciousness of all people. It would seem that Origen's view is that the fall of Adam and Eve symbolizes what happens to all disembodied souls who move away from their original purity. But this is not quite what is going on. He is not saying the embodied Adam and Eve of Genesis symbolize disembodied spirits; he is saying that in the biblical account they *are* disembodied spirits. This is just false, and evidently half the time Origen agreed it was false.

Origen's second symbolic reading of the animal skins is no better than his first. According to the second reading, the skins symbolize the mortality of Adam and Eve since skins come from dead animals. First of all, the skins are not connected with mortality in the Genesis account. It is only after Adam and Eve are given the skins that God decrees they should be thrown out and kept out of the garden of Eden so they cannot eat of the tree of life. Second, putting on animal skins is part of a ritual of rebirth in many cultures. Indeed, Jacob dons a skin before he is blessed by Isaac in the Gen 27 account. It is not surprising that Origen would give a similar interpretation of the two (presumably) leather sandals Moses was wearing in his approach to the burning bush as recounted in Exod 3. These too are taken to be symbols of mortality. In a way, the mortality interpretation fits better in this context than in the garden of Eden episode. But even here it is best to see them as something else, namely, symbols of technology that, as in the case of the original skins, are given to humans as a help in their fallen state. If the burning bush which is unconsumed is understood as a symbol of the world spirit and the area around it amounts to the earthly paradise, we do not need technology in this place, and we have to put off our dualistic consciousness (symbolized by the sandals) to approach the place where all earthly oppositions are reconciled.

The subject of the primordial androgyne has already been broached, and it is the main topic of Elliot R. Wolfson's paper. He begins with an informative and insightful discussion of how certain kabbalists viewed the Godhead and its relation to the world. Along the way he asserts, following Gershom Scholem, that there was a great disagreement between rationalistic philosophers and kabbalists in the Middle Ages over how God should and should not be described and especially over whether any anthropomorphic qualities should be attributed to God. The rationalistic philosophers wanted to eliminate any such language and in effect reduce God to an abstraction (my terminology) while the kabbalists wanted to preserve such language to a certain degree in order to make sense of the view that humans are made in God's image, that is, in order to affirm "the ontological homology between human and divine" (Wolfson, 89). More generally the kabbalists wanted to affirm that there was actually something there from which the universe came. To put it another way, they believed certain descriptions of the Godhead were not mere figurative expressions but actually referred to an "ontic reality," to use Wolfson's phrase (90).

Wolfson quotes a comment by the kabbalist Menahem Recanati to highlight "the kabbalistic rejection of the hyperallegorization of the philosophers," which runs as follows:

> According to the ancient and holy wisdom, everything receives the efflux from what precedes it and overflows to what is beneath it, from the First One, blessed be He, until it reaches us. Not as the reckoning of the philosophers, those of a deficient matter, who deny everything except what is comprehended by their reasoning, which is like an illusion [*ahizat einayam*]. (Recanati, *Perush Hatefillot*, 38a; cited in Wolfson, 91)

Now according to Wolfson, chief among the "exponents of a more rationalistic religious philosophy" was Maimonides (90). If Maimonides and the kabbalists were so much at odds, then with the first sentence of the passage just quoted in mind, it is surprising to find in the *Guide for the Perplexed* (written in the previous century to Recanati's comment) a number of passages containing phrases such as "the Intellect that overflows toward us and is the bond between us and Him, may He be exalted" (3.52). While philosophers like Maimonides may not be on the same page as kabbalists like Recanati, their view of God was not quite as unsubstantial as it might seem from some of these comments and not much different from the kabbalists.

Central to the kabbalists' view of God is their understanding of the *sefirot*. Again, they want to avoid viewing them in a completely abstract way, but rather as in some sense the body of God, or as Wolfson (following Henry Corbin) terms it, the "*imaginal body* ... in order to convey this sense of embodiment that is not material flesh but which is nevertheless a concrete phenomenon and not merely a figure of speech" (92). To begin with, while some commentators refer to the *sefirot* as emanations, this is somewhat misleading. The word *sefirot* literally means numbers or enumerations. The *sefirot* constitute the Godhead and thus the interior life of God as understood by the kabbalists. So rather than follow Recanati in thinking of them as God's garments, as he appears to do based on other comments, we would be better off thinking of them as God's skin, if we wanted to think of them in such a way at all. God as first revealed or manifested is often described in triadic terms, but in this case God is presented as denary or tenfold. The *sefirot* are the aspects or attributes of *Ein Sof*, such as *Chesed* (Mercy or Kindness) and *Gevurah* (Rigor or Judgment), which together make up the archetypal world, the realm of Being, and are thus comparable to the Platonic forms. The good among the forms plays a similar role to *Keter*, the first *sefirah*.

This is not the place for a comprehensive discussion of the *sefirot*. For our purposes it is important to note that all commentators consider two of the ten masculine, namely *Hokhmah* and *Tiferet*, and two of them feminine, namely *Binah* and *Malkut*. This means that God as first revealed has both masculine and feminine aspects. Taken together the *sefirot* are often characterized in kabbalah as being Adam Kadmon (the primordial man). In a way, Adam Kadmon is the first image of God. The being described in Gen 1, which is made in the image of God, can be termed primal man or more neutrally primal Adam, and as Wolfson mentions, it is taken by kabbalists to be the primordial androgyne. It is Adam-Eve and is made in the image of Adam Kadmon, who also has masculine and feminine sides. So it is a true image of the first image. It is not unreasonable to consider the androgyne as the prototype of humans (a personification of divine influence in the world which lacks nothing) rather than an actual complete human being. Wolfson spends the rest of his essay detailing the "subtle nuances of gender politics," which show "androcentrism at play" in kabbalistic interpretations (Wolfson, 98). He discusses the kabbalist's view that the original split of Adam-Eve can be rectified by marriage and sexual relations between men and women. But he does not think their discussions really treat males and females as equals. He uses such expressions as the "androcentric subjugation of the woman" and "the patriarchal stereotype of the wanton woman" (107). He says that it will not do to merely lift the feminine up to the masculine, to make the female male, as it were. What we need is a transcendence of the male-female dichotomy. There is no question, especially after reading all the examples he gives, that kabbalists considered the masculine superior to the feminine. However, kabbalistic ideas about the inner nature of God point us in the right direction. In stressing that God has both masculine and feminine sides, Kabbalism invites us to relate to God in either way or both, and its idea of *Keter* (from which the other sefirot come) induces us to transcend this duality altogether. And this is true of the esoteric side of many spiritual traditions.

Peter J. Forshaw writes about "some continuities and differences between Jewish and Christian *kabbalah iyyunit* or 'speculative kabbalah,' inspired by the Jewish exegetical techniques of gematria, notariqon, and temura" (121). After mentioning Gershom Scholem's dictum that the kabbalists believed that "to know the stages of the creative process is also to know the stages of one's own return to the root of all existence" (see Forshaw, 122), he explains these techniques very clearly, and along the way he describes some of the key ideas of kabbalistic texts such as the Sefer Yetzirah, the Sefer Habahir, and the Zohar, all of which deal with the creative process. He then discusses some of the views of the fifteenth-century philosopher Pico della Mirandola, who is considered the "father of Christian kabbalah." I cannot add much to Forshaw's exposition, but there is one idea of Pico's that is provocative: he evidently equated the Trinity with the first three *sefirot.* He seems to have thought that the latter "form the upper world and are in God" and the other seven *sefirot* "form the middle world from which our sensible world is formed" (Forshaw, 130). It is not his view of the *sefirot* that needs some examination, although it can be said that all of them are in God. Rather it is in his thinking that the first three are comparable to the Trinity.

Kabbalism is not one thing, any more than Judaism, Christianity, Islam, Buddhism, or Hinduism are one thing. Historical development has given us many versions of each, but we sum them up under one "ism." Some kabbalists take *Keter* (the Crown) as a substitute for *Ein Sof,* while others understand it as what I would call Being or the first revelation of the Infinite. In any case, from *Keter* comes *Hokhmah* (Wisdom) and from *Hokhmah* comes *Binah* (Understanding), the mother of all the other *sefirot* and the rest of creation. It is true that if we assume Pico thought God the Father corresponded to *Keter,* then he could argue that, just as in the case of the *sefirot*, the Son is generated or begotten by the Father and the Spirit proceeds from the Father or both the Father and Son. But problems come up with the other two members of the Trinity. According to Forshaw, Pico equated *Hokhmah* with Christ. In only one place in the New Testament is Christ identified as wisdom:

> For Jews demand signs and Greeks desire wisdom, but we proclaim Christ crucified, a stumbling block to Jews and foolishness to Gentiles, but to those who are called, both Jews and Greeks, Christ the power of God and the wisdom of God.... Christ Jesus, who became for us wisdom from God (1 Cor 1:22–24, 30, NRSV).

However, some early church fathers like Gregory of Nazianzus also made this identification. That would leave the Holy Spirit to be equated with *Binah,* and here is where the comparison breaks down. But two out of three is not bad. Perhaps the problem of finding anything comparable to the Holy Spirit in other spiritual traditions is due to the ambiguity of the concept.

Forshaw goes on to expound some of the ideas from Pico's *Heptaplus.* As far as I am concerned, Pico might as well be going off into space. You can prove any text to contain anything you want if you try hard enough. And it must be said that Pico gets his interpretative methods from his kabbalistic sources. There is a point where you are no longer dealing with a sacred text but rather with a shredded version of it. Referring to Pico's goal in one part of the *Heptaplus* where he analyzes the first word of the Bible, *bereshit,* Forshaw writes: "From his kabbalistic analysis of the opening word of the Jewish Old Testament, Pico has extracted confirmation of the Christian message of the New Testament" (Forshaw, 135). He adds that for later Christian scholars as well, "Jewish Kabbalah confirms Christianity from the very first word of the Torah" (136). He goes on to explicate the views of several of these scholars, including Arcangelo da Borgonuovo who claimed that the first three letters of *bereshit* refer to the three persons of the Trinity. Whatever you may think of the kabbalists' interpretive techniques outlined by Forshaw, they were not out to justify their faith; instead they were really trying to uncover a higher message in the text.

Paracelsus's esoteric cosmology is the subject of Georgiana Hedesan's essay. We can see in Paracelsus's cosmology elements of what became modern science, but I will discuss only the esoteric side of his views. The cosmology is enunciated in the book *Philosophia ad Atheniensis*, which, as Hedesan mentions, may very well not have been written by Paracelsus, although all early commentators agreed on its authenticity. But as Hedesan points out, it is the ideas contained in it that matter, and they certainly drew a big response over the hundred years after its first publication. Hedesan goes on to show that divine entities, such as the arcanum and the *mysterium magnum,* which Paracelsus posits "are hard to comprehend through the perspective of established theology or philosophy" and are "idiosyncratic ideas," that may contain inner contradictions (Hedesan, 152).

Most commentators identify Paracelsus's *mysterium magnum* with what since Aristotle has been called prime matter (*material prima).* If some of his ways of describing this *mysterium magnum* seem a little strange, it should be kept in mind that prime matter is not physical matter, even chaotic or completely mixed physical matter. Prime matter is the stuff or substance of all of universal manifestation: the world spirit, the world soul, and finally the world body or physical realm. It is the chaos (waters) mentioned at the beginning of Genesis, a view Hedesan attributes to the sixteenth-century Catholic Old Testament scholar Agostino Steuco. And Paracelsus seems to use the phrase substantial matter (*material substantialis*) to refer to the substance of the physical world, which he says separates out of the *mysterium magnum*. On the one hand, Hedesan mentions that Jacob Böhme interpreted the *mysterium magnum* as the quintessence or fifth element from which the other four come, in other words, the undifferentiated matter out of which the corporeal or physical world is formed. But I believe he confused the *mysterium magnum* with substantial matter. On the other hand, the view of modern scholar Walter Pagel that "the Prime Matter of the world is not matter, but spirit; in fact it is the Word Fiat, the Logos of the Fourth Gospel, the Platonic archetype and idea pattern of the world that is to become a material creation" (Hedesan, 162) equates things that are not the same and seems to be invention rather than interpretation. Perhaps the existence of two such opposing explanations is due to the seeming inconsistency in Paracelsus's description of the *mysterium magnum*.

So let us move on to the arcanum. According to Hedesan,

> Paracelsus postulates that prior to the *mysterium magnum* there is something else, the uncreated 'eternal' arcanum. This is the 'supreme principle,' the 'eternal essence,' the 'goodness of the Creator' or the 'supreme Arcanum.... Paracelsus explains the arcanum thus: 'We do not say that the Arcanum is an essence like the immortal, but that it is this in its perfection'... This 'eternal' does not seem to be God *per se*, who is the 'Author of creation and the Ruler of the eternal' ... but the text sometimes switches ambiguously between the two. (150)

Paracelsus seems to be referring to what I have called Being or the first revelation or manifestation of God. It is Being which polarizes into itself (as Unmoved Mover) and the substance of universal manifestation on which it then acts to bring about the existence of the tripartite world.

Paracelsus seems to posit a third divine entity, namely, "God the Maker and Architect, the 'Author of Creation'" (see Hedesan, 152). This is a most difficult entity to understand, at least as something separate from the other two. God as the great Architect of the world is really an aspect of Being. It is interesting that Paracelsus thinks the present *mysterium magnum* will be destroyed and with it the world, but that there will be a new *mysterium magnum* and world that will never be destroyed. In this he is in agreement with statements found in both the Old and New Testaments about a coming destruction of the world followed by a new regenerated world which will last forever. Furthermore he writes about the "dissolution of matter … through putrefaction" and "the decay of the elements" (see Hedesan, 155). In short, he seems to believe at least partly in the traditional view of cosmic cycles. According to this doctrine, there are cycles of cosmic creation, degeneration, destruction, and regeneration (from a saved remnant). There are four ages in each cycle from a beginning golden age through a silver age and a bronze age to an ending iron age (in Western terminology). There is decay from one to another, and the last age, which humanity is supposedly living through right now, is the shortest and of lowest quality. While the traditional doctrine of ages, which is found around the world, involves a never ending series of degenerating cycles, the Bible seems to posit an end to the series.

The main subject of László-Attila Hubbes's essay is Hamvas's symbolic analysis of the first three chapters of Genesis. It seems to be based on the idea mentioned earlier that there is a correspondence between the heavenly and earthly realms. Only he expresses it in hermetic terms:

> The vision and thinking of historical man relies on logical oppositions; the vision and thinking of archaic man relies on analogy. The main principle of analogy is what the *Tabula Smaragdina* [the Emerald Tablet] expresses this way: "That, which is below corresponds with that which is above, and that which is above corresponds to that which is below."… There is analogy between the way of the stars and human fate; there is analogy between the life of humankind and the life of a single individual; there is analogy between colors and sounds, numbers and bodies. Each is different, still yet each is the same. (*Scientia Sacra* 1.2.3.2; see Hubbes, 203–4)

In trying to understand "as above, so below," we need to add, as Guenon pointed out in a number or works, "but inversely." In other words, what seems the greatest from the earthly perspective is really of little account from the heavenly perspective, and what is of greatest account from the heavenly perspective seems to be of little account from the earthly point of view. It is significant that Hamvas sees numbers as linking the two spheres. The emphasis on numbers in kabbalah—for example, the *sefirot* and by extension the Hebrew letters, which have a numerical value—is due to the fact that numbers seem to exist independently of people thinking of them and writing them down. And they seem to exist eternally and unchanging and are thus comparable to Being. Plato, in the *Republic* puts forward a mathematically oriented curriculum, which is supposed to lift the student's consciousness from the sensible realm to the intelligible realm, the realm of the forms.

Hamvas seems to feel that archaic humans, that is, humans before the fall, were analogical in their thinking. Historical humans, or humans after the fall, think differently. Archaic humans see the connection between things; historical humans see differences. Life before the fall, golden age life, was "whole, total, and unitary" (*Scientia Sacra* 1.1.1.4). Life after the fall, apocalyptic life, is a "fragmentary ... closed existence" (*Scientia Sacra* 1.1.1.5; see Hubbes, 207). Archaic humans felt complete; historical humans always feel incomplete, as if something is not quite right. Archaic humans looked within; historical humans look outside themselves, "in the direction opposite to spirit: towards material nature" (*Scientia Sacra* 1.2.4.5; see Hubbes, 209). Given their perspective, archaic humans looked for analogies between things. But if you notice the list Hamvas presents, not all of these analogies involve the higher and lower, the invisible and visible. For instance, he writes of an analogy between the life of humanity and the life of a single individual. This has nothing to do with above and below. In fact, a number of commentators seem to think that all esoteric symbolism deals with comparing what is below to what is above, to the highest realities. But this is not so. Many esoteric stories deal with what is usually called the spiritual journey of the soul from a fallen state to a restored state. This again is not a matter of above and below.

I cannot say that I completely understand the views of Hamvas as presented by Hubbes. Hamvas does not seem to believe in a complete doctrine of ages. What he calls apocalyptic life, I would call iron age life. It would be better if he did not refer to the original Adam of Gen 1 as Adam Kadmon, since that title is usually reserved for the *sefirot* considered as a whole. It seems at times that he views the original Adam as supernatural, that is, without a body. However, he also seems to think of archaic humans in this way. In that case the fall would have taken place before what is called the fall in Genesis. It was literally a fall into matter by the original humans and the effects of that fall. This sounds very much like something we came across before in considering Origen's account of the story of the fall. As an analysis of Genesis, it therefore leaves a lot to be desired. However, Hubbes makes the following statement early on:

> One thing should be clear from the start: Hamvas never wrote a direct exegesis on Gen 1–3. Rather he was concerned in his work with this founding myth of our world: our creation, our fall, and consecutively,

> our restoration. In fact, he translated for modern Western readers the message, the legacy, and the interpretations of the biblical revelation on the human condition in the created world, based on the best available explanations. (204)

And he adds, “Hamvas, drawing from many archaic traditions, relied steadily on ancient gnosis” (205). So what we have is Hamvas’s own view of the plight of humanity and how it got that way, and not really an explication of Gen 1–3. It is a gnostic view with his own twist that humanity is the corrupter of creation.

As to our restoration from this fallen state, according to Hamvas it depends on love, which he calls “the highest degree of wakefulness.” He links this love with the feminine: “The symbol of salvation: Isis with little Horus in her arms, Magna Mater, holding in her arms the child, which is humanity. The celestial affection awaken in the womanly soul” (*Scientia Sacra* 1.2.6; see Hubbes, 211). Love was there from the beginning of creation, and understood in the way just mentioned it will restore us to the original perfection. By the latter he does not seem to mean the state of Adam and Eve before the fall but of something even higher, which fits in with his idea of when the fall really took place.

> Regardless of the specific interpretations, in all traditions restoration is achieved by a return to the primordial state, to the golden age of creation. In this return to the primordial state, Hamvas elaborates that humanity has an active role to play: “The duty of man is not to wait and contemplate, but to act, to be an active participant in the redemption of the world.” (*Scientia Sacra* 1.3.4.4; see Hubbes, 212)

The idea that human activity is necessary for world redemption reminds us of both Zoroastrianism (copied by Manichaeism) and Kabbalism. How are we to bring about this redemption? By imitating Jesus: “Christianity teaches the restoration of normality through the sacrifice of love, first and irrevocably made by Jesus.” It is rather insightful that “Hamvas insists that Christianity is not meant to be a religion,” with all that is implied by that term (Hubbes, 213). I would put it a little differently: Jesus did not mean for a religion to grow up around what he taught and what he did.

There is not much I can say about Hugh R. Page Jr.’s essay on Africana esotericism, except that little of it touches on esotericism unless one has a very wide definition of the word. There are a number of references to magical practices such as *conjure* and to visions, but these have nothing to do with esotericism. There are several references to the *Rider-Waite Tarot Deck*, which was illustrated by Pamela Colman Smith, but tarot decks originated in Europe. Even if, as Page wonders, "the symbolism of her versions of the Major and Minor Arcana encode her life experiences as a woman of color living in the Diaspora" (Page, 226), this has nothing to do with esotericism nor do the facts that certain of the cards have biblical images and some may allude to the Bible. Page mentions African American Freemasonry, and here they may be an esoteric connection. But there are also a number of references to African Americans who took up Mormonism, one of whom was a follower of Joseph Smith. Indeed Joseph Smith was a Mason and certain Masonic symbols are found in Mormonism, but the meaning of the various symbols has been reworked, so that whatever esoteric teaching was there originally has been erased.

Page also claims that the King James Version of the Bible "must head the list of Africana esoteric texts," because of the impact it has had on Africana life (225). Certainly parts of the Bible carry esoteric symbolism, but Page only cites books that feature the use of the Bible for magical purposes. He mentions Henri Gamache's books, but they too seem to be about the use of magic for one's own purposes. He also adds to the list Elijah Muhammad's *The Mother Plane*. Even though this book alludes to Ezekiel's vision of the celestial chariot, it is as far from being an esoteric work as one can get, unless the word *esoteric* is understood to mean just about anything. In fact, my criticism of Page's approach revolves around what he takes the word *esoteric* to mean. He seems to interpret it as referring mainly to the occult, which includes magical practices. I believe it is important to distinguish between the esoteric and the occult, because the first deals with the spiritual while the second deals with the worldly. Magic is just getting your way by unusual means.

Since I have been so negative up to now, let me try to balance things by presenting a true example of Africana esotericism. I mentioned earlier that one of the symbols of the world spirit or axis is the trunk of the world tree and that in the garden of Eden it is connected with a snake, which symbolizes immortality. In fact, snakes are generally connected with portrayals of the world tree, Yggdrasil from Norse mythology being another example. As it happens, mountains and rainbows have also been used as symbols of the world axis and in one way or another these too are connected with snakes. The link between the world axis and serpents is so strong that there are African spiritual traditions in which the world axis, symbolized by the rainbow, is considered a celestial serpent. In fact, in the Yoruba language, the word for rainbow, *osumare*, contains the word for big snake, *ere*.

Page seems to be much more interested in developments within the African Diaspora than in African religion itself. But one will have to examine the myths and folk tales of Africa, and in general their spiritual traditions, if one wants to find esoteric teachings. There are several, although not enough, books on these subjects, but Page does not list any of them.

Susanne Scholz addresses her paper to the ideas of Emanuel Swedenborg, Rudolf Steiner, and myself. I will concentrate on her explication of the Genesis commentaries of Swedenborg and Steiner. She describes their views in a clear way, which makes them easy to assess. First, a few comments on Steiner's ideas. Steiner wants us to pay attention to the sounds of the Hebrew words, such as the first word of the Bible, because they "tear the soul away from sensory perception" (Scholz, 181). Scholz explains: "We ought to read the text to forget our physicality and to make mental images explicit as they emerge from the texts. In this way, the texts teach about 'our own origin' ([Steiner] 2002, 13), which is spiritual and not physical.… The goal is to develop interiority" (Scholz, 181). Steiner believed that both the earth and humans "emanated from the spiritual to the physical level." He also believed that the sun, moon, and earth were once together, but separated during what he called the Lemurian and Atlantean ages. The earth then began to cool down and thus was able to become "the bearer of human existence" (Scholz, 182). He evidently took the wind and waters of the beginning of Genesis to reflect this reality.

He thought that after the separation of the sun, moon, and earth, many of the soul/spirits went to live on other planets, while "the strongest, toughest human soul/spirits" remained on earth where they were given bodies by the elohim or creative forces (Scholz, 182–83). Not only was the first human androgynous, the first humans were etheric rather than physical. It was only when an advanced form of the elohim developed, namely, Jehovah-Elohim, and imprinted earthly dust into the human body that the denser physical human came into being. Steiner did not believe that humans evolved from lower animals, but that humans arose from crystallization.

There is nothing in Gen 1–3 to justify Steiner's views, except the androgynous Adam of Gen 1 and the idea that humans did not evolve from lower animals. The notion of etheric bodies is muddled at best, but they are a staple of Theosophy as well as of Steiner's Anthroposophy. That humans were originally nonphysical is also a part of theosophical belief.

Elohim and Yahweh (Jehovah) are the two names for God used at the beginning of Genesis, and it is true that Elohim is a plural form. As all Bible scholars know, they come from different written sources, and the name Elohim seems to be based on the name El of a Canaanite god. In English translations, Yahweh and all variations on this name are always translated as "Lord," and Elohim and all variations on that name are always translated as "God," so we can tell which Hebrew name is being used. Thus we get "Lord God" in Gen 2–3 where both names are used together. But there is no indication that the authors of the Bible thought that the God of Gen 1 and the Lord God of Gen 2 were different beings. Nor does Steiner's reading seem to be an esoteric symbolic analysis.

Much more interesting is Swedenborg's reading of Genesis. Swedenborg decried the literalistic interpretation of the Bible and instead sought "the inner meaning of Scripture" (Scholz, 171). He claimed that his knowledge of the inner meaning was revealed to him "by interaction with spirits and angels" (*Secrets of Heaven* §67; see Scholz, 172).Well, what did they reveal? A story that puts forward a doctrine of ages, but with his distinctive views about what each thing symbolizes. Scholz states the following at the outset:

> Swedenborg does not view the Genesis stories as depictions of the exoteric development of life on planet earth. Rather humanity's religious-spiritual development or inner history emerges in four stages. It begins with what he calls the "earliest church," followed by the "ancient church," the "Jewish church," and the "Christian church." Importantly, Swedenborg uses the term *church* not as a reference to the Christian institution but as a term for "the human community sharing particular religious viewpoints." (Scholz, 173)

So the four epochs of humanity's inner development are connected with these four religious viewpoints. It is unclear to me why the Genesis stories could not refer to both the inner developments of humans as well as the outer consequences of those developments. This is certainly the usual way of understanding the doctrine of ages. At any rate, not only did Swedenborg see a degeneration from one of these epochs to another, but there were substages in connection within each "church" so that degeneration took place even within epochs.

What follows seems to be along the lines of standard esoteric explanation. The people of the time of the earliest church were in direct communication with God and other heavenly beings, were focused inward, and could communicate mentally. But this changed with the flood. People of the ancient church were more outwardly oriented and needed to speak in order to communicate. As Swedenborg explains it,

> The states of these two churches were entirely different. That of the earliest church was to receive a perception of good, and so of truth, from the Lord. In the ancient church—"Noah"—the state changed to one of conscience concerning goodness and truth.... The earliest church was heavenly, but the ancient church was spiritual. (*Secrets of Heaven* §597; Scholz, 174)

Originally, people knew right and wrong intuitively; they perceived it, as it were. After the flood "doctrines were grasped through the physical senses, shaped into concrete images in the memory, and then reshaped into ideas," as Scholz puts it. She adds, "At the same time, love ceased to be the most important principle, and the intellect began to dominate" (175). Swedenborg goes on to describe the further spiritual degeneration of humanity in the subsequent churches. His symbolic readings of Genesis tracing the slow but steady degradation of humans turning away from the heavenly and toward the earthly are very insightful, but would take too long to detail in the context of this essay. However, as Scholz points out (178), his views are also sexist and anti-Jewish, so one has to take the good with the bad.

One unusual feature of Swedenborg's doctrine of ages is that the beginning of first epoch seems to predate even the existence of Eve. As he writes:

> When humans received the ability to recognize their own nature—the nature of their good emotions and true concepts—they still sought independence. After all, when people are such that they want to rule themselves, they begin to despise all that the Lord has to offer them, no matter how clearly those things are presented and illustrated for them. (*Secrets of Heaven* §146)

So God built Eve out of Adam's rib. It may seem that the connection between these things is rather forced, but it follows from Swedenborg's view of the feminine.

Scholz gives many examples of how "Swedenborg does not escape privileging maleness and reason" over femaleness and will (178). Nowhere is his negative view of women or the feminine more clear than in his interpretation of the creation of Eve from Adam. He stresses that Eve was not formed from Adam's rib but built from it. "*Building* means reconstructing what has fallen down. A *rib* symbolizes a sense of self devoid of life. A *woman* symbolizes a sense of self brought to life by the Lord. *Bringing her to the human* means giving people a sense of self" (*Secrets of Heaven* §151). So for Swedenborg a woman symbolizes self-will or what we generally term egoism. He goes on: "The fact that the *woman* symbolizes selfhood is indicated by her being the one who was deceived [Gen 3:1–6]. Since nothing ever deceives us besides our self-absorption or, what is the same, love for ourselves and for the material world" (*Secrets of Heaven* §152). Not surprisingly he adds, in his interpretation of Gen 2:24, "*Leaving father and mother* is leaving the inner being behind, as it is the inner being that conceives and gives birth to the outer being. *To cling to one's wife* is to have an inner being within our outer being" (*Secrets of Heaven* §160), which is definitely considered a less spiritual state. To be sure Swedenborg's view of women is complicated by the fact that he sees her symbolizing different things. For instance, he views "the *woman* as the church" (*Secrets of Heaven* §252), the faithful as it were, in all of its ups and downs. But this does not lessen the impact of his negative comments.

Swedenborg realized that his symbolic reading of the creation of Eve was questionable in one respect. If God built Eve from Adam's rib, how could this be seen as negative? Certainly God would not do something evil. Swedenborg's answer is that "the people made Him do it." God yielded to *their* desire for a sense of autonomy. Such an action (or reaction) seems out of character for God and makes this symbolic interpretation questionable. It is obvious that Swedenborg is one of the few esoteric interpreters who does not view the original human of Gen 1 as androgynous. So instead of seeing a neutral separation of Adam-Eve into Adam and Eve in Gen 2, he sees Eve as a production from Adam and thus as a development within Adam of something incipient but not fully realized, namely, self-will or egoism.

Having considered the views expressed in the various essays of this collection, let me conclude with some remarks about modern biblical criticism as it relates to the esoteric approach to the Bible. Esotericists are not concerned with where Bible stories came from or with competing theories of how they were put together. They take Genesis as it is and similarly the whole Bible from Genesis to Revelation. Their only aim is to analyze the spiritual ideas contained in the Bible. If some biblical stories were based on stories from other cultures and were thus derived from other spiritual traditions and if there seem to be alternate versions of narratives and sayings which have been put side by side, this process does not take away from their spiritual symbolism or their power to teach and uplift us. So from the esoteric point of view it is the inner meanings of these texts, the hidden truths they contain, that is of utmost significance.

Works Cited

Augustine. *Confessions*. 1961. Translated by R. S. Pine-Coffin. Baltimore: Penguin.

Guillaumont, Antoine, et al. 1959. *The Gospel according to Thomas*. New York: Harper & Row.

Heidel, Alexander. 1963. *The Gilgamesh Epic and Old Testament Parallels*. Chicago: Phoenix.

Maimonides, Moses. 1963. *The Guide of the Perplexed*. Translated by Shlomo Pines. Chicago: University of Chicago Press.

Philo. *On Flight and Finding, On the Change of Names, On Dreams*. 1968. Translated by F. H. Colson and G. H. Whitaker. LCL. Cambridge: Harvard University Press.

Swedenborg, Emanuel. 2009. *Secrets of Heaven*. Vol. 1. New Century Edition. Translated by Lisa Hyatt Cooper. West Chester, Penn.: Swedenborg Foundation.

Contributors

Samuel D. Fohr is professor emeritus of Philosophy at the Bradford Campus of the University of Pittsburgh. His research centers on Asian spiritual traditions, esoterism, and the spiritual symbolism of Bible stories, myths, and folktales. Among his publications are *Adam and Eve: The Spiritual Symbolism of Genesis and Exodus* (2005), and *Cinderella's Gold Slipper: Spiritual Symbolism in the Grimms' Tales* (2001). He has also edited several translations of the works of René Guénon, including *Symbols of Sacred Science, Initiation and Spiritual Realization,* and *The Great Triad.*

Peter J. Forshaw is a senior lecturer in History of Western Esotericism in the early modern period at the Center for the History of Hermetic Philosophy, University of Amsterdam, the Netherlands, where he specializes in the intellectual and cultural history of learned magic and its relation to religion, science, and medicine. He is editor-in-chief of *Aries: Journal for the Study of Western Esotericism*, editor of *The Word and the World: Biblical Exegesis and Early Modern Science* (2007), and editor of *Laus Platonici Philosophi: Marsilio Ficino and his Influence* (2011). He is currently preparing a monograph entitled *The Mage's Images: Occult Theosophy in Heinrich Khunrath's Early Modern Oratory and Laboratory.*

Georgiana (Jo) Hedesan recently completed her Ph.D. in History at the University of Exeter, UK. In 2013, she was awarded a Cantemir Junior Fellowship at the University of Oxford and a Frances A. Yates Fellowship at the Warburg Institute, University of London. Her interests include early modern alchemical philosophy and its interaction with religion, Jan Baptist Van Helmont, and his intellectual influence, as well as the theme of prolongation of life in an alchemical context.

László-Attila Hubbes is a lecturer in semiotics, rhetoric, and other communication disciplines at the Faculty of Technical and Social Sciences of the Sapientia Hungarian University of Transylvania in Miercurea Ciuc, Romania. His main field of research is apocalyptic studies. His publications include *Visions under the Spell of the End: Apocalypse from a Genre of the Religious Literature to a Way of Artistic Expression* (2008, in Hungarian). He maintains a Hungarian and English bilingual online resource collection on apocalyptic at: www.apokaliptikum.lap.hu. He is presently involved in the research of contemporary myths, online rituals, and discourses of various religious or nationalistic networks and communities, particularly ethnopaganism.

Peter W. Martens is an assistant professor of early Christianity at Saint Louis University. He specializes in the reception history of the Bible in the eastern Mediterranean, with a focus on Origen and the Antiochene tradition. His monograph, *Origen and Scripture: The Contours of the Exegetical Life* (Oxford, 2012), approaches the history of exegesis biographically. It examines Origen's portrait of the ideal (and less than ideal) scriptural interpreter. Martens is currently producing a study, edition, and translation of Adrian's *Introduction to the Divine Scriptures*, a neglected Antiochene textbook on biblical interpretation.

Hugh R. Page Jr. is the dean of the First Year of Studies and an associate professor of Theology and Africana Studies at the University of Notre Dame, Notre Dame, Indiana. His research interests include early Hebrew poetry; ancient myth; and biblical hermeneutics, spiritualities of resistance, and esoteric cosmologies within the Africana world. His major works include *The Myth of Cosmic Rebellion: A Study of its Reflexes in Ugaritic and Biblical Literature* (1996), *The Africana Bible* (as general editor, 2010), and *Israel's Poetry of Resistance: Africana Perspectives on Early Hebrew Verse* (2013).

Elaine Pagels is the Harrington Spear Paine Professor of Religion at Princeton University. Her research interests focus on the early history of Christianity and, in particular, the texts discovered at Nag Hammadi. Besides scholarly articles and textual editions, her major books include *The Gnostic Gospels* (1979), *Adam, Eve, and the Serpent: Sex and Politics in Early Christianity* (1987), *The Origin of Satan: How Christians Demonized Jews, Pagans, and Heretics* (1995), and *Beyond Belief: The Secret Gospel of Thomas* (2002).

Tuomas Rasimus is an Academy of Finland research fellow at the University of Helsinki, Finland and an associate professor at Université Laval, Québec, Canada. He has published on Gnosticism, early Christianity, and Neoplatonism, and his recent works include *Paradise Reconsidered in Gnostic Mythmaking: Rethinking Sethianism in Light of the Ophite Evidence* (2009), *The Legacy of John: Second-Century Reception of the Fourth Gospel* (ed., 2010), *Stoicism in Early Christianity* (ed. with Troels Engberg-Pedersen and Ismo Dunderberg, 2010), and *Gnosticism, Platonism and the Late Ancient World: Essays in Honour of John D. Turner* (ed. with Kevin Corrigan, 2013).

Susanne Scholz is a professor of Old Testament at Perkins School of Theology in Dallas, Texas. Her research focuses on feminist and cultural hermeneutics. Among her publications are *Feminist Interpretation of the Hebrew Bible in Retrospect: Biblical Books* (ed. of vol. 1, 2013), *God Loves Diversity and Justice: Progressive Scholars Speak about Faith, Politics, and the World* (ed., 2013), *Sacred Witness: Rape in the Hebrew Bible* (2010), *Introducing the Women's Hebrew Bible* (2007), *Biblical Studies Alternatively* (ed., 2003), and *Rape Plots: A Feminist Cultural Study of Genesis 34* (2000).

Anna Rebecca Solevåg is a postdoctoral researcher at the School of Mission and Theology, Stavanger, Norway. Among her research interests are gender and its intersection with other axes of power and oppression in the New Testament and early Christian literature. She has recently published a book on the intersection of gender and class in the Pastoral Epistles, the Acts of Andrew, and the Martyrdom of Perpetua and Felicitas: *Birthing Salvation: Gender and Class in Early Christian Childbearing Discourse* (2013). She is currently working on a project about representations of disability in early Christian texts.

Caroline Vander Stichele is *universitair docent* at the Faculty of Humanities of the University of Amsterdam, the Netherlands. Her research and publications focus on the rhetoric of gender in early Christian literature and on the cultural impact of the Bible. Her publications include *Creation and Creativity: From Genesis to Genetics and Back* (ed. with Alistair G. Hunter, 2006), *Contextualizing Gender in Early Christian Discourse: Thinking beyond Thecla* (with Todd Penner, 2009), and *Text, Image, and Otherness in Children's Bibles: What is in the Picture?* (ed. with Hugh S. Pyper,

2012). She is currently preparing a book on Herodias and coediting a volume on film theory in biblical studies with Laura Copier.

Elliot R. Wolfson is the Marsha and Jay Glazer Chair in Jewish Studies and Professor of Religious Studies at the University of California, Santa Barbara. His main area of scholarly research is the history of Jewish mysticism, but he has brought to bear on that field training in philosophy, literary criticism, feminist theory, postmodern hermeneutics, and the phenomenology of religion. He is the author of many publications including *Through the Speculum That Shines: Vision and Imagination in Medieval Jewish Mysticism* (1994), *Language, Eros, and Being: Kabbalistic Hermeneutics and the Poetic Imagination* (2005), *Alef, Mem, Tau: Kabbalistic Musings on Time, Truth, and Death* (2006), *Venturing Beyond: Law and Morality in Kabbalistic Mysticism* (2006), *Open Secret: Postmessianic Messianism and the Mystical Revision of Menahem Mendel Schneerson* (2009), *A Dream Interpreted within a Dream: Oneiropoiesis and the Prism of Imagination* (2011), and *Giving Beyond the Gift: Apophasis and Overcoming Theomania* (2014).

Index of Sources

NEW TESTAMENT

Philo

Greco-Roman Works

Rabbinic, Zoharic, and Kabbalistic Texts

Index of Authors